W9-AVR-043

Contents at a Glance

ABSOLUTE BEGINNER'S GUIDE

TO

Home Networking

Mark Edward Soper

800 East 96th Street,
Indianapolis, Indiana 46240

Absolute Beginner's Guide to Home Networking

International Standard Book Number: 0-7897-3205-X

Library of Congress Catalog Card Number: 029236732059

Printed in the United States of America

First Printing: October 2004

07   06   05   4   3

Trademarks

All terms mentioned in this book that are known to be trademarks or service marks have been appropriately capitalized. Que Publishing cannot attest to the accuracy of this information. Use of a term in this book should not be regarded as affecting the validity of any trademark or service mark.

Warning and Disclaimer

Every effort has been made to make this book as complete and as accurate as possible, but no warranty or fitness is implied. The information provided is on an "as is" basis. The author and the publisher shall have neither liability nor responsibility to any person or entity with respect to any loss or damages arising from the information contained in this book.

Bulk Sales

Que offers excellent discounts on this book when ordered in quantity for bulk purchases or special sales. For more information, please contact:

U.S. Corporate and Government Sales
1-800-382-3419
corpsales@pearsontechgroup.com

For sales outside of the U.S., please contact:

International Sales
international@pearsoned.com

Associate Publisher
Greg Wiegand

Executive Editor
Rick Kughen

Development Editor
Kevin Howard

Managing Editor
Charlotte Clapp

Copy Editor
Nancy Albright

Indexer
Heather McNeill

Proofreader
Leslie Joseph

Technical Editor
David Eytchison

Publishing Coordinator
Sharry Gregory

Interior Designer
Anne Jones

Cover Designer
Anne Jones

Page Layout
Julie Parks

Graphics
Stephen Adams
Tammy Graham
Laura Robbins

Table of Contents

About the Author

Mark Edward Soper, A+, MCP has taught computer troubleshooting and other technical subjects to thousands of students from Maine to Hawaii since 1992. He is the author of *Absolute Beginner's Guide to A+ Certification; Upgrading and Repairing PCs, A+ Certification Study Guide, Second Edition; PC Help Desk; Complete Idiot's Guide to High-Speed Internet Connections; Absolute Beginner's Guide to Cable Internet Connections; Easy Digital Cameras;* and is co-author of TechTV's *Upgrading Your PC*. He has contributed to several editions of *Upgrading and Repairing PCs* as well as multiple other Que titles.

Dedication

This book is dedicated to my wife, Cheryl. She shows the power of human networking in every part of her life.

Acknowledgments

First of all, as always, I must thank Almighty God for the opportunity to write and share what I've learned with you, my readers.

My family is increasingly far-flung, but as their emails and IM chats remind me, home networks bring love home. Thanks to Kate and Hugh, proof that online relationships can turn into tangible results (one grandson and another grandchild on the way!). Thanks to Ed and Erin, Jeremy, and Ian, for reminding me of how technology is fun.

Donnie Owen, the Cisco expert in Evansville, for lending me many of the cool Cisco and Linksys products shown in this book.

Greg Wiegand, who keeps the Que team pointed in the right direction and fields your questions.

Rick Kughen, whose vision for this book helped guide it from start to finish.

Kevin Howard, whose queries, questions, and suggestions helped shape the rough draft into a polished volume.

David Eytchison, whose technical expertise helped improve the final product.

Charlotte Clapp, who kept chapters, artwork, and photos flowing properly throughout the production process.

Nancy Albright, whose sharp eye stopped spelling, grammatical, and punctuation problems from interfering with your enjoyment of this book.

Sharry Gregory, who processed my invoices and shepherded them through the approval process.

The graphics staff, who turned my photos and rough sketches into useful illustrations.

The layout staff, who transformed words, photos, and artwork into an easy-to-use volume.

And all the rest of the Que staff, whose technical books I've relied on over the years for solid information presented in an easy-to-understand form. It's a pleasure to work with all of them.

We Want to Hear from You!

As the reader of this book, *you* are our most important critic and commentator. We value your opinion and want to know what we're doing right, what we could do better, what areas you'd like to see us publish in, and any other words of wisdom you're willing to pass our way.

As an associate publisher for Que Publishing, I welcome your comments. You can email or write me directly to let me know what you did or didn't like about this book—as well as what we can do to make our books better.

Please note that I cannot help you with technical problems related to the topic of this book. We do have a User Services group, however, where I will forward specific technical questions related to the book.

When you write, please be sure to include this book's title and author as well as your name, email address, and phone number. I will carefully review your comments and share them with the author and editors who worked on the book.

Email: feedback@quepublishing.com

Mail: Greg Wiegand
Associate Publisher
Que Publishing
800 East 96th Street
Indianapolis, IN 46240 USA

For more information about this book or another Que Publishing title, visit our website at www.quepublishing.com. Type the ISBN (excluding hyphens) or the title of a book in the Search field to find the page you're looking for.

İNTRODUCTiON

Do You Need This Book?

Home networking has become one of the hottest trends in personal computing. And why not? As broadband Internet access from cable, DSL, and other sources has become more common, the big push is on to share your connection with the rest of the family. But, home networking can do far more than share an Internet connection.

Home networking makes it easier than ever to take work home from the office; help the kids with their homework; enjoy digital music, photos, and video; print and scan from any PC in the home; and even connect console video games in the online world. If some of those uses are news to you, welcome.

Whether you already have a home network, are thinking about getting one, or are trying to get it working, this book has plenty for you:

- If you already have a home network, this book will show you what you can do with it—and how to do it.

- If you're just in the "thinking about it" stages, this book will help you past your fears and show you how to plan your network, step by step.

- If you're confused about wireless networking, this book takes the mystery out of wireless and shows you how wired and wireless networking can work together.

- If you're fighting with problems getting your network to work, this book shows you how to troubleshoot the most common problems so you can enjoy, rather than endure, your network.

How This Book Is Organized

This book is organized into 11 chapters:

- Chapter 1, "What Is a Home Network?" explains what makes home networks similar to and different from business networks and how home networks help your family work and play at the same time.

- Chapter 2, "Building Blocks of the Home Network," covers the hardware, software, and other components used by different networks, including ethernet, wireless ethernet, and others. If you don't understand the difference between a router and a network adapter, relax! This chapter brings you up to speed.

■ Chapter 3, "Planning Your Home Network," helps you determine what the best network is for your home based on how you plan to use it. It also helps you discover what you need to build the network you want and helps you calculate the real cost.

■ Chapter 4, "Choosing a Broadband Internet Access Technology," helps you choose from the most home network friendly options on the market.

■ Chapter 5, "Installing and Configuring a Wired Ethernet Network," helps you build a speedy, low-cost network and hide those pesky cables. Even if you love wireless, you'll want to read this chapter to find out how to put the best of wired and wireless together in a single network.

■ Chapter 6, "Installing and Configuring a Wi-Fi Network," helps you choose from the many flavors of wireless networking, get it working, and enjoy it.

■ Chapter 7, "Home Networks at Play," takes the "work" out of "network." Discover how to add home theater systems, video games, and digital video recorders to your home network. Liberate the digital goodness of family photos and videos and play them back on the big screen TV!

■ Chapter 8, "Home Networks at Work and School," makes working to pay for all that fun gear in Chapter 7 a lot easier to take. Discover easy ways to share information, share printers, and even share that dandy new all-in-one device. Instead of driving back to the office for the files you forgot, connect remotely and securely with VPN or GoToMyPC.

■ Chapter 9, "Home, Sweet, Controlled and Secure Home," shows you how to use popular lighting, HVAC, and home security devices based on X10 or other technologies along with your home network. See what's happening with the kids or turn on the coffeemaker from your office desktop!

■ Chapter 10, "Securing Your Home Network," helps you keep the bad guys away from your home network and your broadband Internet connection. From making your wireless network virtually invisible to war-drivers to figuring out how to spot a bogus email that spells trouble for your personal data, this chapter helps you keep your data, your life, and your family safer online.

■ Chapter 11, "Troubleshooting Your Home Network," shows you common problems and, even better, solutions! From a basic guide to those pesky IP addresses to common-sense solutions to broken network connections and loose cables, this chapter helps you keep your network from becoming a "notwork."

How to Use This Book

If you're completely new to home networking...that makes you an absolute beginner. I was thinking of you the whole time I wrote this book! Even if you're already into home networking, read the whole book cover to cover. The early chapters give you an introduction to terms and concepts that come up again and again in later parts of the book. I saved the most advanced material for last. By the time you get to Chapter 11, you'll be ready for it.

If you'd rather jump around in the book or just read the chapters that are new to you, that's OK too. Review the chapter descriptions in the previous section to zero in on what you don't know. I've added in lots of cross-references to other chapters in case you need more background on a particular topic.

Conventions Used in This Book

Commands, directions, and explanations in this book are presented in the clearest format possible. The following items are some of the features that make this book easier for you to use:

- *Commands that you must enter*—Commands that you need to type are easily identified by special `monospace` format. For example, to view IP configuration information (IP address, subnet mask, and default gateway), I display the command like this: `winipcfg`. This tells you that you need to enter this command exactly as it is shown.

- *Notes*—Information related to the task at hand, or "inside" information, is provided in this format to make it easy to find.

- *Tips*—Pieces of information that are not necessarily essential to the current topic but that offer advice or help you save time are presented as Tips.

- *Cautions*—Notes explaining the need to be careful when performing a particular procedure or task are presented as Cautions.

- *Websites*—These online resources are provided whenever they will help you understand a topic more easily or provide a source for hardware or software you must have to perform a task.

Now that you understand what this book can do for you and how it's designed to help you, it's time to get started. See you in Chapter 1!

PART i

NETWORK YOUR LIFE, NOT JUST YOUR COMPUTERS

1

WHAT IS A HOME NETWORK?

This chapter explains what makes home networks similar to and different from business networks and how home networks help your family work and play at the same time. Consider this chapter to be Networking 101—a course any serious home networker should pass. Even if you've tinkered with networks in the past, you'll be surprised at what you learn here.

What Is a Network?

A network combines two or more connected computers that can share information and resources. However, home networking enables you to do much more than share files and printers. By connecting your home network to broadband Internet access, everyone can access the Internet for homework, research, or entertainment. Add *instant messaging (IM) software,* and you can chat with family and friends without interrupting your work.

Home networking isn't just for PCs anymore. You can connect your TVs and home theater systems to your network so you can enjoy digital music, video, and photos in a big-screen, surround-sound environment. Video gaming, whether you prefer PCs or consoles, is better with a home network: Play against each other or play against distant foes.

Essentially, a home network bridges the gaps between islands of information and recreation. Before home networks, Internet access was available only on one PC. If you didn't have a printer connected to your computer, you had to hand-carry a floppy disk or CD containing your print jobs to the nearest PC with a printer. Digital music, video, and photos could be enjoyed only on the PC storing the files. When you add a home network, every PC and connected entertainment device in your home is more powerful and more versatile. A home network helps you get more work done and have more fun at the same time.

> **caution**
>
> **KEEPING YOUR KIDS OUT OF THE INTERNET'S RED-LIGHT DISTRICT**
>
> In Chapter 10, "Securing Your Home Network," you learn how to filter your kids' Internet access to minimize their chances of getting to the undesirable parts of the online universe.

Similarities Between Home and Business Networks

In business, networks have been used to

- Reduce investments in expensive hardware by sharing a single device, such as a high-quality printer or large hard disk, among multiple computers.
- Improve productivity and profits by providing fast (even real-time) sharing of information between employees.
- Improve productivity and profits by providing faster means to get information from outside sources into users' hands.

Each of these uses has a home networking counterpart:

- Instead of buying a printer for each computer, you can share a single printer. With the money you save through purchasing only one printer, you can buy a faster, higher-quality printer.

- Instead of upgrading several hard disks, share a large hard disk over the network. You save money and you create a single, easy-to-back-up location for documents, music, video, and photo files.

- Instant access to information via IM, email, and shared file storage makes it easy to help the kids with their homework without interrupting your work.

- Networked Internet access means that nobody has to wait in line to get online to check email, access the campus or corporate network, or look up information.

Both business networks and home networks help make users more productive by providing instant access to shared resources, such as folders, printers, and Internet access.

How Do Home Networks Differ from Business Networks?

Although home and business networks both help their users become more productive, they differ in many ways.

The most obvious difference is that a home network can also be used for recreation. From online gaming to streaming video, photo, and audio files, a home network can help everyone relax, kick back, and have fun. If you work with computers as part of your job, you might be wondering whether the process of creating a home network is as painful as building and managing an office network can be. Don't worry. There are several ways in which home networks are different than business networks, and almost every one of those differences makes life easier for you.

Business networks often involve huge collections of wildly dissimilar hardware (Figure 1.1). Business IT personnel often spend a lot of time trying to get mainframe, midsize, and personal computers (PCs) to connect. Because many of these computer systems are quite old in computer terms, some even predating the World Wide Web, getting them to connect isn't easy. And, as Figure 1.1 shows, business networks are often collections of multiple local networks that connect to each other. For security, management, geographical location, and other reasons, different sections of a typical business network will have different settings.

FIGURE 1.1

A typical busi-
ness wide area
network (WAN),
which includes
multiple local
area networks
(LANs).

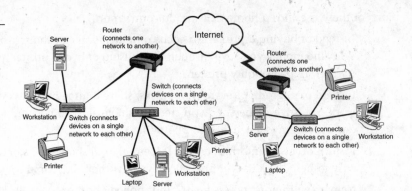

On the other hand, home networks are a lot smaller: a five-station home network
qualifies as "large" in most cases. And, because it's built up with PCs designed to
work on a network or with devices designed to work on a PC network, a home network's far easier to build than a business network (Figure 1.2). Compared to business
networks, most home networks connect all the computers and other network-capable
devices into a single network, so you need to keep track of just one set of configuration options.

FIGURE 1.2

A typical home
network with a
shared printer
and Internet
access.

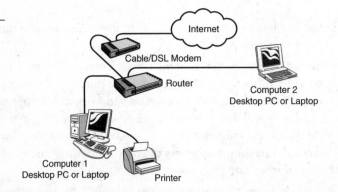

Because business networks are complex, they require full-time management. Home
networks, on the other hand, don't. The automatic configuration options used by
most home networks enable them to work smoothly under normal circumstances.
And if you have a problem, just check Chapter 11, "Troubleshooting Your Home
Network," for expert help.

Business networks are all business: gaming, music downloads, and other recreational activities are actively discouraged by most companies. A home network, on the other hand, is designed for fun as well as hard work (Figure 1.3).

FIGURE 1.3

A home network configured to play digital music, video, and photos through a TV and home theater system.

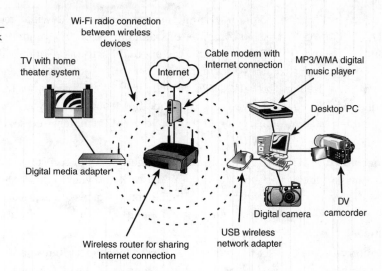

Wi-Fi radio connection between wireless devices

TV with home theater system

Internet

Cable modem with Internet connection

MP3/WMA digital music player

Desktop PC

Digital media adapter

Digital camera

DV camcorder

Wireless router for sharing Internet connection

USB wireless network adapter

With today's smarter networking *hardware* (the devices that connect computers) and *software* (the programs that help connected computers "talk" to each other), you don't need an IT degree to build a home network. All you need is a dream and a bit of cash.

What can you do with a home network? Read the rest of this chapter to find out.

Home Networks for Fun

Home networks help you enjoy your favorite entertainment anywhere in the house. A home network enables you to listen to digital music stored on your PC through your home theater system. You can use your big-screen TV to view digital photos and scanned images stored on your PC. Add broadband Internet access, and a home network enables video game fans to play against each other or against online foes.

Digital Video Recording and Playback

Digital video recording and playback is replacing analog video tape at a rapid clip. However, if you don't have a home network, you still need to carry your video recordings on a DVD or CD from one computer to another, or from your computer to your home theater system. Add a home network, and you can view your digital home movies on any PC connected to the network, and even on your home theater system.

The fun's not limited to your own home movies. Set-top digital video recorders such as TiVo, ReplayTV, and computer-based digital recording solutions such as ATI All-in-Wonder, NVIDIA Personal Cinema, and Microsoft Windows Media Center Edition PCs can be connected to your home network (Figure 1.4). When you network two or more TiVo or ReplayTV DVRs, you can view digital recordings from TV made in one room on the same type of DVR in another room. And, if you have a broadband Internet connection, you can control your DVR remotely and set it to record programs while you're away.

When you add PC-based DVRs to your home network, you can store your recorded TV shows on the biggest hard disk on the network and view your TV shows on other PCs or on your home theater system. Unlike home movies or recorded TV programs on analog tape, digital recordings don't lose quality when copied from one device to another.

Whether you prefer a set-top box or a PC-based video recording solution, your recordings can be viewed anywhere in your home with just a few clicks of a remote control or mouse. If you love TV, the ability to record and share TV programs around your home might be reason enough to build a home network.

FIGURE 1.4

A typical Windows Media Center Edition PC connected to a large-screen TV.

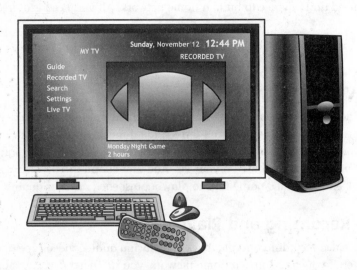

Digital Audio File Sharing and Playback

If you like music, chances are you enjoy converting (*ripping*) your music CDs into digital audio files such as MP3 or Windows Media Audio (WMA). But if you really want to enjoy listening to your digital library, you need a better way than sitting down in front of your computer and putting on earphones or turning on a tiny set of speakers.

With a home network and a home theater system, you can sit in your den or living room with a remote control and media adapter and select your favorite audio tracks. Choose by song title, artist, or genre and the music you select plays through your home theater system. You also can enjoy other family members' digital music collections. Set up a shared music folder on a PC connected to the home network and copy everyone's music files to that folder, and you can enjoy the ultimate mix of digital music from bluegrass to Bernstein in glorious surround sound.

A home network makes creating a music mix CD for playback in your car or portable stereo system easier as well. By putting all your music files into the same location, you simplify the process of selecting the music you want.

When you combine digital music players and adapters (Figure 1.5) with broadband Internet access, music fans can purchase and download favorite digital music tracks online while other family members work, play, or study.

FIGURE 1.5

D-Link's DSM-320 MediaLounge media player enables you to play popular types of audio, video, and digital photos stored on your computers through your favorite TV or home theater equipment. Photo courtesy D-Link Systems, Inc.

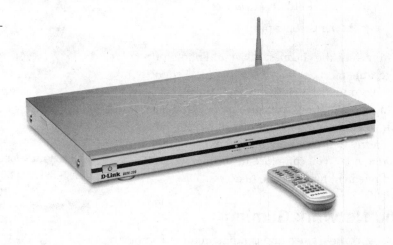

Digital Photo Storage, Viewing and Printing

Whether you prefer to shoot digital photos or scan existing photos, slides, and negatives, digital photography is hot! But viewing your photos on a relatively small computer monitor is not. Whether you're trying to find the best photo for a family greeting card, reviewing vacation photos, or reliving family memories, a home network makes it easy to put your photos on a big screen TV or data projector for better viewing.

Pop some corn and click your way through your family scrapbook. You can zoom in for a closeup and pan your way across your photos with the remote control included with many media adapters. You can even play your favorite music and display your photos at the same time.

If you want to create a portable slideshow of your photos or make prints of your best work, storing your photos in a single shared folder on your home network makes the selecting, editing, and printing processes a lot simpler than going from PC to PC and digging through the My Pictures folder.

By purchasing a single high-quality photo printer that you share through your home network—instead of installing lower-cost, lower-quality photo printers on each PC—you save money two ways:

- Lower overall hardware cost
- Lower cost per print

Ironically, the cheapest inkjet and photo printers cost the most per page because of low-capacity ink tanks and less sophisticated printheads. By spending more up front, you save money in the long run. If you choose a photo printer that can connect directly to the network instead of being shared from a PC, you can place the printer where it's convenient for everyone to access.

note

Most media servers and adapters support JPEG files (the most common file format used by digital cameras), but most also support other types of files. You can use a photo editor such as Adobe Photoshop Elements to convert photos stored in noncompatible formats into JPEG files if necessary.

Online and Network Gaming

Most console video and computer games can be played by just one player. However, it's not nearly as much fun to beat the game's built-in opponents as it is to outsmart other live players. With a home network, you can connect PCs or console games—such as Sony's PlayStation 2, Microsoft's Xbox, or Nintendo's GameCube—for multiroom home gaming against family and friends. You can even host a *LAN party* (a social event in which participants bring their own PCs, connect to a network, and play against other participants).

If you want to beat the world, you can also use shared Internet access and a home network to enable console and PC game players to take on the world while other home network users play or work online.

Home Networks for Lifelong Learning

Whether you're fifteen or fifty, PCs are an integral part of education today. A home network with shared Internet access makes it easy to keep the learning going after school, at night, and on weekends without affecting other home network users.

Research

With a home network and shared Internet access, students can access special databases at local libraries (Figure 1.6) and use online search engines such as Google (www.google.com) to discover the information needed for class assignments.

Certification and Continuing Education

If you're past school age, but involved in an industry that requires or recommends certification or continuing education credits, you can use a home network with shared Internet access to study, find books and other study aids, take practice tests, and schedule your exams.

Distance Education

A home network makes going to college without leaving home easy to do. Distance education, in which you learn through video or computer-presented classes, has become a popular way for older students who work to pick up classes or complete an undergraduate or graduate degree.

tip

GET THE CARD TO GET THE DATABASES

You can research the book holdings of any library with an online catalog from your home network's Internet connection. Similarly, you can find out what databases are offered by a library. However, if you want to check out books or have remote access to the entire collection of online databases, you need a library card for that library system.

Even if your local library is small and has limited resources, cooperative arrangements with other libraries and interlibrary loans can make any library's card a gateway to richer sources of information elsewhere. If you live in a county or state near a library but you don't qualify for a free library card, find out whether you can get a *nonresident card* (also known as a *subscription card*). In some cases, an annual nonresident card is only the cost of a couple of CDs or a hardcover novel—a great bargain!

Reminder to provide library card number when prompted.

FIGURE 1.6

A partial list of the online databases available at the Evansville-Vanderburgh (Indiana) Public Library System. Note that some databases are not available to home users, and others might require you to enter your library card number.

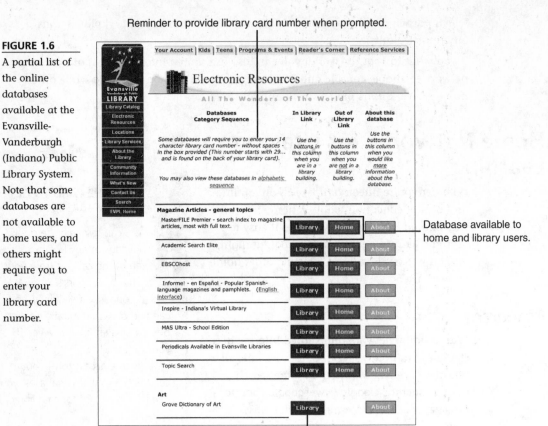

Database available to home and library users.

Database available in library only.

Whether you're in a class conducted on a live basis with videoconferencing or one that uses text chat for interaction between students, you read a lesson delivered by email and take tests, or you take your class in some other fashion, the combination of a broadband Internet connection and a home network assures that study, work, and play using the Internet or your home network can all take place at the same time.

Home Networks for Business

Bringing work home from the office once involved filling up a briefcase or two, spreading paperwork all over the kitchen table, and gathering lots of pencils, pens, erasers, and correction fluid. Today, the briefcase might still be bulky, but a lot of work after hours involves the home PC moonlighting as a part-time corporate asset.

Remote Access to Corporate Networks

Although you can access a suitably configured corporate network with just a dial-up modem, the painfully slow transfer rates and lack of security in traditional direct dial-up access aren't very popular anymore. Using a dial-up modem also prevents others at home from using the telephone while you're connected to your corporate network.

Today, most firms that allow employees access from home use a technology called *virtual private networking (VPN)*. VPN enables you to connect with a corporate network via the Internet, protecting the connection with *tunneling* protocols and encryption. You should contact the IT department at your company to see which products and software it recommends for VPN access.

Although you can access a corporate network through a dial-up Internet connection, sharing the Internet connection with a home network is a much better solution. Most home-network routers support a single VPN connection using *passthrough*. If two or more people in your home need to connect to different corporate networks at the same time, you can get more powerful routers that support multiple VPN tunnels.

With a home network and shared Internet access, you can connect via VPN to your corporate network while other home network users use the network and the Internet for work or play.

Remote access enables you to transfer files between your PC and the office PC or network, print to the office printer, and run applications including email or office suites.

Access to Corporate Email

You can check your email from multiple computers, but if you're not careful, you can wind up with email files on various PCs. Many email clients use the *POP3 protocol,* which stores email on the hard disk of the computer used to retrieve the email. By combining remote-access software with your home network and shared Internet access, you can check your email from home or other locations and keep all your email stored on just one computer.

> **tip**
>
> **UNIVERSAL REMOTE ACCESS WITH GO TO MY PC**
>
> Even if your office network is a small one that lacks VPN capability, you can still enjoy a fast secure connection with secure remote-access software. Go to My PC (www.gotomypc.com) is a long-time favorite of mine. You can use any Web browser (including your home PC and PCs on the road) to connect to the host PC, and multiple PC and enterprise versions are available for larger networks. Go to My PC works great: I've saved many trips to the office by using it while my home network is also being used for other activities.

Conclusion

As you can see, whether it's for entertainment, education, or working from home, home networking makes a lot of sense. But, before you run to the store and fill your shopping cart with network doodads, it's time to take a closer look at the hardware and software used to build a home network. To learn more about these building blocks of the home network, join me in Chapter 2, "Building Blocks of the Home Network."

THE ABSOLUTE MINIMUM

A network combines two or more connected computers that share information and resources.

A home network can contain both PCs and other devices, such as home theater systems, digital video recorders, and console game systems. A home network enables the sharing of information, multimedia files, and printers for both recreational and business use.

As in business networking, home networking enables you to save money by purchasing a single high-performance printer or hard disk upgrade and sharing it among multiple users. Home networks are easier to configure than business networks because the devices in a home network are designed to work with each other.

A home theater system can be connected to a home network to enable digital music files stored on a PC to be played in surround sound. A TV connected to a home network can also be used to play video files or photos stored on a PC. A media adapter or media player interfaces the home theater system and TV to the home network.

Digital recordings made by a network-equipped DVR can be transferred to another DVR of the same type for playback. Digital recordings made with PC-based DVR hardware can be viewed on other PCs or on a TV connected to a home network.

You can play against other network or online players with console games or PCs on a home network equipped with shared Internet access. With a home network with shared Internet access, you have access to school, library, distance learning, and continuing education resources while other users work and play. A home network with shared Internet access can support simultaneous business and recreational uses, including VPN and other types of secure connections and access to corporate email.

2

BUILDING BLOCKS OF THE HOME NETWORK

A home network can connect your computers and home entertainment devices to make them more fun and more powerful. In this chapter, you discover the hardware options you can choose from to make your home network dreams come true.

What Makes a Home Network Work?

In Chapter 1, "What Is a Home Network?" you learned about the many benefits of home networking:

- Interactive gaming
- Enjoying digital media
- Securely working from home
- Learning and education

You explored combinations of computers and other devices that can be connected via a home network. In this chapter, you learn *what* connects the parts of a home network.

Network Types

As you learned in Chapter 1, a network is any collection of computers and devices that share information with each other. There are many different types of networks on the market. The following sections discuss the major features of each type of network.

Wired Networks

Traditionally, the least expensive network to buy has been a wired network. A *wired network* connects its components with some type of signal cable. If you plan to work at home, some types of wired networks also provide the fastest connections possible between computers and devices.

There are three major types of wired networks:

- ethernet
- HomePNA (phoneline)
- HomePlug (powerline)

Ethernet

Ethernet is the oldest network technology suitable for home use; although its earliest form was developed more than 30 years ago for business, Ethernet continues to be the most common wired network in

GIGABIT ETHERNET PLAYS NICE WITH SLOWER SPEEDS

A few new computers include Gigabit Ethernet, which runs at 1,000Mbps, but also works with 10BASE-T and 10/100 Ethernet adapters.

both home and business environments, and it also can be used alongside wireless networks.

Many recent desktop and notebook computers incorporate a 10/100 Ethernet adapter. Depending on the devices it is connected to, this type of Ethernet adapter runs at either 10Mbps (also known as 10BASE-T) or 100Mbps (Fast Ethernet) speeds. If your computer doesn't include an Ethernet adapter, you can add one for less than $50 in most cases.

Ethernet network adapters communicate with each other through a centralized device known as a *hub* or a *switch*. Most network hardware—including broadband Internet access devices, home media players, and network-compatible video games—supports Ethernet.

HomePNA

HomePNA network adapters connect to your home telephone wiring, so you don't need to run additional cables through your home. That feature makes HomePNA attractive, as does HomePNA's capability of working without interfering with normal telephone use (you can plug your phone into the adapter; a separate cable runs from the adapter to the telephone jack in the wall).

However, there are two major drawbacks to using HomePNA as your only network:

■ You need to add HomePNA adapters to your PC; hardly any PCs include a HomePNA adapter.

■ Although you can get HomePNA-compatible routers for shared Internet access, there are very few home entertainment devices that are HomePNA-compatible.

Consequently, I suggest you look at HomePNA primarily as a means of extending the reach of an Ethernet or wireless Ethernet network. Most HomePNA products on the market today support HomePNA 2.0, which runs at 10Mbps; avoid HomePNA 1.0 network adapters, which run at just 1Mbps. Although HomePNA 2.0 runs at only a tenth of the speed of Fast Ethernet, it is fast enough

note

UNDERSTANDING HOMEPNA, DSL, AND DIAL-UP MODEMS

HomePNA, DSL Internet access, and dial-up modem Internet access all use telephone lines, but they're otherwise very different. HomePNA connects computers within your home to each other via the telephone lines in the walls of your home, and it can be used to share various types of Internet access. DSL Internet access piggybacks on the telephone line coming into your home, enabling you to connect to the Internet and talk on the telephone at the same time. Dial-up modems also connect to the Internet, but prevent you from using your telephone while the connection is active.

for accessing shared folders and shared printers and for Internet access.

HomePlug

HomePlug uses the power lines in your home to connect your computers. A HomePlug adapter plugs into an electrical outlet and uses a USB cable to connect to your computer.

HomePlug networks run at a top speed of 14Mbps, slower than Fast Ethernet, but fast enough for accessing shared folders and shared printers and for Internet access.

Like HomePNA, HomePlug can be connected to Ethernet networks through a bridge, so it can be used where Ethernet wiring is not feasible.

Wireless

Networking without wires has become a reality in both home and office environments. Wireless networking isn't much more expensive these days than wired Ethernet, and is the hottest home networking trend today.

Although several types of infrared and radio-frequency networks have come and gone over the years, there are only two major flavors of wireless networking on the market today:

- Wireless Ethernet (often called *Wi-Fi*)
- Bluetooth

Wireless Ethernet and Wi-Fi

Wireless Ethernet (officially known as the IEEE-802.11 family of standards) is the hottest network technology right now, and no wonder. Radio waves carry network traffic hundreds of feet indoors and out, so you don't have the mess or expense of network cable. The same hardware works in home and office wireless networks, so you can use your notebook computer, PDA, or smart phone with wireless Ethernet in both places to connect to the Internet.

"BRIDGING" THE DIFFERENCES BETWEEN HOMEPNA AND ETHERNET

You can interconnect HomePNA and Ethernet networks together with a device known as a *bridge*. A bridge also enables you to add Ethernet-compatible devices to a HomePNA network.

POWERLINE NETWORKING FOR INTERNET ACCESS

In the future, you might also get broadband Internet access through the powerline connection coming into your home. Broadband over Powerline (BPL) is already being tested in some U.S. markets. See Chapter 4, "Choosing a Broadband Internet Access Technology," for more information.

Wireless Ethernet home networking works with game consoles and home entertainment hardware, too, so you can create a 100% wireless home network that covers all your information, entertainment, and education needs.

Because wireless Ethernet is based on Ethernet, it's easy to connect these networks to each other. In fact, most wireless access points (which transmit signals between wireless Ethernet stations) include an Ethernet network switch. My home network includes both wired and wireless connections.

There are a couple of complicating factors to keep in mind when you consider wireless Ethernet:

- Frequencies
- Wi-Fi Certified and noncertified hardware

Wireless Ethernet and Wi-Fi are often considered the same thing. That's not exactly correct. Wi-Fi hardware is wireless Ethernet hardware that has passed the Wi-Fi Alliance (http://www.wi-fi.org) certification tests for interoperability with other brands of hardware. In other words, all Wi-Fi Certified hardware is wireless Ethernet, but not all wireless Ethernet hardware is Wi-Fi Certified. If you want to mix-and-match wireless Ethernet hardware in your home network, or to help assure that you can use the same wireless Ethernet adapter at home and at the office or while traveling, be sure to look for Wi-Fi Certified hardware. Wi-Fi Certified hardware is marked with one of the labels shown in Figure 2.1. The simpler labels in the middle and right of Figure 2.1 have recently been introduced to help users more easily determine which 802.11 standard is supported by a particular Wi-Fi product. The check marks on the label at left indicate which Wi-Fi certifications and frequencies the device supports. The product in the figure supports IEEE 802.11b (11Mbps) speeds and WPA security, but can also connect with IEEE 802.11g (54Mbps) devices because both use the 2.4GHz frequency.

FIGURE 2.1

Typical product box labels indicating Wi-Fi certification.

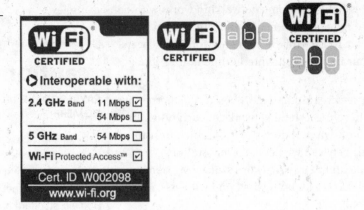

Although there are three different flavors of Wi-Fi, the best one to build your home network around is IEEE 802.11g (Wireless-G). There are several reasons to make this your choice:

- Wireless-G equipment uses the same radio frequency, 2.4GHz, as Wireless-B (B is the original version of Wi-Fi), so G and B equipment works on the same network.

- Wireless-G is up to five times faster than Wireless-B (when you use Wireless-G network adapters and wireless access points), so your wireless network is faster.

- Wireless-G hardware is easy to find at any store that stocks Wi-Fi and wireless Ethernet hardware.

What about Wireless-B? You should consider Wireless-B hardware when Wireless-G hardware is not available for a particular task. For example, although Wireless-G network adapters and wireless access points are widely available, media adapters and other specialized equipment are often available only in Wireless-B speeds. Also, many notebooks with integrated Wi-Fi adapters, such as those equipped with the original version of Intel's Centrino technology, support Wireless-B.

What about Wireless-A? Wireless-A was originally developed to provide better performance and longer range in a corporate environment than Wireless-B. Wireless-A uses a different radio frequency (5GHz) than a Wireless-G or Wireless-B network (2.4GHz), so it can't connect to these networks unless dual-band (A+B or A+G) hardware is used. Dual-mode A+G network adapters enable a computer to connect to home and corporate wireless networks and public hotspots with a single adapter. Linksys has developed dual-band A+G hardware for home networks that routes streaming video and other high-bandwidth traffic over the 5GHz frequency while web surfing and other traffic is routed over the 2.4GHz frequency.

Wi-Fi and wireless Ethernet networks can be configured in a *peer-to-peer mode* for direct connection between computers or devices. However, this mode won't work for Internet sharing or for connections to other networks. Instead, use the *infrastructure mode,* which uses a wireless access point to transfer signals between computers.

Bluetooth

Many PC peripherals—such as printers, mice, and keyboards—and non-PC electronics products—from digicams to cell phones—have built-in Bluetooth capability. Bluetooth capability can be added to other devices.

However, Bluetooth is not a full-blown home network. Bluetooth is used between pairs of devices for data exchange, rather than as a full-blown network with the capability of sharing Internet access, printers, folders, or media files. Its speed is only 500Kbps.

Sharing Broadband Internet Access

As I suggested in Chapter 1, broadband Internet access has become the number one reason for setting up a home network. Instead of fighting over seat time at the PC with the fast Internet connection, you can install a home network and give everybody equal access to home banking, homework sites, digital music servers, movie trailers, weather, online gaming, and much more.

Broadband Internet access is often defined as Internet access with download speeds more than 100Kbps; in practice, most providers support download speeds of 384Kbps or faster (more than seven times faster than the fastest dial-up modem). And, although some older types of broadband Internet access used an ordinary dial-up modem for uploads (tying up your phone line), almost all broadband Internet service today is two-way service, which doesn't interfere with your ability to take or make telephone calls.

A home network designed for sharing broadband Internet access resembles a home network that shares peripherals, but with a couple of differences:

tip

B & G—HAPPY TOGETHER, BUT AT A PRICE

Many Wireless-G wireless access points and routers provide slower performance in networks that have both Wireless-B and Wireless-G hardware. If you're looking for maximum performance in a mixed B/G network, be sure to look at product reviews at sources such as *PC World* (http://www.pcworld .com), *PC Magazine* (http://www.pcmag.com), PracticallyNetworked (http://www.practicallynetworked .com), and others to see which devices provide the best performance in a mixed network.

■ You need a broadband Internet access device.

■ You need to connect the PCs to each other *and* to the broadband access device.

Broadband Internet Devices

The leading broadband Internet service types include cable (brought to you by your friendly cable TV company) and DSL (brought to you in cooperation with your local phone company). However, they're not the only choices. Whether you live in the city, the suburbs, or out in the country, you can get satellite Internet if you have an unobstructed view of the sky toward the equator. Other emerging broadband technologies include wireless and powerline.

Regardless of the type of broadband service you choose, almost all use some type of external device (often called an *XXX* modem—fill in the *X's* with the service type) to make the connection. Figure 2.2 shows a typical cable modem, which connects your computer to the cable TV network.

FIGURE 2.2

A typical cable modem, which can connect to Ethernet or USB ports. Photo courtesy of D-Link Systems, Inc.

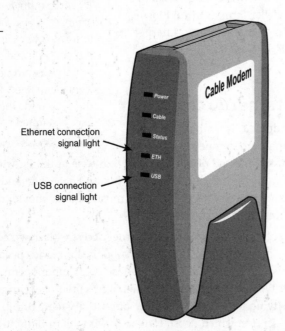

Broadband Internet Access Sharing Methods

Sharing an Internet connection may be the number one reason to build a home network. It's been possible for several years, but as long as the Internet connection was being made with a slow dial-up modem that used the telephone line, it wasn't all that useful to most users.

Dial-up Internet access prevents you from making telephone calls while you use the Internet, and you need special software or updated modems to be able to take telephone calls while you're online. A dial-up connection is painfully slow for a single user, and even slower when two or more users are connecting at the same time.

However, when you combine broadband Internet access with a home network, everybody on the network and every device on the network can connect with the world's largest network without tying up your telephone line.

There are a couple of ways to make the connection between your home network and the Internet:

- You can connect your broadband Internet device to your PC and add a second network adapter to connect the PC to the rest of the network.

- You can connect your network to a router, which detects and routes traffic heading to or from the Internet to the correct computer on the home network.

The first method requires you to install Internet-sharing software on the PC connected to the Internet. Windows 98 Second Edition and later versions, including Windows XP, offer Internet Connection Sharing (ICS). One major drawback of ICS is that when the ICS host PC is turned off or locks up, Internet access fails for everybody on the network.

The second method helps protect all your PCs against intruders and doesn't care which PCs are running at any time. Most routers made for wired Ethernet networks include a switch, so you can replace your switch with a router and use one device for both jobs. Similarly, wireless routers also act as access points, so one device connects the wireless stations to each other and to the Internet. Most wireless routers, such as the one shown in Figure 2.3, also include a switch, so you can network wired and wireless computers together.

Routers are available for all the home networks covered in this book, including Ethernet, Wi-Fi, HomePNA, and HomePlug.

tip

ROUTER OR SWITCH? HERE'S HOW TO TELL THE DIFFERENCE

Routers have a WAN (wide area network) port (Figure 2.3). The WAN port connects the router to the broadband Internet device. It's often located next to the switch ports for each computer (they're usually numbered starting with 1). If you don't see a WAN port, you don't have a router.

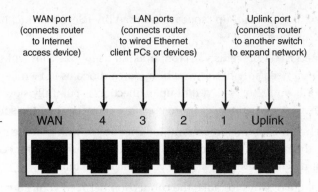

FIGURE 2.3

The rear of a typical router incorporating a four-port Ethernet switch.

Mix-and-Match Networking

As the previous sections suggest, you can mix and match network hardware through the use of bridges, switches, or dual-frequency network adapters. Although it's sometimes easier to run a "pure" network, one that uses only a single network standard, mix-and-match networking can help you

- Bridge coverage gaps in a wireless network.
- Extend an existing network without rewiring.

I show you specific examples of mix-and-match networking to solve these and similar problems later in this chapter.

What You Need to Build Your Home Network

A home network, like any network, has three types of components:

- Network hardware
- Network software
- Network protocols

If any one of these is missing, has failed, or is not configured properly, your home network turns into a disjointed collection of standalone components.

To create a home network, you need to connect the computers and other devices on the network to each other. This requires at least three elements:

- Network adapters (devices to connect each computer to the network)
- A method of transmitting data between computers (cable or radio waves)
- A method of coordinating the exchange of data (a hub, switch, or wireless access point)

Most home networks are used to share Internet access, so two additional components are needed to connect the network to the Internet: a router or gateway, and a broadband Internet access device such as a cable, DSL, satellite, or fixed wireless broadband modem.

Although computers sometimes include a network adapter, you must buy other components to complete your home network, particularly if you want to share Internet access. Network software is provided by the maker of your network hardware if the necessary software is not already part of your version of Windows or other operating system. Network protocols are provided as part of Windows or other operating systems.

It can be confusing to figure out exactly what you need to build the network you have in mind. In the following sections, I'll show you each type of network hardware and provide you with a shopping list for each type of network.

SAVE MONEY WITH COMBINATION DEVICES

Although switches, wireless access points, and routers can be separate devices, you can usually buy combination devices that include multiple functions. For example, most wireless access points made for home networks also include a router, and most also include an Ethernet switch. I recommend using combo devices because they save money and space. A single device is also easier to cable and easier to hide!

Wi-Fi Home Network Components

A Wi-Fi network needs the following components:

- Wi-Fi adapter for each PC or other device on the network

A Wi-Fi network that will be used to provide Internet access also needs:

- Wireless access point (WAP)
- Router (to connect the network to broadband Internet service)

Typically, the WAP and router are combined into a single unit, which might also contain a built-in Ethernet switch.

How do these components fit together? Read on!

Wi-Fi Network Adapters

A *network adapter* is an internal card or external device that enables a computer or other device to connect to a network and exchange data with other computers. A Wi-Fi network adapter must use a standard (Wireless-G, B, or A) that is the same, or is compatible with, other computers and devices on the network.

Figure 2.4 provides examples of different types of network adapters used by Wi-Fi wireless networks.

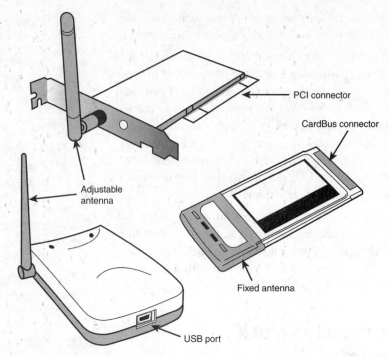

FIGURE 2.4

A PCI card for a wireless Ethernet (Wi-Fi) network (top) compared to a CardBus card (middle right) and a USB adapter (lower left). Photos courtesy D-Link Systems, Inc.

If you're adding a portable computer (laptop or PDA) to your home network, it might already include a built-in Wi-Fi adapter. Check your system documentation to find out whether it does. If your computer doesn't have a Wi-Fi adapter, you need to add one. Table 2.1 reviews your choices.

Table 2.1 Wi-Fi Network Adapter Types

Network Adapter	Connection Type	Computer Type	Notes	Benefits
External USB	USB port	Desktop or notebook PC	USB 2.0 devices; can also work with slower USB 1.1 ports	Easy to move between computers; some also work with console game systems
Internal PCI card	PCI slot	Desktop PC	Requires opening the case	Faster than USB 1.1 adapters
Internal Type II CardBus	CardBus slot	Notebook PC	32-bit (wide, fast connection) version of PC Card	Faster than USB 1.1 adapters

Although you can build a so-called *ad hoc* network by using Wi-Fi adapters, a Wi-Fi network running in *ad hoc* mode doesn't support shared Internet access. To share Internet access, you need a wireless access point and a router, and you need to configure your Wi-Fi hardware to run in *infrastructure* mode.

Wi-Fi Wireless Access Points and Routers

If you want to build a home Wi-Fi network with a potentially global reach, you need to include a wireless access point (WAP) and a router in your network.

A *WAP* transmits radio signals between stations on a Wi-Fi network and can relay signals between the network and a router. A *router* connects one network to another. A WAP and a router can be combined into a single unit. When you have broadband Internet, you have a connection to the world's biggest network (the Internet), and a

FIGURE 2.5

A wireless access point/router that includes an Ethernet switch. Photo courtesy of Linksys, a division of Cisco Systems, Inc.

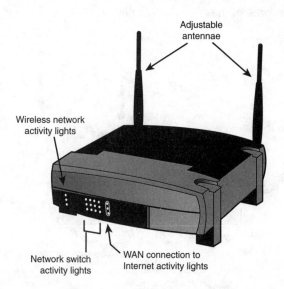

Adjustable antennae

Wireless network activity lights

Network switch activity lights

WAN connection to Internet activity lights

router connects your home network with the Internet. Figure 2.5 shows a typical access point with integrated router and switch.

If parts of your home or property are too far away from a WAP to enjoy a fast or reliable connection, you can add additional WAPs that can relay the signal to the WAP/router or replace the standard antennas on the WAP/router with more powerful versions to improve network performance and reliability.

Specialized Wi-Fi Adapters

Home networking isn't just for PCs anymore, and Wi-Fi networking can be used to connect a wide variety of devices to your home network:

- ▓ *Printers*—Move your printer away from your PC to a more central location by connecting it to a Wi-Fi print server.
- ▓ *Home theater and big-screen TV*—View video or photos or play back digital music in your living room or den by adding a Wi-Fi media adapter.
- ▓ *Console video games*—Play head-to-head or against online foes by adding a Wi-Fi game adapter to the network port on leading console games.
- ▓ *Home security*—Keep an eye on your home with a Wi-Fi video camera or Wi-Fi enabled home security system.

Figure 2.6 illustrates some of these specialized devices.

FIGURE 2.6

Specialized Wi-Fi devices help you connect game consoles, printers, and home entertainment devices to your network and keep an eye on your home. Photo courtesy of Linksys, a division of Cisco Systems, Inc.

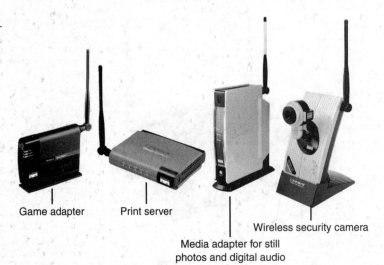

Game adapter   Print server

Wireless security camera

Media adapter for still
photos and digital audio

Diagramming Your Wi-Fi Network

When you take both Wireless-G and Wireless-B devices into account, a Wi-Fi home network can include almost any computing or entertainment device you can imagine. As a consequence, there are many configurations possible. The following sections outline two typical configurations to consider.

Configuration 1: Local Networking with a Media Adapter

In this configuration, you use Wi-Fi strictly for local networking between PCs and add a media adapter so you can play media through your home theater system. Figure 2.7 shows you how this network might look.

FIGURE 2.7

A Wi-Fi home network used to share files between PCs and a home theater system.

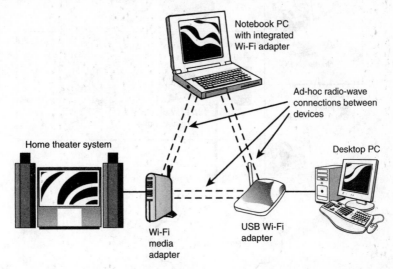

Notebook PC with integrated Wi-Fi adapter

Ad-hoc radio-wave connections between devices

Home theater system

Desktop PC

Wi-Fi media adapter

USB Wi-Fi adapter

Optional components are available. In configuration 1, you can add any other Wi-Fi adapters that can run in ad hoc (peer-to-peer) mode, such as print servers, but you cannot share an Internet connection.

Configuration 2: Shared Internet Access with Print Server

This configuration is great for working and learning at home. By sharing broadband Internet access with the network, everyone can use the Internet for learning, research, and fun. A print server enables you to put the printer where it's convenient for all users. Figure 2.8 shows you how this configuration might look.

Optional components also are available with configuration 2. You can add any other Wi-Fi adapters that can run in infrastructure mode, such as media adapters, game adapters, wireless video cameras, and practically all other Wi-Fi devices.

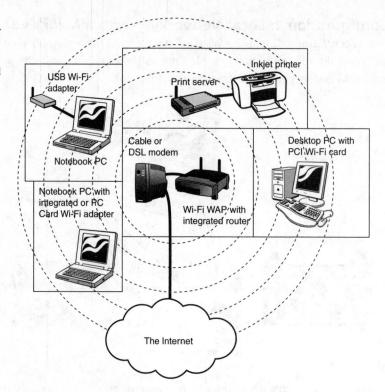

Ethernet Home Network Components

An Ethernet network needs the following components:

- Ethernet adapter for each PC or other device on the network
- A switch or hub to transfer data between each computer or other device on the network
- A CAT5-or-better network cable between each PC and each port on the hub or switch

An Ethernet network that will be used to provide Internet access also needs the following:

- A router (to connect the network to broadband Internet service)

Typically, the router includes a built-in Ethernet switch.

How do these components fit together? Read on!

Ethernet Network Adapters

Although many recent systems have a built-in 10/100 Ethernet adapter (such an adapter runs at 10Mbps or 100Mbps, depending on the switch or hub it is connected to), you might need to add an Ethernet adapter to a PC you want to add to a network.

Most Ethernet network adapters sold today support 10/100 Ethernet; although some vendors now sell Gigabit Ethernet (10/100/1000) adapters, there's no reason to get one unless you're willing to equip your entire network with gigabit adapters and switches.

Figure 2.9 provides examples of different types of network adapters used by Ethernet networks. The PCI card adapter (top left) plugs into an empty PCI card slot in a desktop computer. The USB adapter (bottom left) plugs into the USB port on any recent computer. The PC Card adapter (top right) fits into any notebook computer's Type II PC Card slot. However, most recent notebook computers can use the faster CardBus card (bottom right).

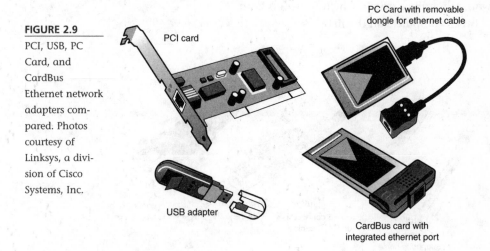

FIGURE 2.9
PCI, USB, PC Card, and CardBus Ethernet network adapters compared. Photos courtesy of Linksys, a division of Cisco Systems, Inc.

PCI card

PC Card with removable dongle for ethernet cable

USB adapter

CardBus card with integrated ethernet port

Ethernet Network Cables

Wired Ethernet networks use Category (CAT) 5, 5e, or 6 cable. This type of cable runs between each PC's network adapter and the hub or switch that relays information between PCs.

Both wired and wireless *routers,* which connect home networks to the Internet, connect to cable modems and other broadband access devices with a CAT 5/5e/6 cable.

The connector on the end of a CAT5/5e/6 cable is known as an RJ-45 connector. It has eight connectors and resembles the RJ-11 connector used by telephones, dial-up modems, HomePNA networks, and DSL internet access. Figure 2.10 compares RJ-45 and RJ-11 connectors to the USB connectors used on some types of network adapters.

Ethernet Switches, Hubs, and Routers

The center of attention in a wired Ethernet network is a hub or switch. A CAT5/5e/6 cable (refer to Figure 2.10) connects each computer on the network to a hub or switch, which transmits data between computers on the network.

note

"WIRELESS" ETHERNET SOMETIMES NEEDS A CABLE

It's often easier to configure a Wi-Fi WAP, game adapter, or other device by connecting it to a wired Ethernet port on a PC. That's one reason why many Wi-Fi devices also have a 10BASE-T or 10/100 Ethernet port.

FIGURE 2.10

From left to right, a telephone cable, a CAT 5 network cable, and both ends of a standard USB cable.

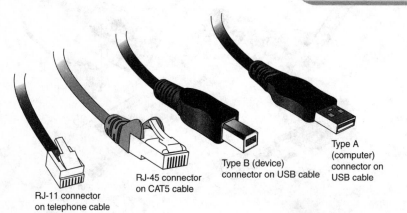

RJ-11 connector on telephone cable

RJ-45 connector on CAT5 cable

Type B (device) connector on USB cable

Type A (computer) connector on USB cable

Although hubs and switches look similar (both have multiple RJ-45 ports on one side of the unit and signal lights on the front or top), they work in different ways. A *hub* broadcasts all the data it receives to all the computers plugged into it; a *switch* sets up a direct connection between transmitter and receiver, making for a faster connection. Switches also support the full speed of the

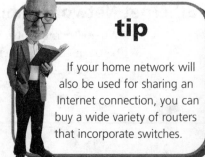

tip

If your home network will also be used for sharing an Internet connection, you can buy a wide variety of routers that incorporate switches.

…e available speed of the network among … time, switches were much more expen- …argely replaced by low-cost switches.

…to share Internet access through an Ethernet network, you should use a router with an *integrated switch* instead of a switch. The WAN port on the router connects to the broadband Internet access device, and the LAN ports on the router connect to the PCs on the home network.

Specialized Ethernet Adapters

Like its wireless sibling, Wi-Fi, Ethernet also offers a host of specialized devices that can spread home networking goodness beyond your PCs. In fact, some print servers, media adapters, and game adapters that are primarily marketed to Wi-Fi users also work with Ethernet networks.

Diagramming Your Ethernet Network

An Ethernet home network can support a wide variety of PCs and other devices. Here are two typical configurations to consider.

note

NETWORK CABLE CATEGORIES

Although CAT5, CAT5e, and CAT6 can all be used with 10/100 Ethernet and Gigabit Ethernet networks and use the same connectors, there are some differences between them. CAT5e supports the same wire speeds as CAT5, but meets certification standards that are not specified for CAT5. CAT6 supports faster wire speeds than CAT5 or 5e, but for home networks all three are essentially interchangeable. Get the technical lowdown on the entire range of network cable standards from the Discount Cables USA Ethernet Cables page at http://discountcablesusa.com/ethernet-cables.html.

Configuration 1: Two-Station Local Network

In this configuration, you use a crossover RJ-45 cable to make a direct connection between two PCs' Ethernet ports. You can't share Internet access or add additional PCs with this configuration, but for simple folder and printer sharing between two computers, it works very nicely.

This configuration has no optional components. You can share additional printers, drives, or similar devices connected to either PC in a two-station network, but you cannot add other computers or network devices. If either computer has an Internet connection (dial-up or broadband), it cannot be shared using this configuration.

Configuration 2: Shared Internet Access with Print Server and Media Adapter

In this configuration, you have a great setup for working and learning at home. By sharing broadband Internet access with the network, everyone can use the Internet for learning, research, and fun.

CROSSOVER AND STANDARD CAT5/5E/6 CABLES

A normal CAT5/5e/6 cable has matching wire pairs at each end. A crossover cable reverses some of the wire pairs. If you build a two-station network similar to the one shown in Figure 2.12 and later decide to expand it with a router or switch, you need to replace the crossover cable with standard cables that run from each PC to the switch. Be sure to mark the crossover cable so you don't mix it up with standard cables.

FIGURE 2.12

A two-station Ethernet home network used to share files and printers between PCs.

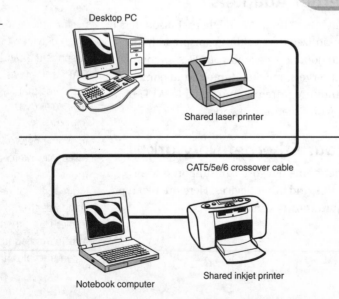

Desktop PC

Shared laser printer

CAT5/5e/6 crossover cable

Notebook computer

Shared inkjet printer

A print server enables you to put the printer where it's convenient for all users, and a media adapter allows you to play audio and other types of media through your home theater system. Figure 2.13 shows you how this configuration might look.

FIGURE 2.13

An Ethernet home network with shared broadband Internet access, a print server, and a media adapter.

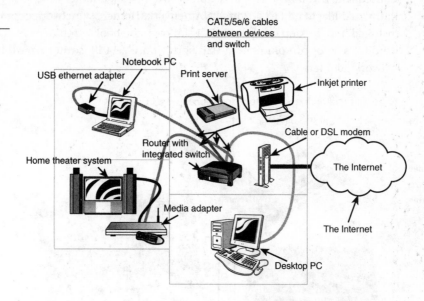

Optional components are available in configuration 2. You can add as many computers or other devices as you want—including game systems, projectors, and others—by connecting them to the appropriate Ethernet adapter. If you need additional ports for new devices, you can add a switch to the uplink port on the router's integrated switch.

HomePNA Home Network Components

A HomePNA network needs the following components:

■ One HomePNA adapter for each PC or other device on the network

A HomePNA network that will be used to provide Internet access also needs the following:

■ A router (to connect the network to broadband Internet service)

Keep reading to see how the pieces of a HomePNA network fit together.

HomePNA Network Adapters

It's extremely rare for a computer to include a HomePNA network adapter. Consequently, you need to add a HomePNA network adapter to virtually any PC that you'd like to add to a HomePNA network. HomePNA network adapters can be installed in a desktop computer's PCI slot or a notebook computer's PC Card or CardBus slot, or can plug into a USB port. Figure 2.14 illustrates typical HomePNA network adapters.

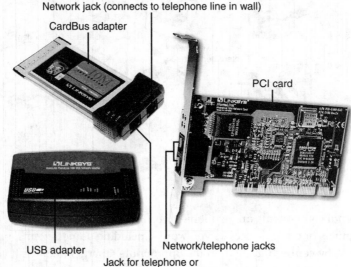

Network jack (connects to telephone line in wall)

CardBus adapter

PCI card

USB adapter

Network/telephone jacks

Jack for telephone or additional HomePNA adapters

FIGURE 2.14

Typical HomePNA network adapters. Photos courtesy of Linksys, a division of Cisco Systems, Inc.

Unlike Ethernet, which requires a hub or switch if more than two computers are used, a HomePNA network uses daisy-chaining to connect to the rest of the network. A HomePNA 2.0 network can handle up to 50 HomePNA network adapters using up to 1,000 feet of telephone cable—far more than enough for the typical home network.

If all you want is to share files and printers, you're set.

HomePNA Routers

As with other types of home networks, a router is necessary if you want to use your HomePNA network to share an Internet connection. A HomePNA router resembles an Ethernet router, but it includes one or more HomePNA ports.

Some routers made for HomePNA networks can also connect to Ethernet networks. These routers have a single LAN port, which must be connected to an external switch.

Specialized HomePNA Adapters

Unlike Ethernet and Wi-Fi, HomePNA product offerings are generally limited to adapters for PCs and routers. There are few digital entertainment products available for HomePNA.

However, you can bridge an Ethernet network to your HomePNA network. This enables you to use Ethernet-based home entertainment, gaming, and multimedia adapters with your HomePNA network.

Diagramming Your HomePNA Network

There are two basic configurations possible in a pure HomePNA network.

Configuration 1: Local Network

In this configuration, your HomePNA network is used for file and printer sharing. Figure 2.15 shows you how this configuration might look.

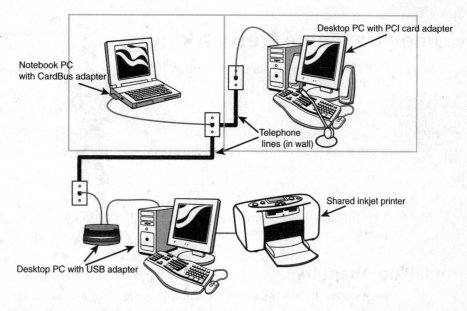

FIGURE 2.15

A three-station HomePNA home network used to share files and printers between PCs.

Notebook PC with CardBus adapter

Desktop PC with PCI card adapter

Telephone lines (in wall)

Shared inkjet printer

Desktop PC with USB adapter

Optional components include other HomePNA adapters, including media adapters.

Configuration 2: Shared Internet Access

In this configuration, everyone can use the Internet for learning, research, and fun. Figure 2.16 shows you how this configuration might look.

FIGURE 2.16

A HomePNA
home network
with shared
broadband
Internet access.

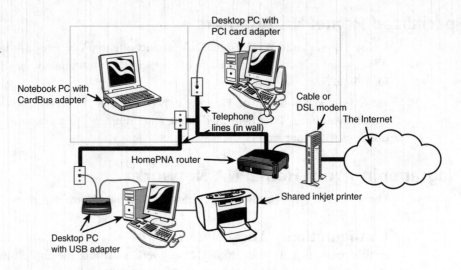

FIGURE 2.16
A HomePNA home network with shared broadband Internet access.

Optional components include other HomePNA adapters, including media adapters.

HomePlug Home Networking

A HomePlug home network needs the following components:

- One HomePlug adapter for each PC you want to add to the network

If you want to share an Internet connection, you also need the following:

- A router

To learn more about HomePlug hardware, read on.

tip

MIXING HOMEPNA WITH OTHER NETWORKS

For more information about using HomePNA with other networks, see "Building a Mix-and-Match Network," p. **xxx**, later in this chapter.

HomePlug Adapters

HomePlug adapters plug into the AC wall socket. They connect to both desktop and notebook computers through USB ports. Figure 2.17 shows a typical HomePlug adapter.

HomePlug, like HomePNA, uses a peer-to-peer connection between computers. Thus, if you don't need shared Internet access, a HomePlug adapter for each PC is all you need to create a home network.

FIGURE 2.17
FIGURE 2.17
A typical
HomePlug
adapter. Photo
courtesy
GigaFast.

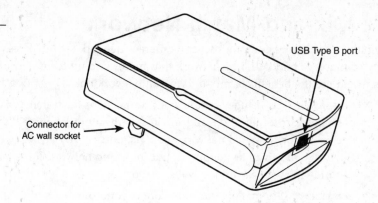

USB Type B port

Connector for
AC wall socket

HomePlug Routers

If you want to share Internet access on a HomePlug network, you need a router that is compatible with HomePlug, or one that can connect to a HomePlug network. Although several vendors make HomePlug-to-Ethernet bridges that can be used to connect HomePlug networks to an Ethernet-based router, routers with built-in HomePlug support are also available. A HomePlug router resembles an Ethernet router, but it includes a HomePlug connection to an AC power line.

Some of these routers also include an Ethernet switch, enabling you to connect Ethernet and HomePlug networks to the same broadband Internet connection.

Specialized HomePlug Adapters

HomePlug is the newest home network technology on the market, and so far it is being used only for PC-to-PC connectivity. However, you can bridge an Ethernet network to your HomePlug network. This enables you to use Ethernet-based home entertainment and multimedia adapters with your HomePlug network.

Diagramming Your HomePlug Network

A HomePlug network uses a peer-to-peer connection similar to a HomePNA network, except that HomePNA uses the telephone lines in your walls and HomePlug uses the AC power lines. Refer to Figures 2.15 and 2.16 for examples of typical configurations.

tip

MIXING HOMEPLUG WITH OTHER NETWORKS

For more information about using HomePlug with other networks, see the next section, "Building a Mix-and-Match Network."

Building a Mix-and-Match Network

Although this chapter examines several different network technologies, it's increasingly common to build a home network that mixes and matches network technologies. What are the benefits of mix-and-match networking?

■ *Cost savings*—By using wired network connections for systems or devices that are near your router and using wireless connections for more distant devices, you save money. Wired network adapters, particularly Ethernet, are less expensive than wireless adapters, but installing network cable, particularly if you hide the wire within the walls, can be costly.

■ *Convenience*—If parts of your home are beyond the reach of your WAP, it can be easier to use HomePlug or HomePNA to bring the network within reach of certain rooms or locations than to try to use multiple WAPs or other methods to boost range.

Here are examples of two typical mix-and-match network configurations. Configurations similar to these might help you conquer a tough network job in *your* home

FIGURE 2.18

A mixed Ethernet/Wi-Fi home network with shared Internet access.

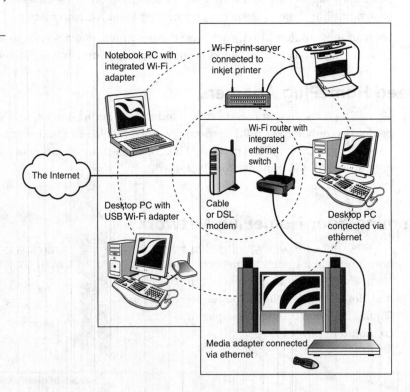

Notebook PC with integrated Wi-Fi adapter

Wi-Fi print-server connected to inkjet printer

Wi-Fi router with integrated ethernet switch

The Internet

Desktop PC with USB Wi-Fi adapter

Cable or DSL modem

Desktop PC connected via ethernet

Media adapter connected via ethernet

Configuration 1: Ethernet + Wi-Fi for Extra Speed in Video Playback

In this configuration (refer to Figure 2.18), the computer located next to the wireless router connects via its Ethernet port to the router's built-in switch, and other computers use Wi-Fi access. The media adapter also connects via Ethernet, but the print server uses Wi-Fi. By putting the computer storing streaming media and the media adapter on Ethernet connections, the connection has more than enough speed to handle streaming video (which requires higher speeds than still photos or audio).

Ethernet or Wi-Fi devices of all types are available as optional components.

Configuration 2: Wi-Fi + HomePlug to Cover Blind Spots

In this configuration (see Figure 2.19), a HomePlug network helps cover a part of the home where the Wi-Fi signal from the WAP/router is too weak for good coverage. This can happen because of building construction (brick or concrete walls can block Wi-Fi signals), antenna placement, or distance.

Wi-Fi or HomePlug adapters and devices are available optional components.

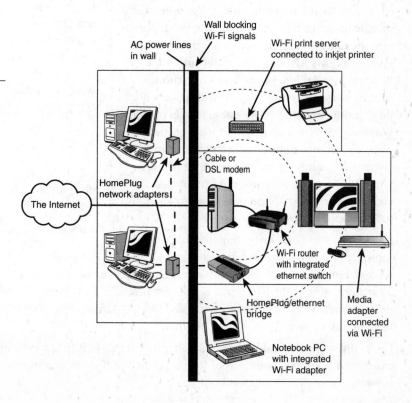

FIGURE 2.19

A mixed Wi-Fi/HomePlug home network with shared Internet access.

Network Software

Windows, MacOS, and Linux operating systems are all network-ready as installed. You don't need to install any third-party network software unless you want to improve security or add compatibility with a corporate network.

When you connect your computer to the home network, you might need to insert your operating system CD to install driver files or to enable file (folder) or printer sharing for a particular PC.

Network Protocols

You probably know that the Internet is the world's largest network. What's even more amazing is that there's no requirement that you have a specific brand or type of computer or use a particular operating system to access the Internet. The latest Windows XP-based computer running a Pentium 4 or Athlon 64 process can exchange instant messages, email, or files with a low-end iMac running MacOS or an aging laptop running Windows 95. When your web browser requests a web page from a computer a continent away, the computer hosting the website could be running Linux, Unix, or some other operating system you've never heard of and might be big enough to fill a walk-in closet.

tip

USE YOUR HOME NETWORK TO BRING OLD PCS UP TO DATE

Starting with Windows 98, Microsoft has offered Windows and driver updates via Windows Update, a free online service. Windows Update is one of the best ways to add security updates and other improvements to Windows. However, many users don't use Windows Update regularly because their computers connect to the Internet via a slow dial-up connection or don't have any Internet connection. When you add your PCs to a home network with a broadband Internet connection, be sure to use Windows Update on each PC to download security and other patches and improvements. It will take some time the first time you do it, but your PCs will work better and be more secure.

How is this seamless connection possible between radically different types of computers and hardware? Every device (computers, routers, home media players, and so on) that accesses the Internet must use a common "language" called *Transport Control Protocol/Internet Protocol (TCP/IP)*. TCP/IP does the hard work of enabling Windows, MacOS, Linux, and other operating systems to talk to each other via the Internet.

Generally, when you add a network adapter to a PC, TCP/IP components are installed automatically as part of the process. Non-PC devices that work on home networks have TCP/IP support built in.

Home network hardware is designed to make TCP/IP configuration relatively simple when everything works as it ought to (the details are covered in the chapters on setting up each network). However, if you have problems, be sure to check out Chapter 11, "Troubleshooting Your Home Network," for troubleshooting help and more background about TCP/IP.

Now that you understand the components used by each type of home network, it's time to find out which network is best for you. See you in Chapter 3.

THE ABSOLUTE MINIMUM

You can install a wired home network, a wireless home network, or a mix-and-match network, which has both wired and wireless components.

Wired networks include Ethernet, HomePNA, and HomePlug.

Wireless networks include wireless Ethernet (Wi-Fi) and Bluetooth.

Ethernet uses unshielded twisted-pair (UTP) cables between each PC or device and a central switch.

HomePNA uses existing telephone lines between PCs.

HomePlug uses existing AC power lines between PCs.

Wi-Fi refers to wireless Ethernet devices that have passed certification tests for operation with other brands of hardware.

Wi-Fi includes Wireless-B, Wireless-A, and Wireless-G standards, of which Wireless-G is the best choice for home use.

Wireless-G and Wireless-B use the same frequency (2.4GHz) and can work together on the same network, but Wireless-A uses a different frequency (5GHz).

Bluetooth is not designed for sharing Internet access.

You can share broadband Internet access by using one PC as a gateway for the rest of the network, or by using a router.

A router can include a wireless access point or a switch, or both.

A Wi-Fi network used for Internet sharing needs a Wi-Fi adapter for each PC or other device, a wireless access point (WAP), and a router.

An Ethernet network used for Internet sharing needs an Ethernet adapter for each PC or other device, a switch, and a router.

continues

A HomePNA network used for Internet sharing needs a HomePNA adapter for each PC and a router.

A HomePlug network used for Internet sharing needs a HomePlug adapter for each PC and a router.

You can use Ethernet bridges to connect Ethernet or Wi-Fi networks to HomePNA or HomePlug networks.

Windows, MacOs, and Linux all include network protocols, but you might need to add additional software for security or to connect with corporate networks.

3

PLANNING YOUR HOME NETWORK

Now that you know what a home network can do and what it takes to build a home network, it's time to decide which home network is the right one for you. In this chapter, you find out how to

- Match what you want your home network to do with the home network that does it best.
- Select the best broadband Internet service type for you.
- Learn which computers are ready to network and which ones need network adapters.
- Figure out what your home network is going to cost.

At the end of this chapter, you'll be ready to start shopping and making your home network a reality. So, let's get started.

Goals for Your Home Network

Before you buy a single network adapter or cable, you should ask yourself one simple question:

- What do I want my home network to do?

The answer (or answers) you provide to that question will guide you toward the network type and performance level you need. As you read the following sections and discover which situation best fits your needs, you will also learn which network, or networks, will be the best fit for you.

Recreation

Networked computers are fun! Some of the most popular recreational uses for home networks include

- Playing network or Internet games
- Viewing or listening to online media content
- Using IM or other chat services
- Sharing computer-based media files with others via a home theater system
- Searching the Web

Why look at recreational uses first? Although any home network can do these jobs, some are better than others. And, a home network that can handle any recreational task you can think of is more than equal to handling any other task you can throw at it. For example, if your idea of online gaming is turn-based, slower networks—such as phoneline, powerline, or wireless—will be fine. However, if you're itching to play 3D deathmatches online, your home network needs to be as fast as possible, and 10/100 Ethernet's the best choice, with the fastest wireless network (802.11g) being a good alternative.

Table 3.1 compares suggested network and broadband Internet connection types suitable for different recreational uses.

Table 3.1 Popular Recreational Uses for Home Networking

Activity	Recommended Wired Networks	Recommended Wireless Networks	Recommended Broadband Services
Web surfing	Any	Any	Any
Turn-based and RPG network and online gaming	Any	Any	Any
3D network and online gaming	10/100 Ethernet	802.11g	Cable; DSL
Online streaming audio	Any	802.11g, 802.11b	Cable; DSL
Online streaming video	10/100 Ethernet	802.11g, dual-band 802.11a+g	Cable; DSL
Playback of PC-hosted audio or still photos	Any	802.11b/g	—
Playback of PC-based video	10/100 Ethernet	802.11g, dual-band 802.11a+g	—
Instant messaging (IM)	Any	Any	Cable; DSL
Video chat, Voice over (VoIP)	10/100 Ethernet	802.11g, dual-band 802.11a+g	Cable; DSL

Education

If the computers on your home network are there mainly to improve your mind (or your childrens' minds), a variety of home network and broadband connections can do the job for you. However, as with recreational tasks, some types of educational uses put more stress on a home network than others. See Table 3.2 for details.

tip

GAMING? GET A FAST UPSTREAM CONNECTION!

If you're playing interactive 3D games, consider opting for cable or DSL services that offer faster upload speeds than the usual 128KBps speed. See Chapter 4, "Choosing a Broadband Internet Access Technology," for details.

Table 3.2   Popular Educational Uses for Home Networking

Activity	Recommended Wired Networks	Recommended Wireless Networks	Recommended Broadband Services
Web surfing	Any	Any	Any
Online streaming audio	Any	802.11g, 802.11b	Cable; DSL
Online streaming video	10/100 Ethernet	802.11g, dual-band 802.11a+g	Cable; DSL
Playback of PC-hosted audio or still photos	Any	802.11b/g	—
Playback of PC-based video	10/100 Ethernet	802.11g, dual-band 802.11a+g	—
Network printing	Any	Any	—
Network folder sharing	Any	Any	—
Educational gaming (turn-based)	Any	Any	Any
3D educational gaming	10/100 Ethernet	802.11g	Cable; DSL
Virtual private networking (VPN) access to campus network	10/100 Ethernet	802.11g	Cable; DSL

Business

If your home network is also your business network, don't cut corners. Go for the fastest network and Internet connections you can afford, especially if you need to perform a lot of file transfers:

- For broadband Internet access, go with DSL or cable where available.
- For wireless networking, insist on 802.11g. If you plan to stick with the same brand of hardware across the board, a souped-up version of 802.11g is also suitable.
- For wired networking, 10/100 Ethernet is king. You can build a mix-and-match network that combines 10/100 Ethernet and wireless ethernet clients.

caution

SHARING VPN SUPPORT

Most routers designed for use on a home network can handle only one VPN connection at a time. If you expect that two or more users will need VPN connections at the same time (many campuses and corporate networks use VPN connections for remote users), select a router with support for multiple VPN tunnels. See Chapter 8, "Home Networks at Work and School," for details.

Mixed-Use Networks

Although the previous sections describe three distinct uses for a home network, chances are very good that *your* home network will be used for a mixture of recreational, educational, and business uses. In such cases, keep in mind that your home network and broadband Internet connection should meet your requirements for the fastest uses you have in mind. If you build one that's fast enough for the most demanding tasks you have in mind, it will be more than fast enough for the rest.

tip

UPLOADING? GET A FAST UPSTREAM CONNECTION!

If you plan to upload large files (1MB or larger) via email or FTP, or use videoconferencing, consider opting for cable or DSL services that offer faster upload speeds than the usual 128KBps speed. See Chapter 4 for details.

Finding the Best Home Network for You

Now that you've compared the tasks you want your home network to do with the home networks on the market, it's time to review the best features of each home network. As you review the following sections, keep in mind that it's no longer necessary to build a "pure" home network that is based on a single network type.

In my home, for example, I run a mixture of wired and wireless ethernet (802.11g Wi-Fi) because it makes sense. It would be silly for me to install a wireless ethernet network adapter in a computer that's less than 5 feet away from my wireless access point (which also contains a router and switch). However, it's equally silly for me to run more than 100 feet of CAT5/5e/6 cable to an upstairs workroom when I can connect wirelessly. I use 10/100 Ethernet downstairs, and Wi-Fi wireless ethernet upstairs.

You might find that your home (or small office, for that matter) can be networked more easily with a different network or mix of networks than I use. Just be sure to keep in mind that the greater the number of network types you connect, the more complicated your task of managing them will be. Remember that the only help desk you have at home is the one you're sitting at now.

Wi-Fi Pros and Cons

"Look, Ma! No wires!" If your biggest desire in home networking is to "cut the cable" that ties you to your desk or your kitchen table, Wi-Fi (the popular name for IEEE 802.11 wireless ethernet) is the home network for you. Wi-Fi offers these advantages:

■ *No wires means "freedom!"*—As long as you can pick up a signal from your wireless access point (WAP), you can plop down in an easy chair with your laptop or PDA, head out to the pool or the deck, or nod indulgently as your teenager sprawls across the bed to do homework online.

■ *PC + Home Theater + TV = Entertainment*—An increasing number of wireless devices exist to help you play your favorite digital music and view your favorite videos and photos through your home theater system and big-screen TV.

■ *Share the wireless joy*—Wi-Fi also works with printers, webcams, and video games.

■ *Stick with one brand of hardware for easy setup*—For example, if you use Linksys-brand Wi-Fi hardware, you can create an easy-to-use passphrase you can type to access a secure network instead of memorizing a finger- and brain-busting WEP key.

■ *Wi-Fi inside?*—If you bought a laptop since mid-2003, you might already have a Wi-Fi adapter built in, saving you money. Any laptop featuring Intel's Centrino technology includes Wi-Fi, as do many others based on both Intel and AMD processors.

■ *Easy mix-and-match networking*—Most Wi-Fi routers include ethernet switches, so it's easy to build a mixed ethernet/Wi-Fi network.

But, before you decide that Wi-Fi's the way to go, keep in mind these limitations:

■ *Wi-Fi = insecure by default*—Wi-Fi devices out of the box are inherently insecure. If you can access your home network, so can anyone else *if* you don't enable security settings. See Chapter 6, "Installing and Configuring a Wi-Fi Network," for basic wireless ethernet security settings and Chapter 10, "Securing Your Home Network," for advanced strategies and tools.

■ *Wi-Fi security is a work in progress*—Expect to upgrade firmware and drivers a couple of times to implement the latest security features such as Wi-Fi Protected Access (WPA) or 802.1x authentication. If you don't, your Wi-Fi network isn't as secure as it could be.

■ *Wi-Fi connections are rarely (make that never) as fast as advertised*—For example, in tests performed by *PCWorld* magazine for its July 2004 issue, the typical throughput of 802.11b wireless networks was just 4.5Mbps (the rated speed is 11Mbps). 802.11g wireless networks, which are rated to provide 54Mbps, provided throughput of just 18Mbps.

- *Distance = slowdowns*—The further you are from the WAP or router that distributes Wi-Fi signals, the slower the throughput. Brick or concrete walls can also absorb Wi-Fi signals, slowing throughput or blocking signals entirely.

- *Different brands bring Wi-Fi headaches*—Although Wi-Fi certification indicates that different brands of wireless access points and adapters should be able to "play well with others," differences in how security settings work can cause headaches you can avoid if you buy the same brand of hardware.

- *No cabling doesn't mean cheaper*—Although you don't have the expense of cabling, Wi-Fi adapters and WAPs are more expensive than most other network hardware *unless* your computers already have Wi-Fi adapters included.

- *Wi-Fi (often) not included*—Almost all desktops and most laptops, particularly those built before mid-2003 or low-end models, need Wi-Fi adapters.

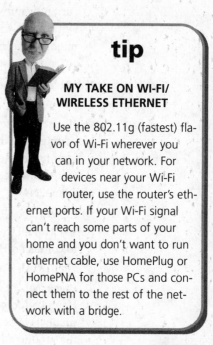

tip

MY TAKE ON WI-FI/ WIRELESS ETHERNET

Use the 802.11g (fastest) flavor of Wi-Fi wherever you can in your network. For devices near your Wi-Fi router, use the router's ethernet ports. If your Wi-Fi signal can't reach some parts of your home and you don't want to run ethernet cable, use HomePlug or HomePNA for those PCs and connect them to the rest of the network with a bridge.

HomePNA Pros and Cons

If your home has a telephone jack in every room, you already have a home network wired up and ready to go. The missing link? A HomePNA adapter. HomePNA strong points include

- *No rewiring*—The phone jacks *are* the network, so you don't need to put crayon-colored wires all over the place.

- *No security worries*—Your telephone wiring is a closed network.

- *Easy setup software*—Run the software included with the adapters and away you go!

Despite its strong points, you should think twice before making HomePNA your only network. Here's why:

■ *HomePNA's a slowpoke compared to other networks*—Most HomePNA products currently correspond to version 2.0 (10Mbps). Although a faster (128Mbps) version 3.0 was approved in June 2003, it looks as if version 3.0 hardware might never make it to market. The original version of HomePNA, HomePNA 1.0, ran at just 1Mbps!

■ *HomePNA = more money, less availability*—HomePNA network adapters are almost as expensive as Wi-Fi adapters, and are harder to find at retail stores.

■ *HomePNA's mostly for PCs*—Most media adapters are designed to connect between your home theater system and ethernet (wired or wireless) networks, not HomePNA.

■ *Expect to buy a bridge*—A relatively expensive HomePNA-Ethernet bridge is required to connect a HomePNA network to an ethernet or wireless ethernet network.

■ *HomePNA.org's website needs work*—The HomePNA.org website's list of compatible products is not well maintained. Many of the product links are not working, and many of the products listed are no longer available (or might never have been produced).

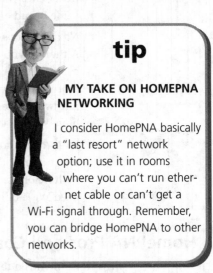

tip

MY TAKE ON HOMEPNA NETWORKING

I consider HomePNA basically a "last resort" network option; use it in rooms where you can't run ethernet cable or can't get a Wi-Fi signal through. Remember, you can bridge HomePNA to other networks.

HomePlug Pros and Cons

Although HomePlug powerline networking isn't as well-known as some other network types, it provides features similar to HomePNA, but works in any room that has an electrical outlet. HomePlug's strong points include

■ *Built-in encryption*—Snoopy neighbors can't get to your data.

■ *No rewiring*—The AC power lines in the wall *are* the network.

■ *Easy network connections*—The only network connection you add to your PC is a small device about the size of an AC briquette power adapter that plugs into the AC wall socket (no surge protectors, please) and your computer's USB port.

■ *HomePlug is more popular than HomePNA*—Many mail-order and online stores offer HomePlug hardware and an increasing number of vendors produce HomePlug network hardware.

Nevertheless, you should think twice about making HomePlug your only network for these reasons:

■ *HomePlug's a slowpoke*—Although HomePlug's rated speed is 14Mbps, its real-world performance is about the same as 11Mbps 802.11b wireless networks. If you want to use it for streaming video, HomePlug is too slow.

■ *HomePlug's just for PCs*—Current media adapters don't support HomePlug, so you need to use an ethernet/HomePlug bridge to connect a media adapter to a HomePlug network.

tip

MY TAKE ON HOMEPLUG

HomePlug is a good option for networking PCs for web-surfing and printer-sharing if Wi-Fi or ethernet isn't feasible. Use a bridge to connect a HomePlug network to an ethernet or Wi-Fi network.

Ethernet Pros and Cons

Ethernet, the built-in network adapter found in most recent desktop and notebook PCs, has four big advantages:

■ *Low cost*—Most recent PCs have an ethernet (RJ-45) port built in. Add a low-cost router to your broadband Internet access device (cable, DSL, and so on) and a cable for each device and you have a network with Internet sharing.

■ *High performance*—Almost all routers, switches, and network adapters used on ethernet home networks these days support a feature called *full duplex* (simultaneous read/write). Full duplex support makes a 100Mbps ethernet connection run at 200Mbps!

■ *Versatility*—Many specialized network adapters, such as print servers, media adapters, and others, even if sold primarily for Wi-Fi use, also have ethernet ports.

■ *Mix and match with Wi-Fi*—Most Wi-Fi routers incorporate an ethernet switch, making it easy to build a mixed ethernet/Wi-Fi network.

With ethernet's many advantages, why not use it for everything? Keep in mind these drawbacks:

- *Network cable expense*—Long cable runs can be costly, especially between far-flung rooms or from one floor of your home to another.

- *Network cable esthetics*—Your home might look like somebody's been drawing on the baseboards with crayons unless you take time and spend money to hide the cables or standardize on neutral cable colors such as white or light gray.

tip

MY TAKE ON ETHERNET

Connect close-in computers and devices with ethernet (especially if you can hide those cables!) and use Wi-Fi for more distant areas of your home.

Evaluating Your Current Hardware for Network Capabilities

Before you can build a home network, you ought to take a few minutes to see whether your PCs and other devices are ready to network, and what type(s) of networks they support.

Examining Your PCs

You can use an RJ-45 connection for ethernet networking, and a USB port for any home network discussed in this book. Figure 3.1 illustrates typical ethernet (RJ-45) and USB ports on the rear of a typical desktop PC.

RJ-45 port for ethernet

FIGURE 3.1

RJ-45 (ethernet) and USB ports on the rear of a typical desktop PC.

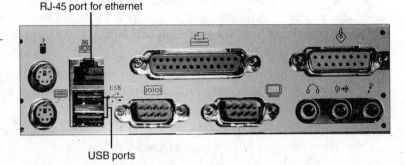

USB ports

If you have a notebook or laptop computer, you might find these ports on the rear or sides of your PC. Figure 3.2 compares USB, RJ-45 (ethernet), and RJ-11 (modem) ports on the rear of a typical notebook computer.

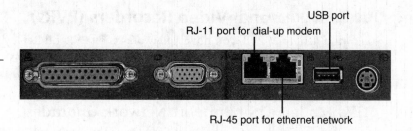

FIGURE 3.2

Modem, ethernet, and USB ports on the rear of a typical notebook PC.

RJ-45 port for ethernet network

As you can see from Figures 3.1 and 3.2, it's easy to determine whether you have an ethernet port or a USB port. However, it can be harder to tell whether your notebook computer already has wireless ethernet (Wi-Fi) installed.

Here are some ways to determine this information:

- Computers with Intel Centrino technology incorporate built-in Wireless-B (802.11b) Wi-Fi networking.

- Stickers on the outside of the computer might indicate the presence of built-in Wi-Fi adapters.

- Find the specific model number of your computer (look for a sticker on the back or bottom of the PC) and check the vendor's specification sheet to determine whether it has Wi-Fi on board. For example, an IBM ThinkPad G40 2384EHU does not have on-board Wi-Fi, but a G40 2384B9U supports Wi-Fi (802.11b and 802.11a standards).

- Open the Network Connections dialog in Windows 2000 or Windows XP to see whether a wireless network adapter is present: Right-click on the My Network Places icon on the Windows Desktop or Start button and select Properties.

To learn how to add your PC to an ethernet home network, see Chapter 5, "Installing and Configuring a Wired Ethernet Network." To learn how to add your PC to a Wi-Fi home network, see Chapter 6, "Installing and Configuring a Wi-Fi Network."

tip

CHECK THE CARD SLOTS, TOO!

If you don't find RJ-45 or USB ports next to other ports as in Figure 3.1, check the card slots (located to the right of these ports). Some systems use an ethernet or USB card to provide these ports.

Checking Out Your Personal Video Recorders (PVRs)

If you own a ReplayTV PVR, you have a network-ready PVR; all ReplayTV PVRs have included a 10/100 Ethernet port from the beginning. If you have a TiVo, check Table 3.3 for a list of network-compatible TiVo models.

Table 3.3 TiVo Models That Support Network Upgrades

Vendor	Model	Service Upgrade Required
Toshiba	SD-H400	TiVo Plus*
Pioneer	DVR-810H, DVR-57H	TiVo Plus*
TiVo	Series 2	—

TiVo Plus brings the TiVo features in third-party units up to the level of the standard TiVo service provided with TiVo Series 2 PVRs.

To learn how to add TiVo to your home network, see Chapter 7, "Home Networks at Play."

Evaluating Your Game Systems

The Microsoft Xbox has a built-in 10/100 Ethernet port. You can also add a wireless ethernet game adapter to the ethernet port. However, the Sony PlayStation2 and Nintendo GameCube don't have any on-board network support.

If your Sony PlayStation2 was purchased as part of a bundle with the Sony Network adapter, the Network adapter can be installed to provide 10/100 Ethernet network support for your console. Otherwise, you can purchase the Sony Network adapter separately. To add the Nintendo GameCube to a home network, purchase and install the Nintendo Broadband adapter; this adapter provides 10/100 Ethernet network support. After 10/100 Ethernet adapters are installed in the PlayStation2 or GameCube, you can add a wireless ethernet game adapter.

To learn how to install these adapters and connect any of these game systems to ethernet or Wi-Fi networks, see Chapter 7.

Costing Out Your Network

Now that you've compared the home network candidates and made your selections, it's time to figure up how much your home network is likely to cost. I know you're itching to get started, but here's why you should take time to add up the cost first:

■ You probably have a budget, and calculating the cost of the network you want helps you see whether your budget will handle all the network features you want.

■ By calculating the cost of the network in specific detail, you can determine what types of networks to use in different parts of your home and where to use them.

Because of the wide variety of home network and broadband Internet access options available, the following sections include budget worksheet templates you can use to calculate how much your network will cost, regardless of which network hardware you choose or how many PCs and other devices you add to your home network.

You can use them with a trusty calculator, or use them as a model to build a worksheet in Microsoft Excel, Quattro Pro, Lotus 1-2-3, or other spreadsheet programs. By using a spreadsheet, you can provide instant "what-if" analysis by changing options.

To help you use these templates, I've provided simple examples of each one with sample data. The prices in each section are typical of what you might pay, but you can probably find even better prices if you do some shopping around.

Broadband Internet Access

If you don't have broadband Internet access already, use Table 3.4 to calculate how much your preferred solution will cost. Table 3.5 shows you a sample calculation.

Table 3.4 Calculating Broadband Internet Costs

Item	Includes	One-Time Charge (A)	Monthly Charge (B)	Carryover from Cols A & B
Equipment purchase			—	
Installation			—	
Monthly service		—		
		Up-front Total (Col A + Col B)		
		Monthly Charge (Col B)		

Table 3.5 Sample Calculation of Broadband Internet Costs

Item	Includes	One-Time Charge (A)	Monthly Charge (B)	Carryover from Cols A & B
Equipment purchase	Cable modem	$90	—	$90
Installation	Split existing cable TV service	$10	—	$10
Monthly service	Cable Internet service	—	$40	$40
		Up-front Total (Col A + Col B)		$140
		Monthly Charge (Col B)		$40

As you can see from the example in Table 3.5, you can use the template in Table 3.4 to calculate both the up-front cost and continuing monthly expense of any broadband Internet service you choose.

Network Wiring

Network wiring is a factor in your installation only if you decide to install an ethernet network. The template in Table 3.6 can be used to calculate the lengths and prices for pre-assembled patch cables; see Table 3.7 for a sample calculation.

Table 3.6 Calculating Pre-assembled Cable Requirements

Patch Cables Between Device and Router	Device to Connect	Cable distance[1]	Assembled Cable Length[2]	Assembled Cable Cost
Device #1				
Device #2				
Device #3				
Device #4				
				Total

[1] Not straight-line distance; distance required to run cables behind furniture, along baseboards, and around doorframes.

[2] Based on commonly available lengths of CAT5/5e/6 network cable.

Table 3.7 Sample Calculation of Pre-assembled Cable Requirements

Patch Cables Between Device and Router	Device to Connect	Cable distance	Assembled Cable Length	Assembled Cable Cost
Device #1	Desktop PC in living room	5 feet	7 feet	$8
Device #2	Media adapter on home theater system in living room	10 feet	14 feet	$15
Device #3	Desktop PC in home office	20 feet	25 feet	$25
Device #4	Laptop PC in bedroom	40 feet	50 feet	$30
			Total	$78

You might prefer to build your own cable as described in Chapter 5. Use Table 3.8 to calculate the cost of supplies (bulk cable, connectors) and Table 3.9 to calculate the cost of each cable as built. Tables 3.10 and 3.11 show sample calculations.

Table 3.8 Determining Unit Cost of Bulk Patch and Wall-Mount Cable Components

Item	Package Price (P)	Quantity (Q)	Unit Cost = P/Q	Notes
Bulk CAT5/5e/6 cable				
RJ-45 connectors				Two connectors needed for each patch cable
RJf-45 wall plate kit*				Two kits needed for cable installed in wall*

* Some wall plate kits include a keystone jack for direct wiring; some include a coupler for connecting two standard RJ-45 cables.

Table 3.9 Calculating Custom-Assembled Cable Requirements

Cable Location	Cable Type	Bulk Cable Length[1]	Extended Cable Cost (E)	Unit Cost of Connector or Jack/Wall Plate[2]	Extended Parts Cost (U×2=P)	Total Cable Cost (E+P)
						Total

[1]For wall cable, this distance is often significantly shorter than for patch cable.

[2]Use RJ-45 connector cost for patch cable or for wall cable that uses a coupler-type wall plate; use keystone jack and wall plate unit cost for wall cable that does not use a coupler.

Table 3.10 Sample Calculation of Bulk Cable Unit Cost

Item	Package Price (P)	Quantity (Q)	Unit Cost = P/Q	Notes
Bulk CAT5/5e/6 cable	$100	1000 feet	$.10/foot	
RJ-45 connectors	$7	20	$.35	Two needed (one each end) for patch cable
RJ-45 and wall plate kit	$5	1	$5	Two needed (one each end) for wall cable; use patch cable between wall jack and device*

*Some wall plate kits include a keystone jack for direct wiring; some include a coupler for connecting two RJ-45 cables. Adjust your cost calculations according to the wall plate kit type you purchase.

Table 3.11 Sample Calculation of Custom-Assembled Cable Requirements

Cable Location	Cable Type	Bulk Cable Length[1]	Extended Cable Cost (E)	Unit Cost of Connector or Jack/Wall Plate[2]	Extended Parts Cost (U×2=P)	Total Cable Cost (E+P)
Living room PC to router in living room	Patch cable	5 feet	$.50	$.35	$.70	$1.20

Cable Location	Cable Type	Bulk Cable Length[1]	Extended Cable Cost (E)	Unit Cost of Connector or Jack/Wall Plate[2]	Extended Parts Cost (U×2=P)	Total Cable Cost (E+P)
Living room home media adapter to router	Patch cable	10 feet	$1.00	$.35	$.70	$1.70
Living room to bedroom	Wall cable	30 feet	$2.40	$5	$10	$12.40
PC in bedroom to bedroom wall jack	Patch cable	3 feet	$.30	$.35	$.70	$1.00
					Total	$15.30

Ethernet cable runs can be unsightly. If you want to use the methods discussed in the section "Hiding Your Cables," in Chapter 5, p. 122, to hide cables in walls or inside cable-management systems, use Table 3.12 to calculate these costs. See Table 3.13 for a sample calculation.

Table 3.12   Calculating Cable-Hiding/Management Costs

Item	Unit Cost (U)	Quantity (Q)	Extended Cost (U×Q)	Notes
		Total		

Table 3.13   Sample Calculation of Cable-Hiding/Management Costs

Item	Unit Cost (U)	Quantity (Q)	Extended Cost (U×Q)	Notes
Series 375 1-piece raceway 5ft	$6	3	$18	http:// cableorganizer.com
Series 375 inside corner	$2	2	$4	
End caps for Series 375 raceway	$2	2	$4	
		Total	$26	

Network Adapters for PCs

No matter what network you choose to install, in most situations you will need to install network adapters in at least some of your PCs. Use Table 3.14 to help plan these purchases.

Table 3.14   Planning Network Adapter Purchases

System Type	System Location	Network Type	Network Adapter Type	Brand/Model	Price	Where Purchased

Table 3.15 provides a sample used to plan a mix-and-match network.

Table 3.15   Sample Network Adapter Purchase Planner Worksheet

System Type	System Location	Network Type	Network Adapter Type	Brand/Model	Price	Where Purchased
Desktop	Living room near router	ethernet	Built in to PC	—	—	—
Laptop	Moves between office/home office	802.11g/a	CardBus	Brand A, Dual-Mode AG	$90	Mail order PC stuff
Desktop	Den	802.11g	PCI	Brand B, PCI-G	$50	Big-box Store
Laptop	Moves between kids' bedroom/school	802.11g	Built in to PC	—	—	—
Desktop	Spare bedroom	HomePlug*	USB	Brand C, HomePlug NIC	$60	Bigger-box store

*Must be bridged to ethernet network (see Tables 3.16 and 3.17).

Routers, Switches, and Bridges

Although a few DSL modems have built-in routers, most of the time you will need to connect a router to your broadband Internet access device in order to share the Internet with your home network. If you don't have enough ethernet ports in your router, you might need to add a separate switch to your router to handle additional stations (such as for a LAN party). If you use HomePNA or HomePlug network adapters for some computers, you will need to use a bridge to connect them to your ethernet or Wi-Fi network. Use Table 3.16 to cost out these items.

Table 3.16   Planning Router, Bridge, or Switch Purchases

Device Type	Device Location	How Used	Network Type(s) Supported	Brand/Model	Price	Where Purchased

Table 3.17 provides a completed sample.

Table 3.17   Sample Router, Bridge, or Switch Purchase Worksheet

Device Type	Device Location	How Used	Network Type(s) Supported	Brand/Model	Price	Where Purchased
Router	Living room near cable modem	Shares Internet with home network	802.11g, 10/100 Ethernet	Brand B, 54GB Router	$80	Big-box store
Bridge	Living room near router	Connects HomePlug to ethernet	HomePlug, 10/100 Ethernet	Brand C, HomePlug bridge	$70	Bigger-box store

Specialized Network Adapters

Use Table 3.18 to plan your purchases of specialized network adapters such as print servers, network adapters for games, media adapters, and so forth.

Table 3.18 Planning Specialized Network Adapter Purchases

Device Type	Device Location	How Used	Network Type(s) Supported	Brand/Model	Price	Where Purchased

Table 3.19 provides a completed sample.

Table 3.19 Sample Specialized Network Adapter Purchase Worksheet

Device Type	Device Location	How Used	Network Type(s) Supported	Brand/Model	Price	Where Purchased
Video game adapter	Den	Connects Xbox to Wi-Fi network	802.11g	Microsoft Xbox wireless adapter	$70	GameWorld
Print server	Home office	Connects laser and inkjet printers to Wi-Fi network	802.11g	Brand B Wi-Fi Print Server	$90	Big-box store
Media adapter	Living room home theater network	Connects home theater to ethernet	10/100 Ethernet, 802.11g	Brand B Home Media Adapter 888	$170	Electronics cosmos

Bringing Your Network Online in Stages

As you plan your home network, keep in mind that you don't need to network everything at once. Look carefully at your goals and budget your time and money appropriately. For example, you should probably build a home network to provide broadband Internet access for your PCs first. Later, you can add console games, home media, or other specialized features to your home network.

The Absolute Minimum

The tasks you want your home network to perform help you decide which home network and which type of broadband Internet access you should choose.

Cable or DSL are the best choices for broadband Internet access because they support all business, recreational, and educational uses.

802.11g wireless network and 10/100 Ethernet are the best choices for a home network because they are fast enough to support all types of business, recreational, and educational uses.

Wi-Fi's most obvious benefit offers you the ability to network without wires, but it also supports many non-PC devices and has built-in connections to 10/100—ethernet networks.

The most desirable "flavor" of Wi-Fi to use in a home network is 802.11g, which runs at 54Mbps.

HomePNA networking can be used in any room with a telephone jack, but it isn't well supported by non-PC network adapters.

HomePlug networking can be used in any room with AC electrical outlets, but it's much slower than 802.11g wireless networks.

Ethernet works well with Wi-Fi because routers often incorporate Wi-Fi WAPs and ethernet switches, and you can use bridges to connect ethernet to HomePNA or HomePlug networks.

Most PCs include ethernet ports, but other types of network adapters must be added to most PCs.

Many notebook computers built since mid-2003 include Wi-Fi adapters, but Wi-Fi is still rare on desktop computers.

ReplayTV PVRs have built-in 10/100 Ethernet networking.

TiVo Series 2 and some third-party TiVo devices support USB network adapters.

Of the major game systems, only Microsoft's Xbox has built-in networking (10/100 Ethernet).

You should calculate the total cost of your network, including broadband Internet access devices, network adapters, routers, bridges, and adapters for specialized uses.

Calculating the total cost of your network helps you plan your network budget and decide which type(s) of networks to use and where to use them.

PART

Building Your Home Network

4

CHOOSING A BROADBAND INTERNET ACCESS TECHNOLOGY

Sharing a broadband Internet connection is one of the leading reasons to build a home network. However, some broadband Internet technologies are better choices than others. In this chapter, you learn about the major options and how to choose the right one for you.

Understanding Broadband Internet Access Types

What is broadband Internet access? Recall from Chapter 2, "Building Blocks of the Home Network," that, typically, broadband Internet access refers to Internet access that has the following features:

- Download speeds more than 300Kbps
- Upload speeds more than 100Kbps
- Telephone lines available for ordinary phone calls
- "Always on" or quick-connect access to Internet

There are four major types of Internet access that satisfy this definition of broadband:

- Cable
- DSL
- Satellite
- Wireless

In the following sections, you learn more about the features of each one.

Cable Internet

Your friendly local cable TV company's digital network brings more than Animal Planet and Saturday Night Live reruns to millions of households across the world: it also brings broadband Internet service. Often called *cable modem* or *cable broadband service, cable Internet* is the most popular form of broadband Internet service in the United States and is among the leaders worldwide.

Although a few cable TV companies brought Internet access to their subscribers over now-outdated all-coaxial networks a few years ago, in virtually every case today cable TV companies don't offer cable Internet service to a particular locality until they have upgraded their networks to use fiber-optic lines and digital channel options.

Compared to an all-coaxial network, fiber-optic cable networks can carry many more channels of TV, movies, and music. And, there's plenty of room for channels carrying broadband Internet signals to and from subscribers.

Cable Internet Hardware

A device known as a *cable modem* connects to the cable line coming into your home. If you also have cable TV, a *splitter* is used to provide separate connections to your cable modem and to your set-top box (Figure 4.1). Originally, cable modems connected to the RJ-45 port on an 10BASE-T or 10/100 Ethernet card, or built-in Ethernet port. However, some cable modems connect to the USB port or offer both port types. Thus, you can connect a cable modem to virtually any recent desktop or notebook computer.

Figure 4.2 shows the rear of a typical cable modem after connecting power, RJ-45 Ethernet, and coaxial cables.

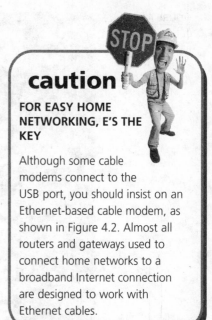

caution

FOR EASY HOME NETWORKING, E'S THE KEY

Although some cable modems connect to the USB port, you should insist on an Ethernet-based cable modem, as shown in Figure 4.2. Almost all routers and gateways used to connect home networks to a broadband Internet connection are designed to work with Ethernet cables.

FIGURE 4.1

A typical cable modem and cable TV nstallation.

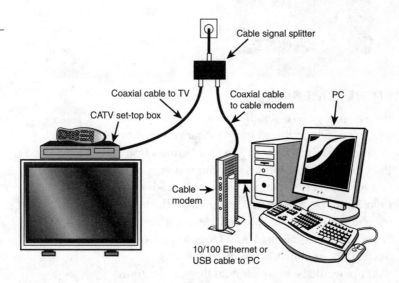

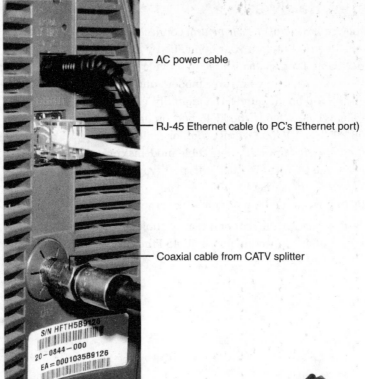

— AC power cable

— RJ-45 Ethernet cable (to PC's Ethernet port)

— Coaxial cable from CATV splitter

Cable Internet Speeds

Unlike other types of Internet service, many cable Internet providers like to make rather vague download speed claims, such as "up to fifty times faster than dial-up." This sounds very impressive, until you remember that dial-up download speeds vary from 31.6Kbps to 53Kbps, sometimes on the same telephone line in a short period of time. Then, the "up to fifty times faster" claim looks suspiciously flexible. For example, a download speed of 834Kbps would be more than 26 times faster than 31.6Kbps but only 15 times faster than a 53Kbps dial-up connection. A download speed of 2580Kbps is more than 81 times faster than a 31.6Kbps dial-up connection. However, it falls a bit short of the "fifty times faster" goal at 49 times faster.

note

KBPS VERSUS MBPS

Kbps indicates kilobits per second. If you're trying to compare online services that measure speed in Mbps (megabits per second), multiply the Mbps by 1,000 to get the corresponding Kbps speed. For example, 1.5Mbps equals 1,500Kbps.

Why don't cable Internet companies guarantee a particular speed? The short answer is, "they can't." Here's why: A cable Internet connection to a particular neighborhood is shared among multiple users (the exact number varies with the ISP and the location). Consequently, during peak times (such as early evening, when most users are online), speed for each user drops. At off-peak times (such as midday or after midnight), with fewer users using the connection, the available bandwidth for each user is higher and speed increases. Major fluctuations, particularly in download speed, can take place in a short time period. For example, I used the BroadbandReports.com speed test one morning to check the speed of my cable modem connection. At 7:37 a.m., my download speed was 2,736Kbps, but my upload speed was only 53Kbps. A few minutes later at 7:44 a.m., my download speed dropped to 2,133Kbps, but my upload speed increased to a still modest 91Kbps.

Why are upload speeds so slow? As with most other broadband solutions, cable Internet service's upload speeds (the speeds at which outgoing emails and web page requests travel) are limited by the way the service is configured. A maximum rate of 128Kbps is typical, and real-world results can be slower. Because fast uploads speeds are important to users who sent a lot of information (such as website designers, users of video conferencing, file-sharing fans, and online gamers), some cable ISPs offer premium service options that increase maximum upload speeds to 384Kbps.

> **tip**
>
> **GET REAL-WORLD RESULTS BEFORE YOU BUY**
>
> Instead of depending on a vague promise of speed, I suggest you check out real-world speeds for the cable ISP you're considering. One of the best sources is BroadbandReports.com (formerly known as DSLReports). You can search by provider, service type, or ZIP Code to see real-world speeds, reviews of service quality, and many other useful shopping tools and tips. Speed tests list ZIP Code, date, and time, so you can see the variables that affect real-world speeds.

Cable Internet Ordering and Pricing

To order cable Internet service, check with your local cable TV provider(s). If you have more than one serving your area, be sure to check with all providers to get the best deal.

Expect to pay about $40 to $50 per month in the United States for typical cable Internet service. Expect to pay about 50% more to get upload speeds up to 384Kbps (when available). You can lease a cable modem for about $10/month. Does it make sense to lease? See "Equipment Cost per Month" p. 88, this chapter, for the answers.

Some vendors provide free installation, and others might charge you for installation. Although cable Internet's biggest rival, DSL (see next section) can often be self-installed, cable Internet rarely offers this option.

DSL

In the U.S. market, *digital subscriber line (DSL)* runs a strong number two to cable; worldwide, DSL is often more popular than cable. As the name suggests, DSL service is provided in conjunction with (and sometimes by) your local telephone company through the telephone line that runs to your home. Unlike cable Internet, which is available to anybody in a neighborhood served by the provider, the availability of DSL service at a particular location is affected by two factors:

- The quality of the telephone line going to the location
- The wire distance between the location and the phone company's central switch (the location where DSL connections are made to the Internet)

Unlike cable Internet, which integrates perfectly with digital cable TV, residential DSL service runs over a telephone system that was usually installed long before digital services were contemplated. Because of various shortcuts that local telephone providers (known as telcos) have used over the years to expand local service without full-scale rewiring, it's possible that some homes in the same block might qualify for DSL service but others don't have telephone lines of sufficient quality to handle the high-speed digital signals used by DSL.

A second barrier to universal DSL service is the effect that longer wire distances have on DSL speeds. Wire distance refers to the length of the wire(s) used to connect the location to the central switch. The longer the wire distance, the slower the DSL service that's possible to a particular location. Because of how wires are routed aboveground or underground, locations that are within the theoretical radius of DSL service might not qualify for the fastest DSL speeds or for DSL service at all.

There are two major types of DSL service:

- *ADSL (Asymmetric DSL)* is sold primarily to home and small-business users. Upload speeds are much slower than download speeds. ADSL can be run over high-quality existing phone lines and can often be self-installed.
- *SDSL (Symmetric DSL)* is sold primarily to medium and large businesses. It supports identical upload/download speeds. SDSL usually requires a new telephone line to the location and must be professionally installed.

Table 4.1 compares the effect that greater wire distance has on ADSL upload/download speeds offered. The data in Table 4.1 is drawn from various vendors' ADSL service offerings.

Table 4.1   Typical DSL Service Distances/Speeds

ADSL (Download/Upload) Service Speeds	Maximum Wire Distance (ft.)
768/128Kbps	16,200
1,500/768Kbps	12,000
768/384Kbps	12,000

DSL Hardware

A device known as a *DSL modem* connects to the telephone line coming into your home. Most DSL providers include the DSL modem as part of DSL service. Depending on the provider and package you choose, the DSL modem might include a built-in router with support for wired or wireless Ethernet networking.

Because DSL signal quality can be degraded by interference from other telephone-based devices (including answering machines and fax machines), some DSL providers run a separate line exclusively for DSL from the outside phone connection into the home. If you install your own DSL service, an option offered by many DSL vendors, devices known as microfilters must be connected between telephones and other telephone devices to prevent interference. See "Self-installing DSL," p. 92, this chapter, for typical examples.

Most DSL modems connect to the computer through an RJ-45 Ethernet port, but a few offer both USB and Ethernet, or only a USB port. For easy home networking, insist on a DSL modem that plugs into an Ethernet port.

tip

SAVE A BUNDLE WITH A NETWORK BUNDLE

If you're already planning to create a home network to share your DSL connection, check to see whether your vendor offers a network-ready DSL modem. If you can get a DSL modem that includes a router with an Ethernet switch or a wireless Ethernet access point (or both) included as part of your plan—or for less than $50 more than a plain-vanilla DSL modem—it's a great way to save money on networking. You also avoid a lot of support headaches because your DSL vendor knows the hardware you're using.

DSL Speeds

When you order ADSL service, you might be able to select from two or more speed plans, depending upon your location. The most common DSL speed plans include 384/128Kbps, 768/128Kbps, and 1,500/128Kbps. Generally, upload speeds above

128Kbps are less common and are more expensive. Unlike cable Internet service speeds, which can be greatly affected by subscriber usage, actual DSL speeds are generally very close to those advertised on properly working phone circuits.

ADSL Pricing

Traditionally, ADSL and cable modem services have been similar in price per month ($40 to $50). However, many regional telephone companies are making a big push for ADSL subscribers, often offering pricing less than $30/month plus package deals on DSL modems and other options. Keep in mind that although ADSL speeds are more consistent than cable, cable often offers a much higher peak download speed at a given price point. DSL modems are usually bundled with the service; check with the vendor to determine whether you are purchasing or leasing the modem.

tip

DSL SPEED DROP? LOOK FOR WIRING PROBLEMS

Because DSL requires high-quality phone lines to operate, problems with phone lines running to your home or in your home could cause drops in speed. Check for loose connections, frayed or broken phone wires, or problems with microfilters if your DSL speeds suddenly drop. Call the vendor for help if you can't find the problem yourself.

Satellite

Lucky city dwellers and suburbanites often have two or more cable or DSL vendors fighting over them. However, if you live beyond the reach of cable or DSL, you still have broadband options, assuming you can see the equatorial sky (the southern sky for those of us in North America). If you have a clear view, or if you already have satellite TV, you can probably get broadband Internet as well, and from a choice of companies.

Keep in mind that satellite Internet service is slower than cable or DSL and can suffer from slower or lost connections during stormy or very cloudy weather. Consequently, you should consider satellite only if cable or DSL service is not available in your area.

Two vendors provide satellite Internet service:

- DirecWAY (formerly DirecPC)
- StarBand

Satellite Internet Hardware

Both DirecWAY and StarBand use external devices known as *satellite modems* to connect an individual PC to a satellite dish. A satellite modem connects to the computer's USB or Ethernet port (depending on the modem). Coaxial cable runs from the satellite modem to a satellite dish, which is aimed at a designated geosynchronous satellite. These satellites orbit the equator at a distance of about 22,500 miles, which places them over the same ground location at all times. The satellites transmit page requests to large satellite dishes connected to Internet backbones and operated by each service. Web pages, email, and other online content are transmitted back up to the satellite, which transmits the data back to the individual ground station that requested it (Figure 4.3).

tip

CHECK ALL THE VENDORS FOR THE BEST DEAL ON DIRECWAY

DirecWAY is also sold by AgriStar, EarthLink, and NRTC. The DirecWAY website provides links to these and other vendors. Because offer details and prices might vary from vendor to vendor, be sure to shop around for your best deal.

FIGURE 4.3

By using a special satellite dish, you can receive satellite Internet and satellite TV with a single dish.

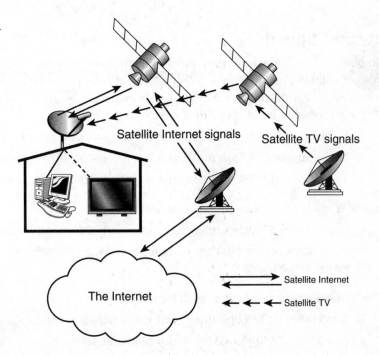

Satellite Internet signals

Satellite TV signals

The Internet

→ Satellite Internet
◄ ◄ ◄ Satellite TV

Because the dish must be aimed precisely, self-installation is not available; the dish must be installed and aimed by a professional installer. Both DirecWAY and StarBand offer optional satellite dishes that can be used to pick up both satellite Internet and TV programming. DirecWAY can be used with DirecTV, and StarBand can be used with Dish Network; separate subscriptions and receivers are required.

If you want to use a router for networking with satellite Internet, you need to specify a service plan that includes a satellite modem made for network operation. DirecWAY plans now feature the DW6000 satellite modem, which has a 10/100 Ethernet port (but no USB port) and can be connected to a router. New StarBand small-office customers can get the StarBand 484 satellite modem, which includes a four-port Ethernet switch and router.

note

ALREADY HAVE SATELLITE INTERNET? ASK ABOUT UPGRADES

If you have older USB-based satellite modems and you want to share your Internet connection with a home network, ask your vendor about upgrading to a satellite modem that offers an Ethernet port or Ethernet switch.

Satellite Internet Speeds

Although the applied science that makes satellite Internet access is breathtaking, the speeds available through current satellite Internet services are far more modest than those available with cable Internet, and are similar to those available with low-end ADSL packages. StarBand offers three service packages:

- Residential (500Kbps maximum download/50Kbps maximum upload)
- Telecommuter (750Kbps maximum download/100Kbps maximum upload)
- Small Office (1,000Kbps maximum download/100Kbps maximum upload)

DirecWAY offers two service packages for the home user:

- Home service (500Kbps maximum download/50Kbps maximum upload)
- Professional service (500Kbps maximum download/50Kbps maximum upload for up to two users)

DirecWAY also offers two higher-speed business plans:

- Small office (1,000Kbps maximum download; up to three concurrent users)
- Business (1,000Kbps maximum download; up to five concurrent users)

All DirecWAY plans are subject to various FAP limits on continuous downloading.

Satellite Internet is slower than other broadband solutions in another way: latency (also known as *lag time*). *Latency* refers to how quickly remote sites respond to a request for information and send it back to the requesting computer. This takes much longer with satellite Internet than with ground-based services because of the distance between the satellite (22,500 miles) and the ground facilities. It takes four(!) 22,500-mile trips for a single page request:

- 22,500 miles (PC to satellite)
- 22,500 miles (satellite to service center)
- Various distances (service center to remote server and back)
- 22,500 miles (service center back to satellite)
- 22,500 miles (satellite back to PC)

For this reason, satellite Internet is *not* recommended for the following:

- Gaming
- Teleconferencing

Satellite Internet Ordering and Pricing

The basic order process for either satellite Internet service works like this:

1. Check the pricing and availability of each service.
2. Contact the vendor via its website or toll-free number.
3. Select the equipment (dish, satellite modem) that meets your needs.
4. Schedule installation.

Purchasing satellite Internet service can be almost as confusing as selecting a cell phone service because of the wide variety of service plans and commitment time

tip

SATELLITE IS *NOT* ALL-YOU-CAN-EAT BROADBAND

FAP is DirecWAY's Fair Access Plan, a controversial feature that limits download speed when more than a specified amount of data has been downloaded. For example, if a Home service user downloads more than 169MB of data within 4 hours, FAP slows the download speed drastically for up to 12 hours. Other plans offer various higher FAP limits. According to DirecWAY, FAP is designed to prevent a small number of users from hogging the satellite connection.

StarBand's Acceptable Use Policy also prevents bandwidth hogging, but does not specify how much use is "too much."

Many satellite Internet users recommend using Internet Download Manager (http://www.internet-downloadmanager.com/; $29.95 with free trial available) because it is designed to prevent you from exceeding FAP limits when downloading large amounts of data.

required. Typically, you can choose from plans with a high up-front price for equipment and installation (as much as $700) and a lower monthly service charge ($60–70/month is typical) or plans that charge a low up-front charge (as little as $100) but spread the cost of installation and equipment over the life of the contract with a higher monthly service charge (typically around $100/month). Contracts are usually for 12 months, although some special pricing plans might require a longer term. Keep in mind that most plans charge anywhere from $100 up to as much as $700 in early termination fees (amounts depend upon your contract) if you opt out before your contract's over.

The bottom line? Make sure you really want satellite Internet service before you sign up for it.

Satellite Internet is the most expensive type of Internet access available for widespread home use.

Wireless

Wireless Internet, unlike its distant sibling, satellite Internet, uses ground-based stations to relay its signals to and from users. There are two distinct types of wireless Internet access:

- Fixed-base wireless
- Wireless Ethernet (Wi-Fi)

caution

NETWORK-FRIENDLY? YES, *IF* YOU GET THE RIGHT EQUIPMENT

DirecWAY service now features the DW6000 satellite modem, which features an Ethernet port and can be used with both Windows PCs and Macs. You can also connect the DW6000 to a router for easy home networking. StarBand has switched to Ethernet-based hardware for its telecommuter (481, one Ethernet port) and business plans (484, which includes a four-port Ethernet switch and router). Residential customers can save money with the 360 modem (requires Windows) or opt for the more expensive but more flexible 481 satellite modem.

Fixed-base wireless service is usually provided by companies that specialize in providing wireless cable TV service to rural areas as much as 30 miles or more from the microwave transmitter. This type of service is often called *MMDS wireless*. Some types of fixed-base wireless service are two-way, using the wireless antenna to send and receive signals. However, if the location is beyond the range of two-way wireless signals or a direct line of sight is not available, reflectors (sometimes called *benders*) can be used to bounce the signal from the tower to the antenna; a regular dial-up modem is used to upload information.

The rise in popularity of wireless Ethernet (Wi-Fi) has led to the development of a second type of wireless Internet access, *Wi-Fi access,* which uses the same Wi-Fi network adapters used to connect to Wi-Fi networks in homes and offices. Most Wi-Fi hot spots are located in businesses such as airline terminals, hotels, coffee shops, restaurants, and truckstops. Access is provided on a daily or hourly basis, or by means of a monthly or yearly contract. However, some communities now provide Wi-Fi access for specific neighborhoods or entire cities. Wi-Fi access is also available in many public buildings, such as libraries. Community-based Wi-Fi access might be free, require free registration, or be provided as a commercial service by a public utility.

Wireless Hardware

MMDS wireless networks use a small antenna that is aimed at the microwave tower used to distribute the signals. Coaxial cable runs between the antenna and a device known as a *wireless broadband router (WBR).* WBRs resemble cable modems. Some WBRs feature a nine-pin port that can connect the WBR to an analog dial-up modem for use with a one-way system (see Figure 4.4).

FIGURE 4.4

A typical wireless broadband router (WBR). This WBR can be connected to an external analog (dial-up) modem for use in a one-way environment.

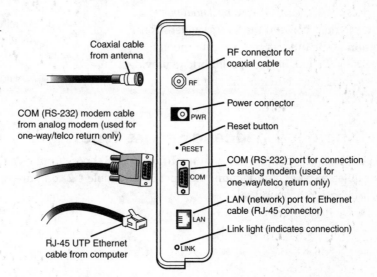

Coaxial cable from antenna

RF connector for coaxial cable

RF

COM (RS-232) modem cable from analog modem (used for one-way/telco return only)

Power connector

PWR

Reset button

RESET

COM (RS-232) port for connection to analog modem (used for one-way/telco return only)

COM

LAN (network) port for Ethernet cable (RJ-45 connector)

LAN

Link light (indicates connection)

LINK

RJ-45 UTP Ethernet cable from computer

Wi-Fi broadband Internet access typically uses the most common form of the three Wi-Fi specifications (802.11b) and uses the same type(s) of Wi-Fi hardware (USB, CardBus, or PCI card Wi-Fi adapters) as those used on home or office networks.

Wireless Pricing and Availability

For pricing and availability of wireless Internet access in your area, contact your local wireless cable TV or public utilities.

Powerline (BPL)

Broadband over powerline (BPL) is a promising alternative to point-to-point broadband technologies such as satellite and fixed-base wireless because it uses the existing power grid to carry network signals. However, amateur radio buffs and radio astronomers have expressed concern that BPL might interfere with the signal frequencies they monitor and use. Several pilot programs are underway across the United States and Europe in various markets.

HomePlug (powerline) and Wi-Fi adapters are used at each residence to transfer data from the BPL network to each computer in the home. Devices such as *couplers* and *backhaul points* transmit data between the BPL provider's connection to the Internet and neighborhoods served by the BPL line. A special bridge provides BPL service to each neighborhood in the service network.

tip

KEEPING YOUR EYE ON BPL DEVELOPMENTS

Current Communications Group, LLC, has several BPL projects underway. See how BPL is doing by checking out its website at http://www.currentgroup.com/.

Comparing Different Broadband Service Types

Depending on where you live, you might be able to choose from as many as three or four different types of broadband Internet access. Table 4.2 compares the major features of each broadband solution.

Table 4.2   Comparing Broadband Internet Access Types

Service Type	Download Speed Range	Upload Speed Range	Speed Affected by Other Users	Availability	Network Support
Cable	Up to 3,000Kbps	Up to 128Kbps or 384Kbps	Yes	Most areas served by digital cable TV providers	Yes
DSL	384Kbps; 768Kpbs; 1,500Kbps	128Kbps; 384Kbps	No	Most city/suburban areas with DSL-ready infrastructure	Yes
Satellite	Up to 500Kbps[1]	Up to 128Kbps	Yes	Any location with an unobstructed view of the satellite(s) used by the service; contact vendor for details	Varies
MMDS Wireless	Up to 3,000Kbps[2]	Up to 128Kbps or 384Kbps	No	Requires unobstructed line of sight with transmitter; maximum distance usually 30 miles	Yes
Wi-Fi Wireless	Varies with connection to the Internet used by network[3]	Varies	Yes	User must be within range of a Wi-Fi access point and have the proper credentials to use it	Yes

[1] Speeds up to 1,000Kbps (1Mbps) available with small-business plans or by upgrading to a newer satellite modem; contact vendors for details.

[2] Many wireless vendors provide multiple tiers of performance starting at 128Kbps download speed; consult vendor for available speeds.

[3] Although the maximum speed of Wi-Fi (wireless Ethernet) network connection is 11Mbps (802.11b) or 54Mbps (802.11g/a), the actual throughput speed is controlled by how the Wi-Fi network connects to the Internet. Contact the vendor for actual throughput speeds.

Choosing the Right Service for You

As you can see, choosing the right broadband Internet service can be complicated. However, by breaking down the essential features of each service option that's available to you, it's easy to see which service or services are most likely to satisfy your needs.

Service Cost per Month

The most obvious place to start is with the monthly rate you pay for Internet access. Although there are many variables (including speed, upload speed, additional features, and geographic location) that affect the cost per month, typical plans can be ranked as shown in Table 4.3. The least expensive plans are shown at left, with more expensive plans at right. Wireless and powerline broadband plans are not included because their pricing varies widely according to the individual market and they are not available in many areas.

Table 4.3 Comparing Broadband Internet Service Plans

Least Expensive per Month	Mid-Range	Most Expensive per Month
128Kbps DSL	384 or 768Kbps DSL	
	Cable modem	Satellite

Although Table 4.3 provides general guidance for pricing, check with the vendors available in your area for the latest pricing information before you make a decision.

Equipment Cost per Month

The next variable to consider is equipment cost. Typically, cable Internet vendors give you the option to lease a cable modem (about $10/month) or provide your own (you can buy one from various electronics and computer stores for about $70–90). Unless you're planning to move in the near future to a location that doesn't offer cable Internet service, you should buy your cable modem. At current rates, you'll spend the equivalent of its purchase price in nine months or less if you lease it. And, keep in mind that if you sign up for cable Internet service through a store that works with local suppliers to provide one-stop signup (Circuit City and Best Buy are two chains that offer this option), you might get the cable modem free after rebate.

By contrast, most DSL suppliers bundle the cost of the DSL modem and other hardware into the service charge. Because of the lack of a unified standard for DSL hardware, DSL modems are not sold separately at this time.

Satellite vendors, as you learned earlier in this chapter, offer you the option to buy the equipment up front or pay a higher monthly service charge to spread out your payments. Keep in mind that the already-steep cancellation fees get even steeper if you bail out of this type of service plan.

Wireless vendors who use MMDS or other point-to-point microwave transceivers also bundle the cost of the WBR into the monthly service cost.

The best hardware deal is available to those who live in an area with Wi-Fi wireless Internet access. For $40–80 to purchase a Wi-Fi adapter (if you don't already have one), you're ready to connect.

Powerline broadband Internet access (BPL) is still in its infancy, but I expect that the equipment will be leased as part of the monthly service charge, at least for the foreseeable future.

Other Up-Front Costs

Up-front costs in addition to hardware cost can be trivial to free (with cable, DSL, or Wi-Fi service) or can amount to major amounts of money (satellite, MMDS, or other fixed wireless). Don't forget to shop around for the best deal. For example, if your area is served by two cable Internet vendors, play them against each other. If DSL service is available to your address, you don't have to use the telephone company's service; a third-party service might save you money.

With satellite and fixed wireless services, professional installation (which includes a site survey) might be part of the initial startup costs or be a separate line item.

tip

LOOK FOR THE CABLE LABS CERTIFIED LABEL

It's usually safe to buy a cable modem instead of renting it because almost all cable systems today use cable modems that are Cable Labs Certified. Also known as DOCSIS (data over cable service interface specification), this certification assures that all cable modems and cable services that support DOCSIS will work with each other. If you are shopping for a cable modem, make sure you can use a Cable Labs Certified/DOCSIS cable modem with the cable service, and look for models that support the most recent DOCSIS standard available (1.1 or greater). I suggest using modems that use an Ethernet connection to your computer. See http://www.cablemodem.com for more information about Cable Labs Certified cable modems.

Cost per Kbps

No matter what else is true about a particular broadband Internet access service, what you're paying for, mainly, is download speed. How expensive is that speed? You can find out easily by calculating the cost per Kbps of download speed, using this formula:

cost per Kbps (cents) = service cost per month / Kbps (download speed) * 100.

> *Example 1: DSL (various telcos)*
>
> Service cost per month = $39.95 Speed = 768Kbps
>
> Cost per Kbps (approximately) = 5.2 cents/Kbps
>
> *Example 2: Cable modem (various providers)*
>
> Service cost per month = $39.95 Speed 2,000Kbps
>
> Cost per Kbps (approximately) = 2 cents/Kbps
>
> *Example 3: DirecWAY*
>
> Service cost per month = $59.95 Speed 500Kbps
>
> Cost per Kbps (approximately) = 12 cents/Kbps

If you want to include up-front costs in your calculations, take the up-front cost, divide it by 12 (if you plan to keep the service at least one year), by 24 (2 years) or by 36 (3 years). Add the result to the monthly service charge and perform the rest of the calculation. These calculations will help you determine which service provides the best "bang for the buck."

caution

$AVE MONEY WITH U$ED EQUIPMENT? MAYBE!

Some satellite services allow you to provide equipment you have purchased from another user and offer special rates for activation and service schedule. Before you buy used equipment, check with the vendor to see whether the equipment is still supported and what download/upload speeds it supports. Recent performance upgrades enabled by new satellite modems used by both DirecWAY and StarBand make non-current hardware less desirable—and keep in mind that professional installation is still required.

Upload Speeds

Most broadband service plans support upload speeds up to 128Kbps. However, if you need to upload web pages, use teleconferencing, play online games, or perform a lot of file transfers, you might want faster upload speeds. Faster speeds cost more, but may be worthwhile if you upload a lot of data.

Support for VPNs

If you're planning to work from home and access your corporate network, remember those three little letters from Chapter 1, "What Is a Home Network?": *VPN*. Recall that a VPN (virtual private network) is a method for using the public Internet to access a secured network. VPNs work by using so-called *tunneling protocols* to encrypt data at the transmitting end and unencrypt data at the receiving end of the connection. Tunneling protocols (IPSec is the most common) also encrypt the sending and receiving IP addresses for additional security.

Most broadband services support VPN, but VPN performance is much better with DSL or cable than with satellite. Satellite VPN performance usually drops to dial-up speeds because of the long latency inherent in satellite Internet service and because the encryption used by VPN disables the normal speedup methods used by satellite modems to speed up non-VPN traffic.

tip

DOING YOUR OWN SITE SURVEY

To avoid sticker shock from additional installation charges, check your site for a clear view to the satellite or transmission tower. To avoid the expense of a tower, opt for a roof mounting, if possible, if you need to raise your antenna or satellite dish.

Note that some vendors might charge a nonrefundable site survey charge if you ask for an installation at a site that doesn't have a clear view of the satellite or transmission tower. And, expect to pay more if a tower is needed.

Network-Friendliness

At one time, cable and DSL were the best choices if you wanted to connect your system to a home network. Both services typically use external Ethernet-based modems. However, the recent introduction of satellite modems with Ethernet ports (DirecWAY DW6000 and StarBand 481 and 484 series) brings satellite Internet into a network-ready mode. MMDS (fixed-base wireless), Wi-Fi, and powerline networks are inherently network-ready.

Although most broadband Internet services are network-friendly, you'll enjoy better performance and fewer setup hassles with a non-satellite service. Satellite Internet's throughput isn't high enough to support a lot of downloading, and there's always the danger of exceeding the explicit or implicit download limits of these services. For details about connecting various services to a home network, see Chapters 5, "Installing and Configuring a Wi-Fi Network," and 6, "Installing and Configuring a Wired Ethernet Network."

tip

DETERMINING REAL-WORLD SPEEDS FOR YOUR CALCULATIONS

If you're considering two or more services with similar cost per Kbps based on their *published* speeds, check Broadband Reports (www.broadbandreports.com) or other test sources to find out the average speed that users in your area are experiencing. If you live near a friend who uses the service you're considering, ask him or her to run the speed test at Broadband Reports a couple of times at different times of the day. Use real-world figures to perform your calculations for a more accurate cost per Kbps.

Self-installing DSL

If you decide that DSL is right for you, your DSL provider might offer you the opportunity to install DSL service yourself. It's fairly simple, especially if you have a 10/100 Ethernet port already built into your PC—and, self-installation saves you the cost of professional installation.

tip

AVOIDING VPN DISAPPOINTMENT

To prevent a mismatch between the VPN support provided by your company and what your broadband service provides, check with your IT department to see what type of VPN software it uses. You also need this information to determine that routers or other home networking hardware you buy will work properly with the service.

Figure 4.5 shows you the contents of a typical DSL self-installation kit:

- DSL modem
- Line splitter
- Microfilters
- Wall mount filter
- DSL data cable
- Ethernet cable
- Installation software

Some kits might also include a 10/100 Ethernet PCI (for desktop PCs) or PC Card (for notebook PCs) network adapter. However, most recent systems have a 10/100 or 10/100/1000 Ethernet port already built in. Buying a kit that contains a network adapter makes sense only if your computer doesn't have one already.

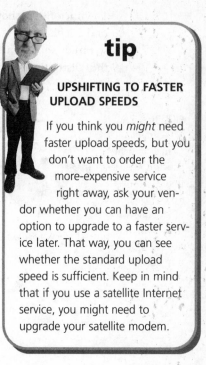

tip

UPSHIFTING TO FASTER UPLOAD SPEEDS

If you think you *might* need faster upload speeds, but you don't want to order the more-expensive service right away, ask your vendor whether you can have an option to upgrade to a faster service later. That way, you can see whether the standard upload speed is sufficient. Keep in mind that if you use a satellite Internet service, you might need to upgrade your satellite modem.

FIGURE 4.5

Contents of a typical DSL self-installation kit. The network adapters (shaded area) are optional items not necessary if your computer already has an Ethernet port.

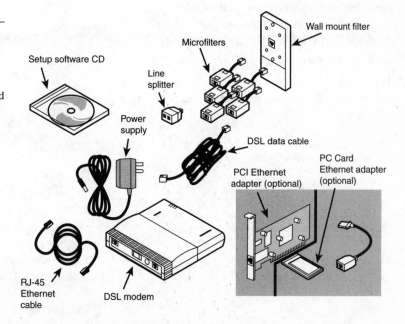

The microfilters shown in Figure 4.6 must be connected between each phone line and telephone or telephony-based device (answering machines, fax machines, and so on) as shown in Figure 4.6. Telephones and similar devices can cause interference that disrupts the high-frequency signals used by DSL. If you have a wall-mounted phone, use the wall-mount filter between the current wall socket and your phone.

FIGURE 4.6

A DSL microfilter (center) attaches between the telephone jack (left) and a telephone or other device to prevent interference with the DSL signal.

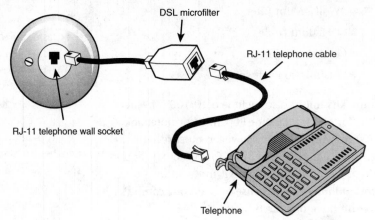

DSL microfilter

RJ-11 telephone cable

RJ-11 telephone wall socket

Telephone

After the microfilters are in place and the DSL modem is connected to the computer via the Ethernet port (Figure 4.7), run the software included with the kit to configure your service.

Figure 4.8 shows a typical DSL connection after all components have been connected and configured.

note

NO SLOTS LEFT? ADAPT USB TO ETHERNET!

Many vendors make Ethernet adapters that plug into USB ports. You can use such an adapter to enable a system without an Ethernet port or a place to install an internal adapter to use an Ethernet-based DSL modem. For the best performance, look for adapters that support Hi-Speed USB (USB 2.0) and plug them into a Hi-Speed USB port.

FIGURE 4.7

Attach the Ethernet cable (left) between the Ethernet port on the PC (after installing an Ethernet adapter if necessary) and the Ethernet port on the DSL modem (not shown).

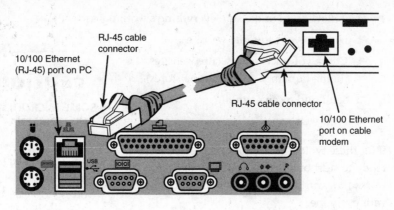

RJ-45 cable connector

10/100 Ethernet (RJ-45) port on PC

RJ-45 cable connector

10/100 Ethernet port on cable modem

USB

FIGURE 4.8

A completed DSL installation using a microfilter, two-line splitter, and an external DSL modem.

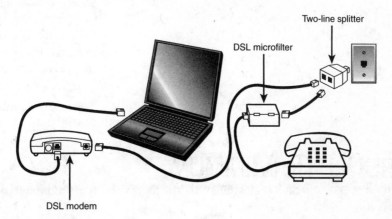

Two-line splitter

DSL microfilter

DSL modem

Testing Your Broadband Connection

Before you build your home network around your broadband Internet connection, make sure your connection works properly. Although home networking is easier than ever, installing a home network before you know whether your broadband Internet connection works makes it much harder to figure out what's causing a problem with your connection.

caution

DON'T "FILTER" OUT YOUR DSL SIGNAL!

Don't attach an inline microfilter or wall socket microfilter to the line connected to your DSL modem. Doing so will prevent the DSL modem from working.

Try the following to make sure everything's working correctly:

- Look up your favorite websites.
- Check your access to secure websites (home banking, email, online stores).
- Send and receive email.
- Print web pages.

If all these typical tasks work properly, you're ready to start building your choice of home networks that can share the broadband goodness with everyone.

> **caution**
>
> **SOME MICROFILTERS AND HOMEPNA DON'T MIX**
>
> If you're planning to use HomePNA (phoneline) networking to share your connection, make sure the microfilters you use are HomePNA-compatible. Incompatible microfilters will prevent a HomePNA network from working. Check the microfilter's packaging or contact your DSL provider to determine this information.

The Absolute Minimum

Cable, DSL, satellite, and wireless are the four major types of broadband Internet access.

Cable Internet is provided by cable TV companies, usually over a digital fiber-optic network.

Cable Internet offers download speeds as high as 3,000Kbps, but maximum speed varies greatly because multiple homes share a single connection.

DSL is provided through telephone lines by the local telephone company or a third-party provider.

Line condition and distance affect your ability to get DSL and the service speeds you can choose from.

DSL modems are leased from the vendor.

DSL download speeds range from 384Kbps to 1,500Kbps, and are more consistent than cable modem speeds.

Satellite Internet is available almost anywhere, including places where cable or DSL is not available.

Satellite Internet is much slower than cable and somewhat slower than DSL, offering download speeds up to 500Kbps for home and up to 1,000Kbps for small-office plans.

Satellite Internet is not suitable for gaming or teleconferencing because of long latency.

Wireless Internet comes in two forms: fixed-base wireless (provided by wireless cable TV companies, mostly to rural areas) and Wi-Fi, available in some cities as well as public hot spots around the country.

Fixed-base wireless uses a small microwave antenna and a device similar to a cable modem called a wireless broadband router.

Powerline Internet (BPL) is an emerging broadband technology now being tested in several markets.

DSL and cable Internet access are the least expensive in terms of equipment and monthly charges; satellite is much more expensive.

You can self-install DSL in many situations using a kit provided by the DSL vendor.

If you already have an Ethernet port in your PC, DSL installation is very simple.

Before you set up a home network to share your broadband Internet connection, test it to make sure it works correctly.

5

INSTALLING AND CONFIGURING A WIRED ETHERNET NETWORK

Wired ethernet is the oldest network you can use at home. However, it's still one of the best choices, especially if you plan to network just one or two rooms. Wired ethernet also works well as part of a mix-and-match network with wireless ethernet (Wi-Fi).

From installing adapters and building network cable to configuring your router and hiding your cable, this chapter is your guide to fast, inexpensive home networking with wired ethernet.

Why Wired Ethernet Still Makes Sense

Wired ethernet (which includes 10BASE-T, Fast Ethernet, 10/100 Ethernet, and Gigabit Ethernet) doesn't have the sex appeal of its wireless sibling, but if you're looking for the cheapest, fastest, and easiest-to-configure home network around, wired ethernet's worth considering.

What makes wired ethernet so inexpensive? First of all, consider the fact that most desktop and notebook computers built in the last couple of years include a 10/100 Ethernet (RJ-45) port, as you learned in Chapter 3, "Planning Your Home Network." Even if your computer lacks an ethernet port, you can add one for less than $50. Second, 10/100 Ethernet routers (the devices that connect your network with the Internet) have never been cheaper, with many brands selling for around $50. Almost all routers include a switch, so you can use a single device to connect your computers to each other and to the Internet. Even if you decide to install a wireless ethernet(Wi-Fi) router incorporating a 10/100 Ethernet switch (perfect for building a mixed wired/wireless network), you won't spend much more.

Wired ethernet is blazing fast. The standard 10/100 Ethernet adapters and ports run at 100Mbps (Fast Ethernet speed) unless your network has some of the old 10BASE-T (10Mbps) network hardware. Even then, network switches create high-speed connections between 100Mbps devices. Better still, most recent 10/100 Ethernet network adapters and switches support full duplex. Some new computers feature Gigabit Ethernet (1000Mbps), which is also backward-compatible with 10/100 Ethernet.

Finally, wired ethernet is easy to configure. Run the Windows Home Networking wizard or manually configure a simple TCP/IP option called *dynamic host configuration protocol (DHCP)* on each computer, and each station on the network gets a unique IP address. Networking in business can be complicated, but ethernet networking at home is simple.

FULL DUPLEX FOR SUPER-FAST ETHERNET SPEED

Ethernet speed ratings assume half duplex operation: Each network adapter is reading data from another network station or sending (writing) data to another network station. When enabled, full duplex network hardware performs simultaneous read/write operations, pushing the effective speed of a 10/100 Ethernet network with Fast Ethernet hardware to 200Mbps, a cool 8×-or-more faster than the real-world speed of typical 802.11g Wi-Fi wireless nets. To maintain full duplex performance, always use a switch, never a hub, to add additional ports to your network.

So, what's the big rap against wired ethernet? The wires, of course. Long wire runs can add up to some serious bucks if you buy pre-built wire, wire colors are refugees from a crayon box, and they can be hard to run through walls. None of these are fatal objections, though. If economy, speed, and fixed locations are your goals, wired ethernet is your network, and this chapter will show you how to do it.

Adding Network Adapters to Your Hardware

If some of your notebook or desktop PCs don't have on-board ethernet adapters, the following sections show you how to get your systems ready to join a wired ethernet network.

If all the hardware (PCs, home entertainment devices, video cameras, and so forth) is ethernet-ready, skip to "Hub, Switch, or Router? Making the Right Connectivity Choice" (p.109, this chapter) to continue.

tip

MIX-AND-MATCH FOR ECONOMY AND PERFORMANCE

In my own home network, I take full advantage of the mix-and-match capabilities of a wireless router, which also includes a switch. I run cables to close-in locations, and use the wireless feature for roving PCs such as my notebook computer. The techniques covered in this chapter work with both "pure" wired ethernet networks and with the wired component of a wired ethernet/Wi-Fi network.

Adding Wired Ethernet Adapters to Your PCs

Most, but not all, recent PCs already have a 10/100 Ethernet port. However, if your PC doesn't, there are several ways to connect it to an ethernet network, as Table 5.1 reveals.

Table 5.1 Ethernet Adapters for PCs

Computer Type	Adapter Type	How Added	Benefits	Drawbacks
Desktop	PCI	Installed into open PCI slot	Faster connection than USB or Hi-Speed USB port; lowest-cost adapter type	Requires opening PC; difficult to move between systems
Notebook	PC Card	Installed into open PC Card or CardBus Type II slot	Easy to install	PC Card slot is slower than CardBus slot; card becomes useless if dongle is lost or damaged; can't be used with desktop PCs

Table 5.1 (continued)

Computer Type	Adapter Type	How Added	Benefits	Drawbacks
Notebook	CardBus	Installed into open CardBus Type II slot	Easy to install; faster than PC Card	More expensive than PC Card; can't be used with desktop PCs
Desktop or Notebook	USB 1.1	Connects to open USB 1.1 port	Easy to install or move; works in any system with a USB 1.1 port	Slower than CardBus or PCI; more expensive than PCI card
Desktop or Notebook	Hi-Speed USB (USB 2.0)	Connects to open USB 2.0 or 1.1 port	Easy to install or move; works in any system with a USB port	Requires Hi-Speed USB port for best performance; more expensive than PCI card

Which solution is right for you? From the standpoint of performance, choose these:

- Desktop or notebook PC with Hi-Speed USB port: Hi-Speed USB (USB 2.0) adapter.

- Desktop with open PCI card slot (but no Hi-Speed USB port): PCI card adapter

- Notebook with open CardBus slot (but no Hi-Speed USB port): CardBus adapter

Although USB 1.1 adapters can be used with virtually any PC built in the last 5 or 6 years, the maximum speed of the port is just 12Mbps. PC Card adapters work in both recent notebooks and old models (CardBus slots also take PC Cards), but the PC Card's 16-bit data bus limits performance compared to CardBus's 32-bit data bus. Figure 5.1 shows typical examples of Hi-Speed USB, PCI, and CardBus 10/100 Ethernet network adapters.

note

THE PROCESS IS SIMILAR WITH OTHER ADAPTER TYPES

Because other types of network adapters use similar installation processes, I'll provide cross-references to this section in other chapters. After you complete these steps, return to the appropriate chapter for additional steps to follow to complete the installation process.

FIGURE 5.1

A typical
CardBus (left),
PCI card (top
center), and USB
adapter (right)
for 10/100
Ethernet net-
works. Photos
courtesy D-Link
Systems.

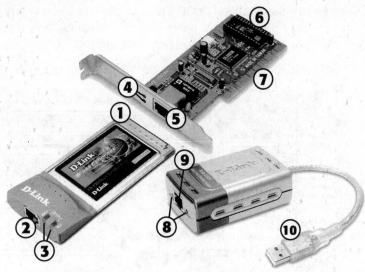

1. CardBus connector
2. RJ-45 port
3. Link/activity lights
4. Link/activity lights
5. RJ-45 port

6. Boot ROM socket
7. PCI connector
8. Link/activity lights
9. RJ-45 port
10. USB Type A connector

Installing a USB Adapter

If your system has a USB port, installing a USB ethernet adapter is far and away the simplest way to connect it to a wired ethernet network. Here's how to do it:

1. Install the driver disk or CD for your USB adapter. Although USB is widely praised as a "plug-and-play" technology, plug-and-play assumes that your computer already "knows" about the device category and specific require-ments of a given USB device. If you don't install drivers for a specific USB device first, the system won't recognize it, or might try to use an existing driver that won't work.

2. Attach the USB cable to the adapter if necessary. Some ethernet adapters use a removable USB cable, and others use a built-in USB cable.

3. Plug the device directly into a USB port on your PC, or into a powered hub (Figure 5.2). USB ports in your PC output the full 500mA power requirement used by some USB devices, but USB ports in keyboard or other bus-powered hub usually provide only 100mA per port.

4. Provide the Windows CD if requested. This step is necessary if your system needs additional USB support from the Windows CD or if the necessary network protocols are not already installed.

USB ports (2)

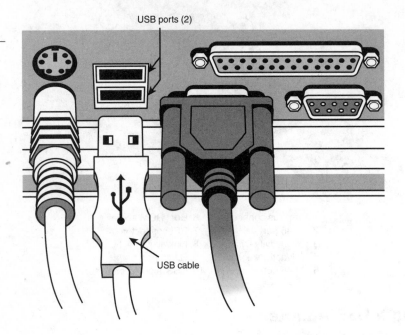

USB cable

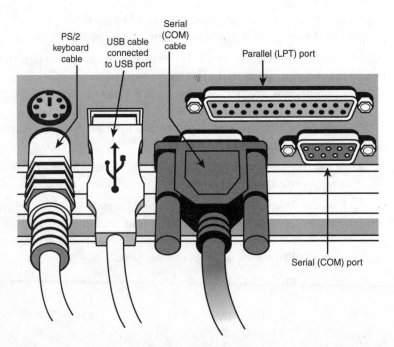

PS/2 keyboard cable

USB cable connected to USB port

Serial (COM) cable

Parallel (LPT) port

Serial (COM) port

FIGURE 5.3

A warning triggered by plugging a Hi-Speed USB (USB 2.0) network adapter or other device into a USB 1.1 port on a system running Windows XP.

Installing a PC Card or CardBus Adapter

Most recent notebook computers have one or two Type II CardBus slots. These slots can also handle PC Card devices. After you determine which type of card your system uses, the remainder of the installation process is almost identical:

1. Determine whether your notebook computer has CardBus or PC Card slots. To find out which type of card slot your notebook computer uses, check your system documentation or use Windows Device Manager (Figure 5.4) to see whether your system has a CardBus controller.

2. Insert the CardBus or PC Card into the appropriate slot. Note that if your system has only one CardBus or PC Card slot and you are already using it, you must eject the card first before you can insert another card. Use the Safely Remove Hardware utility in the Windows System Tray to stop the other card before you eject it.

3. Install the required drivers. Use the CD or floppy disk provided with the adapter, or point the installation program to updated drivers you have downloaded.

note

DON'T PANIC IF YOU MISMATCH HI-SPEED USB AND USB 1.1

Windows XP will pop up a warning (Figure 5.3) if you connect a Hi-Speed USB device to a USB 1.1 port. Your device will work, but its speed will be limited by the slower speed of the port.

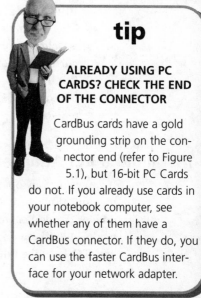

tip

ALREADY USING PC CARDS? CHECK THE END OF THE CONNECTOR

CardBus cards have a gold grounding strip on the connector end (refer to Figure 5.1), but 16-bit PC Cards do not. If you already use cards in your notebook computer, see whether any of them have a CardBus connector. If they do, you can use the faster CardBus interface for your network adapter.

CardBus and PC Card controllers are listed under the
PCMCIA adapters category in Device Manager

FIGURE 5.4

Using Windows
XP's Device
Manager to
determine
whether a
portable com-
puter has a
CardBus con-
troller on board.

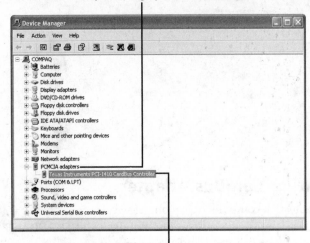

Device Manager listing for a typical CardBus controller

4. Provide the Windows CD if requested. If your system hasn't already been connected to the Internet or to another network, you might need to provide the
Windows CD so that Windows can install the appropriate network protocols.

5. If the card is equipped with a dongle,
connect it after the card is installed.
Many older PC Card-based 10BASE-T,
10/100 Ethernet, or combo
ethernet/modem cards use a removable
dongle to connect standard cables to the
narrow edge of a Type II card (Figure
5.5). If the dongle is lost or damaged,
the card is useless until the dongle is
replaced.

tip

**HANDLING THE
WINDOWS/DRIVER
CD-SWAP BLUES**

If you need to remove your
network driver CD and insert
your Windows driver CD
during installation, your
system might "forget" what
folder to use for files. If this hap-
pens, use the Browse button on
the dialog box and navigate to the
appropriate folder on the
Windows or driver CD.

Installing a PCI Adapter

If you've already opened your system to install a
memory, drive, or video card upgrade, installing
a network adapter won't be hard. However, if
you're embarking on your first journey inside
your PC, keep the following in mind:

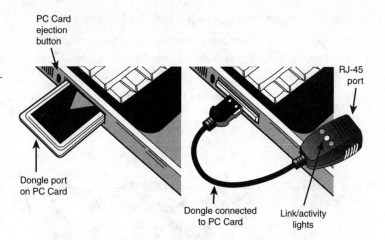

PC Card
ejection
button

RJ-45
port

FIGURE 5.5

Inserting a typical Type II PC Card 10/100 Ethernet adapter, which uses a dongle.

Dongle port
on PC Card

Dongle connected
to PC Card

Link/activity
lights

■ You need a Phillips screwdriver or hex driver to open your system and remove a card slot cover. As long as you keep your driver away from floppy or Zip disks, it's OK to use a magnetic-tipped tool.

■ To avoid ESD (electrostatic damage), be sure to touch a metal part of the case *before* you open your PC. And, keep one hand on the power supply or another metal part while the system is open. Or, use a wrist strap.

To install a PCI card in a desktop computer:

1. Take ESD precautions. Touch a metal part of the PC or use a wrist strap.

2. Turn off the system and unplug it. Run the Windows Shutdown procedure to shut down your system. If your power supply has a power switch, turn it off before you unplug the power cord.

3. Remove the screws holding the cover in place. Some systems use separate panels for each side of the cover, and others use a one-piece cover for the entire system.

4. Remove the cover. Some cases lift off the frame in one piece or in sections, and others slide off.

tip

A WRIST STRAP'S THE WAY TO KEEP THE ESD BLUES AWAY

A commercial anti-ESD wrist strap uses an alligator clip to connect to a metal part of the PC to prevent the buildup of static electricity. You can buy them from a variety of computer-tool vendors, or you might find one included in a computer toolkit.

5. Locate an empty PCI expansion slot. See Figure 5.6 (top).

6. Remove the slot cover corresponding to the expansion slot. In most cases, the slot cover is held in place by a screw. However, some systems use a snap-out slot cover that might be disposable.

7. Line up the PCI card with the PCI slot and push it into place. See Figure 5.6 (bottom).

Screw covering slot cover

FIGURE 5.6

Locating an empty PCI expansion slot (top) and installing the network card (bottom).

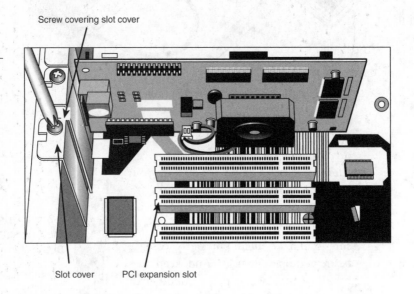

Slot cover   PCI expansion slot

Screw securing card bracket

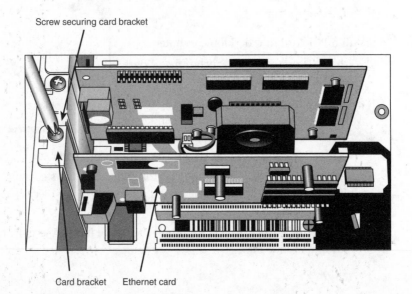

Card bracket   Ethernet card

8. Fasten the card bracket to the case with the screw removed in step 5. See Figure 5.6 (bottom).

9. Close the case. If the case was removed in sections, be sure to reinstall case sections in the correct order.

10. Plug in the power supply and restart the system. If the power supply is turned off, turn it on before attempting to restart the system.

11. Provide the Windows and network adapter driver disk(s) or CDs when prompted. You might not need to provide disks or CDs with newer versions of Windows.

Adding Home Entertainment Devices to Your Network

You can connect home entertainment devices such as home theater systems, stereos, TVs, personal video recorders, and video games to a wired ethernet network.

To add home theater systems, stereos, or TVs to your network, connect them to a media adapter. These devices include software that enables the device to connect with a PC that contains the photo, video, or music files you want to play and a remote control for selecting and playing the files. Although most media servers are marketed to users of Wi-Fi (802.11) wireless networks, the vast majority of them also support 10/100 or 10BASE-T wired Ethernet networks.

TiVo Series 2-compatible personal video recorders feature a USB port that can be used for ethernet or other types of USB network adapters. ReplayTV personal video recorders feature a built-in ethernet port.

The Microsoft Xbox is ready to connect to a wired ethernet network as soon as you take it out of the box. However, if you want to add a Sony PlayStation 2 to an ethernet network, you need to use Sony's PlayStation 2 broadband adapter (included in recent systems or available separately) or a PlayStation 2-compatible USB to ethernet adapter. Similarly, you need the Nintendo GameCube broadband adapter if you want to connect a GameCube system to your network.

For more details about adding home entertainment hardware to any type of home network, see Chapter 7, "Home Networks at Play."

Hub, Switch, or Router? Making the Right Connectivity Choice

Stations on a 10/100 or 10BASE-T Ethernet network do not connect directly to each other. Instead, they are connected through a centralized device that receives and sends signals between the stations (Figure 5.7).

FIGURE 5.7

A typical home network using wired ethernet hardware.

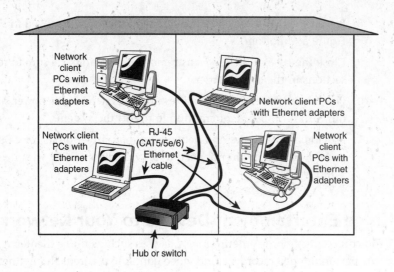

Hub or switch

There are three types of devices that can be used to make the connection between stations in a wired ethernet network:

- *Hub*—Simplest of the three devices, a hub broadcasts to all devices on the network and subdivides the bandwidth of the network among connected devices. Thus, a 10/100 Ethernet network with four 100Mbps stations connected through a hub has an effective speed of 25Mbps (100/4).

- *Switch*—The switch creates a direct (one-to-one) connection between sending and receiving computers and provides full network speed for all stations. Most switches also provide full-duplex support.

- *Router*—A router connects one network (such as a LAN) to another (such as the Internet). Almost all routers made for home networking include a switch. Otherwise, a router can be connected to a switch or hub.

If your network is used to share an Internet connection, you need a router, preferably with an integrated switch. Even if your home network doesn't include Internet access now, the small price

note

SIMPLIFYING TERMS

Although some wired ethernet home networks still use hubs, I will use the term *switch* in the remainder of this book to refer to the connection between PCs on a wired ethernet network. Because almost all routers contain integrated switches, I will use the term *router* to refer to a router that has an integrated switch or is connected to a separate switch.

premium for routers with integrated switches over switches alone makes using a router preferable. Routers also provide IP addresses to the computers connected to them, making network setup relatively simple.

How can you tell whether a device is a hub, switch, or router? Table 5.2 provides a quick reference to the features of each type of device. Figure 5.8 compares these devices. In most cases, the signal lights shown in Figure 5.8 are on the front of each device, and the ports are on the rear of each device. Note that the switch has signal lights for full duplex, and the router has a WAN port and separate signal lights for the WAN connection to the Internet.

The Uplink ports shown in Figure 5.8 are used to connect the device to another device (see Figure 5.9 for an example).

FIGURE 5.8

A hub (top) compared to a switch (center) and a router with an integrated switch (bottom).

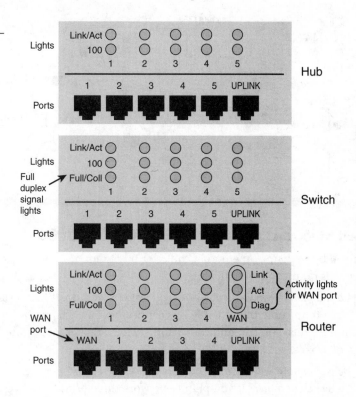

Table 5.2   Hub, Switch, and Router Feature Comparison

| | Features | | | |
Device Type	LAN Ports & Signal Lights	Full Duplex Indicator	WAN Port & Signal Light	Uplink Port
Hub	Yes	—	—	Optional
Switch	Yes	Yes	—	Optional
Router	Yes*	Yes	Yes	Optional

A router with an integrated switch will have four or more LAN ports. A router without an integrated switch will have one LAN port to connect it to a hub or switch.

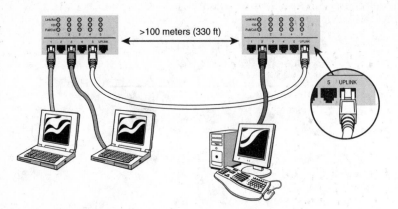

FIGURE 5.9
To add extra ports or to boost distances beyond 100 meters, connect a second switch on your network via its Uplink hub (right) to a LAN port on the first switch.

Building Versus Buying Ethernet Cables

Should you build your own ethernet cables or buy them? The answer to that question depends on the following factors:

- *Do you plan to run your cables through walls?* If you do, it's easier to snake raw cable than cable that already has connectors on each end. After the cable is in the walls, you can add connectors or, for a neater job, connect the ends to wall boxes.

- *Do you plan to network three or more devices at distances greater than 100 feet to the switch or router?* If you plan to network three or more devices, especially with relatively long cable runs, it can make more sense economically to build your own cable. As an alternative, also consider building a mix-and-match network that uses wired ethernet for close-in devices and wireless ethernet (Wi-Fi) for longer (over 100 feet) distances. This is the approach I use in my home network.

However, if your home network includes only a couple of devices and you don't need (or don't want) to snake your cable through walls, you can save yourself a bit of trouble by using assembled cables.

Assembled Cable Benefits and Drawbacks

There are advantages to buying pre-assembled ethernet cable:

- *Availability*—You can buy ready-to-use CAT5/5e/6 Ethernet cable at office-supply, electronics, and discount stores. CAT5 is all you need for a 10/100 Ethernet network, but 5e and 6 provide higher signal quality.
- *Color-coding*—You can use a different cable color for each station on the network: blue, red, gray, black, purple, clear, and others.
- *Snagless connectors*—Almost all pre-assembled ethernet cables feature a cover over the locking tab on each end of the cable. This so-called *snagless boot* helps prevent cable tangles and damage to the locking tab. See Figure 5.10.

Of course, there are disadvantages to pre-assembled cable as well:

- *Cost per foot*—Short cables (under 25 feet) are very expensive. Expect to pay $2–$3/foot or more.
- *Difficulty in running cables through walls*— The connectors at the end of each cable make snaking the cable through walls or ceilings more difficult and require larger holes than raw cable does.

tip

MONEY-$AVING TECHNIQUES FOR CUSTOM CABLING

Ethernet cables and connectors aren't expensive, but high-quality crimping tools (refer to Figure 5.11) can be more than $50. If you have friends or acquaintances who have already built ethernet cable, see whether you can borrow their tools, or buy them dinner and ask them over to help!

tip

CABLE TOO SHORT? COUPLERS TO THE RESCUE

If your network cable is too short to reach a particular station but it's difficult (or impossible) to rerun a longer cable, buy an inline coupler. An inline coupler (Figure 5.10) connects to the end of one network cable and enables another cable to be plugged into the other end. Make sure the coupler is CAT5 compatible; some older couplers support CAT3 (10Mbps) signals only.

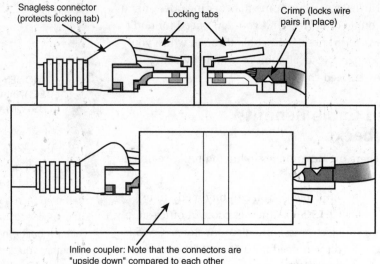

Snagless connector
(protects locking tab)

Locking tabs

Crimp (locks wire
pairs in place)

Inline coupler: Note that the connectors are
"upside down" compared to each other

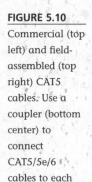

FIGURE 5.10
Commercial (top left) and field-assembled (top right) CAT5 cables. Use a coupler (bottom center) to connect CAT5/5e/6 cables to each other.

Building and Running Your Own Ethernet Cables

If you want to build your own ethernet cables, you should decide whether you want to build cables with standard ends (such as the ones shown in Figure 5.10) or if you want to build cables that connect to a wall plate.

There are two ways you can use to connect cables to a wall plate. One method uses a keystone jack, which is an RJ-45 port that fits into a wall plate. You wire one end of the cable directly into the keystone jack. The other end of the cable can be wired into another keystone jack or can use a standard RJ-45 connector. An RJ-45 patch cable from a network adapter plugs into the keystone jack. The other method uses a wall plate that uses a snap-in coupler. The coupler works like the in-line coupler shown in Figure 5.10, enabling you to use standard RJ-45 connectors to build all of your cables.

Whether you use a keystone jack/wall plate assembly or a snap-in coupler/wall plate assembly, using a wall plate provides a more professional look to your network, but it also requires you to cut a hole in the wall. Table 5.3 breaks down the supplies needed for each type of cable, and Table 5.4 lists the tools needed for each type of cable.

Table 5.3   Supplies Needed for Building Ethernet Cables

Item	Quantity Needed	Connection Type	Options	Notes	Refer to Figure #
Bulk Ethernet cable	250 feet or longer	All	Color, type (solid or stranded)	Solid is stiffer and thus easier to run through walls.	Figure 5.11, Figure 5.20
RJ-45 standard connectors	Two per cable (one at each end) for standard cables; one per cable for keystone cable	Standard, in-line coupler	Snagless connector cover	Snagless connector cover should be color-matched to cable color.	Figure 5.12, Figure 5.20
RJ-45 keystone jack[1]	One per each end of cable	Keystone, in-line coupler	—	8-wire keystone jacks work with RJ-45.[2]	Figure 5.13, Figure 5.14
Wall plate with keystone jack or snap-in coupler	One per each end of cable	Keystone, snap-in coupler	Number of ports (1–6)	Wall plate can also support RJ-11 telephone, RG-6 cable TV, and so on.	Figure 5.13, Figure 5.14[1]
Mounting bracket	One per wall plate	Keystone, snap-in coupler	Match size of wall plate	Enables mounting of keystone jacks with wall plate without a wall box	Figure 5.14
Wall box	One per wall plate if mounting bracket is not used	Keystone, snap-in coupler	Match size of wall plate	Enables mounting of keystone jacks with wall plate to a stud	—

[1]These figures show wall plates with keystone jacks.

[2]8-wire keystone jacks work with RJ-45. Do not try to use 2-wire, 4-wire, or 6-wire keystone jacks. Those types are used with RJ-11 telephone cable.

FIGURE 5.11

Bulk CAT5 solid Ethernet cable (top left) and an RJ-45/RJ-11 crimper (bottom). The crimper also includes a wire cutter/stripper.

Solid CAT5 Ethernet cable

Wire cutter/stripper

RJ-45 crimper

RJ-11 crimper

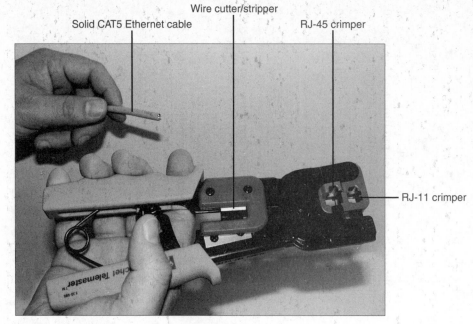

FIGURE 5.12

A typical RJ-45 connector. The wire pairs are inserted through the end of the connector (left).

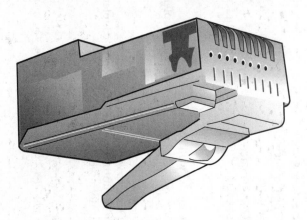

FIGURE 5.13

A two-jack wall outlet with one keystone jack already inserted (top left).

FIGURE 5.14

A mounting bracket with a CAT5 cable, keystone jack, and two-hole wall plate.

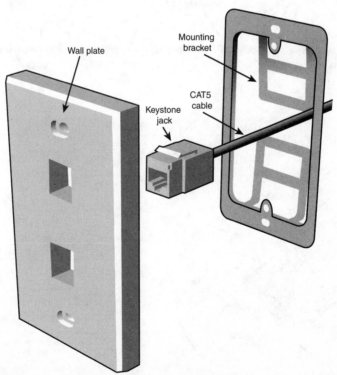

Wall plate

Mounting bracket

Keystone jack

CAT5 cable

Table 5.4 Tools Needed for Building Ethernet Cables

Item	Connection Type	Notes	Refer to Figure #
Crimper	Standard	Models with RJ-45 and RJ-11 crimps can also build telephone cables. Models with integrated wire stripper can be used to prepare wire for use. Creates more durable and reliable cables than pliers.	Figure 5.11, Figure 5.20
Punchdown tool	Keystone	Punches wire pairs into the keystone jack	Figure 5.15
Utility knife	Both	Strips outer jacket and wire pairs	Figure 5.16
Wire fish	Both	Pushes unfinished cable through walls and along studs	Figure 5.17
Diagonal cutters	Both	Cuts cable and trims wire pairs to correct lengths	Figure 5.18

FIGURE 5.15

A typical punch-down tool.

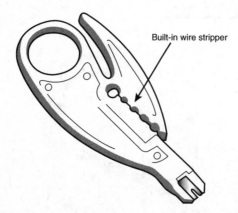

Built-in wire stripper

FIGURE 5.16

Using a utility knife to strip off the outer wire jacket from the CAT5 cable.

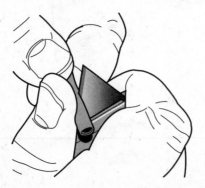

FIGURE 5.17
A typical wire fish. The unfinished cable end is connected to the end of the wire fish, which pushes it through the wall and past obstacles to its destination.

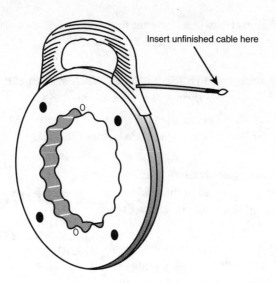

Insert unfinished cable here

FIGURE 5.18
Using a typical pair of diagonal cutters to trim off the end of CAT5 cable. The wire pairs must be the same length for proper crimping.

Building a Standard Cable

Whether you're building a new ethernet cable from components or replacing a broken connector, the process works like this:

tip

FIX IT, DON'T TOSS IT!

You can also use some of the tools and supplies shown in Tables 5.3 and 5.4 and their companion figures to repair CAT5/5e/6 cables with broken connectors. Bent or broken locking tabs are the most frequent type of connector damage.

1. Run the cable from the switch or router to the location where you plan to place the computer or device. See "Hiding Your Cables," p. 122, this chapter, for details.

2. Allow a couple of feet of additional cable for slack at each end. Make sure your cable run is no more than 100 meters (about 328 feet).

3. Cut off the end of the cable or the broken connector with a diagonal cutter (refer to Figure 5.18). Make sure the cut is straight.

4. Measure and mark slightly more than one-half inch from the end of the cable. The outer jacket of this cable is removed in the next step.

5. Use a utility knife to remove the outer jacket of the cable with the utility knife or wire stripper, as marked in step 4 (refer to Figure 5.16).

6. Check the wire pairs for nicks or cuts. Redo steps 3–5 if any nicks or cuts are noticed.

7. Arrange the wires to match the EIA 568B standard as shown in Table 5.5 and in Figure 5.19.

8. Flatten the cable slightly.

caution

BUILD THE RIGHT KIND OF CABLE FOR THE JOB

If you are building a cable with a standard connector on one end and a keystone jack on the other end, perform steps 3 and above *only* on the end of the cable that will have the standard connection.

Table 5.5 EIA 568B Standard for UTP Cable

Wire #	Color
1	White-Orange
2	Orange
3	White-Green
4	Blue
5	White-Blue
6	Green
7	White-Brown
8	Brown

9. Trim the wires so that they are slightly less than one-half inch longer than the outer wire jacket.

10. Push on the RJ-45 connector with the locking tab facing away from you until the end of the outer jacket is lined up with the shoulder of the connector. Figure 5.19 shows the top and profile view of a typical cable before and after the RJ-45 connector is inserted.

FIGURE 5.19

UTP wire pairs arranged to match the EIA568B standard (top) and inserted into an RJ-45 connector (middle and bottom).

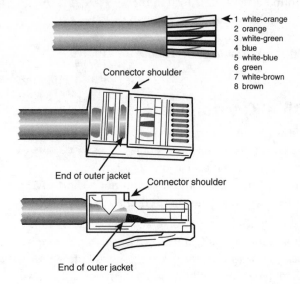

1 white-orange
2 orange
3 white-green
4 blue
5 white-blue
6 green
7 white-brown
8 brown

Connector shoulder

End of outer jacket   Connector shoulder

End of outer jacket

11. After inspecting the wire pairs and the position of the outer jacket, insert the end of the cable into the RJ-45 crimper (Figure 5.20).

12. Squeeze the crimper handle tightly (using both hands if necessary) to crimp the outer jacket and wire pairs in place.

FIGURE 5.20

Crimping the connector.

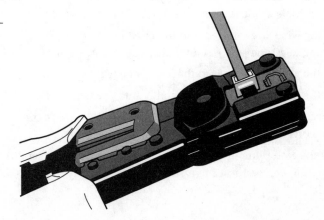

If you use wall plates with snap-in couplers, use this same method to build your cables. Connect the wall-mounted cable connector to the inside end of the coupler, snap it into the wall plate, and use the mounting bracket described in the next section to fasten the wall plate to the wall. Connect a standard RJ-45 cable from the network adapter to the outside end of the coupler to finish the job.

> **tip**
>
> **DON'T TRUST—VERIFY**
>
> A well-crimped cable is difficult to pull apart by hand unless you really stress your muscles. If a gentle motion pulls the connector off the cable, you didn't crimp the cable properly.

Building a Cable with a Keystone Jack

If you want to put your cable in the wall and don't want to use snap-in couplers, a keystone jack enables you to create the most elegant installation possible. After the keystone jack is installed, you run a short CAT5/5e/6 patch cable to the jack in the wall to make your connection.

Instead of using a male RJ-45 connector, a keystone jack assembly for home and small office environments uses a female RJ-45 connector, a wire holder known as a *keystone plug* (packaged with the keystone jack), a wall plate (buy the same brand as the keystone jack to avoid compatibility problems), and either a wall box or a mounting bracket. The mounting bracket's bendable tabs enable the assembly to be secured to existing drywall.

To build the cable, follow steps 1–9 in the preceding section. Then, continue with the following:

10. Insert each wire into the keystone plug according to the EIA 568B standard listed in Table 5.5. Use your hands or the punchdown tool.

11. After the wires are inserted into the keystone plug, make sure the keystone plug and keystone jack resemble those shown in Figure 5.21.

12. Snap the keystone plug into the keystone jack (Figure 5.22).

13. Snap the keystone jack/plug assembly into the rear of the wall plate.

14. Connect other cables desired (telephone, coaxial, and so forth) to the appropriate ports in the wall plate.

15. Screw the wall plate into the wall box or mounting bracket already attached to the wall *after* you test the installation.

Hiding Your Cables

There are a variety of ways to make ethernet cable less obtrusive. Some of the methods you can use include

FIGURE 5.21
Keystone plug (top) and keystone jack (bottom).

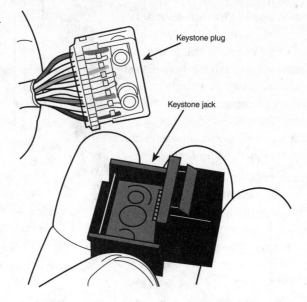

Keystone plug

Keystone jack

FIGURE 5.22
Snapping the keystone plug into the keystone jack.

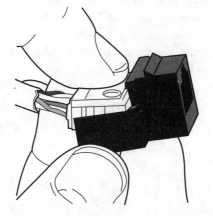

- Running cables behind furniture
- Running cables along the edges of carpet or baseboards
- Drilling holes in walls and running the cable through the walls
- Installing various types of wire management systems

Which one is right for you?

- Wire-management systems can be built in to new construction, retrofitted behind the baseboards of existing baseboards, or attached to the sides of existing walls. External wire-management systems are also known as *cable raceways*. When repainted to match the wall, cable raceways harmonize with your existing décor. Wire-management systems can reduce the cabling costs of your network by enabling you to use shorter cable lengths, but the overall cost of your network is higher because of the cost of the wire-management solution you choose. Figure 5.23 shows how the WireTracks wire management system can be retrofitted to an existing room.

- Running cables behind furniture or along existing baseboards, windows, and door-frames can increase the costs of your network because of the longer cable runs required. However, this is the easiest way to install network cable in an existing home or office.

- Running cables through walls provides the shortest possible cable runs, but it also requires you to use unfinished cable and add connectors after it is installed. You can run the cable directly out of the wall to your device. However, if you want to create a more finished installation, you can connect your cable to a keystone jack and snap it into a wall box as described in the previous section. Then, you can use a short patch cable between your device and the wall box.

> **tip**
>
> **CHOOSE CABLE COLORS CAREFULLY**
>
> If you're planning to run your network cable along the baseboards or edges of a room, choose a cable color that blends into the wall or baseboard color if possible. Of the standard colors, gray is a good choice for many rooms.

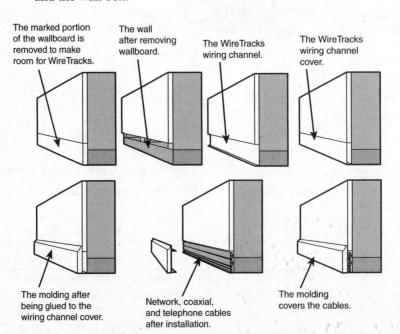

FIGURE 5.23
Installing WireTracks wire-management systems into existing construction.

The marked portion of the wallboard is removed to make room for WireTracks.

The wall after removing wallboard.

The WireTracks wiring channel.

The WireTracks wiring channel cover.

The molding after being glued to the wiring channel cover.

Network, coaxial, and telephone cables after installation.

The molding covers the cables.

Running Network Cable

As Figure 5.7 shows, each station on a 10/100 Ethernet network connects to a switch. If your computers and other devices are in the same room or nearby rooms and you can hide the cable behind furniture or run it along baseboards, you might be satisfied to buy appropriate lengths of pre-built cables to run between each device and the switch. However, if you are building a home network that will have stations in several rooms in your home or have stations on two or more floors, how you buy and how you route your cabling can become critical issues.

Whether you decide to buy pre-assembled cables or build your own, keep these basic rules in mind:

■ *Keep network cables away from interference sources such as fluorescent lights, electric motors, and so on.* The cables used by ethernet are sometimes referred to as unshielded twisted pair (UTP) cables, and that lack of shielding can lead to transmission problems if you don't route them properly.

■ *Keep network cables off the floor if possible, or protect them if they run across the floor.* Network cables are vulnerable to crush damage (the wire pairs inside the outer jacket are made of very fine wire). You can use cable runners to protect network cable if you need to run it across the floor. However, it's better to run cable around the doorframe if possible.

■ *Color-code or mark your cables so you know which cable goes to a particular system.* If you buy pre-built cables, you can use different colors for this purpose. Otherwise, you can use a label-maker.

> **note**
>
> **TRACKING DOWN WIRE-MANAGEMENT SYSTEMS**
>
> Some of the leading vendors for wire-management systems include
>
> - WireTracks (www.wiretracks.com)
> - LanShack (www.lanshack.com; also sells bundled network, coax, and fiber-optic cables)
> - HomeTech (www.hometech.com/techwire/wiremgmt.html)
> - CableOrganizer (http://cableorganizer.com/)
>
> Most of these vendors also sell bulk network cable, cable-building tools, and other supplies you will find useful.

Cable Distance Limits

You can run UTP Ethernet cable up to 100 meters (more than 300 feet) between a switch and a network client (PC or device). If you need a longer run, run a cable from one LAN port on the original switch to the uplink port on the remote switch, and then connect additional computers to the remote switch's LAN ports. Refer to Figure 5.9.

Using HomePlug or HomePNA as an Alternative to Rewiring

As you can see from the preceding sections, one of the most challenging parts of a wired ethernet network is the wiring itself. As you will learn in Chapter 6, "Installing and Configuring a Wi-Fi Network," you can build a network that mixes Wi-Fi (wireless ethernet) and wired ethernet as one method for bridging longer distances. However, you can also use the existing telephone and power lines in your home to extend your home network beyond the convenient reach of wired ethernet.

> **tip**
>
> **REDUCING YOUR CABLE RUNS AND AVOIDING HEADACHES**
>
> If you have two or more stations that are close to each other but are a long distance away from the switch, consider installing a switch in a convenient location to both systems and run your cables to the switch. Then, run a single cable between the switch and the central switch or router.

HomePlug network adapters connect to a standard outlet and to your computer's RJ-45 Ethernet port. HomePNA uses your phone lines to carry computer data as well as telephone calls; HomePNA adapters can connect to your computer's USB port, PC Card slot, or PCI slots. As with HomePlug, you use a HomePNA adapter for each PC. How do HomePlug and HomePNA compare to each other and to 10/100 Ethernet? Table 5.6 lines up the facts for you.

Table 5.6 HomePlug, HomePNA, 10/100 Ethernet Compared

Network Type	Rated Speed	Typical USB Adapter Price	Wiring Type Used	Notes
10/100 Ethernet	100Mbps	$35	CAT5/5e/6 UTP	Directly compatible with ethernet routers and switches
HomePNA 2.0	10Mbps	$50	Phoneline	Requires bridge to ethernet network
HomePlug	14Mbps	$60	Powerline	Requires bridge to ethernet network

Although the rated speeds of HomePNA 2.0 and HomePlug are far slower than 10/100 Ethernet, any of these standards are far faster than the fastest broadband Internet connections currently available (4Mbps cable modem).

Bridging Ethernet to Other Network Types

To connect HomePlug stations to a wired ethernet network, connect a HomePlug-to-Ethernet bridge to a LAN port on your network's switch or router. To connect HomePNA stations to a wired ethernet network, connect a HomePNA to ethernet bridge to an ethernet switch or router on your home network.

By incorporating an ethernet bridge in your home network, HomePlug or HomePNA and ethernet-based computers can connect with each other as part of a single network. Figure 5.24 illustrates a network with HomePlug and ethernet adapters and a HomePlug-to-Ethernet bridge.

ADAPTER AND BRIDGE?

Some vendors sell a single HomePlug device that functions as an adapter and an ethernet bridge, and others sell separate adapters and ethernet bridges. Be sure to check the specifications of the device you use.

FIGURE 5.24

Using HomePlug network adapters and a HomePlug-to-Ethernet bridge to connect to a wired ethernet network.

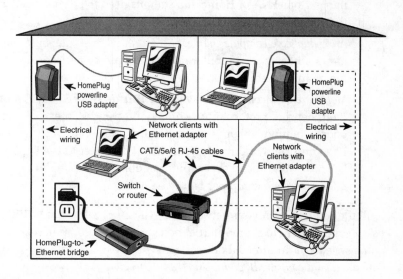

Configuring Your Ethernet Network

After you connect your computers to the hub/switch/router, it's time to configure them. In the past, network configuration has been a hair-pulling problem for many computer users. It required you to assign settings to each PC manually, and there was a high probability of network failure if you slipped up somewhere. However, starting with Windows 98, Microsoft Windows has included various versions of a home networking wizard, culminating with the Windows XP version.

Before we cover how to use the Windows XP Home Networking wizard, it's important to understand the keys to successful home networking:

> **tip**
>
> **USE THE WINDOWS XP WIZARD FOR EASY HOME NETWORKING**
>
> If you have even one Windows XP CD handy, you can use its home networking wizard to configure your entire home network (if everybody uses Windows 9x/Me/XP). Windows XP's home networking wizard is easier to use than previous versions.

- *Make sure everybody is part of the same workgroup.* With most versions of Windows, sharing printers or folders is more difficult if different workgroups are in use. Every network station needs to be configured to use the same workgroup name. HomePNA or HomePlug stations need to be connected via a bridge to the ethernet network.

- *Avoid duplicate computer names.* Although all computers use the same workgroup name, each computer needs a unique name. You can use the location, the main user, the computer brand or model, and so on.

- *Make sure each computer has a unique IP address.* The TCP/IP protocol is the main network protocol in use today. You can assign each computer its own IP address manually, but doing so requires you delve deep into the intricacies of IP address rules and regulations. It's a *lot* simpler to use DHCP. A DHCP server is built in to virtually every router, enabling the router to provide a unique IP address to each computer on the network.

If all the computers on your network use Windows 98/Me/2000/XP *and* you're not using your network to share Internet access or for noncomputer devices such as game systems or multimedia devices, you can use a feature built in to Windows called *automatic private IP addressing (APIPA)* to create a network without a router or other device to provide unique IP addresses. Each computer chooses its own unique IP address. For more information, see "Creating a Strictly Local Network with APIPA," p. 138, this chapter.

Configuring a Router for Broadband Internet Sharing

If you already have a wired ethernet network but don't have shared Internet access yet, you can provide shared Internet access to your network with this process:

1. Connect one computer directly to the broadband Internet device and configure it to connect to the device. Depending on the service, you might do this by running a configuration program from a CD or by setting the computer to receive its IP address automatically from the device.

2. Test the connection. If you can connect to the Internet, continue. If not, troubleshoot your connection. See Chapter 11, "Troubleshooting Your Home Network," for details.

3. To use a router to share your Internet access, you need to duplicate the settings used by your computer in the router's configuration. To view these settings, use Winipcfg (Windows 9x/Me) or IPConfig (Windows XP and Windows 2000). To run Winipcfg, click Start, Run, type winipcfg, and click OK. Select your network adapter and click More. To run IPConfig, click Start, Run, type cmd, and click OK. Type IPConfig/all at the command prompt. Type EXIT to close the command prompt when you're done. Refer to Figure 5.25.

FIGURE 5.25

Using IPConfig/all (top) and Winipcfg (bottom) to view the network settings used by a particular computer.

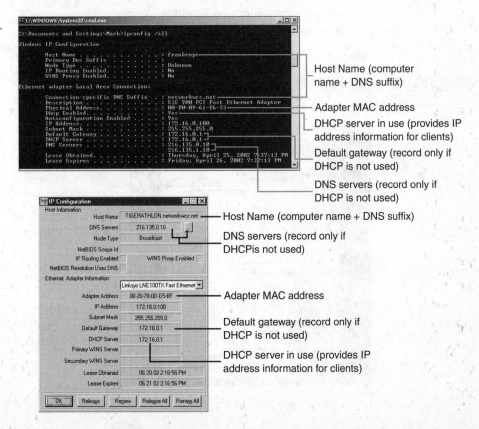

Host Name (computer name + DNS suffix)

Adapter MAC address

DHCP server in use (provides IP address information for clients)

Default gateway (record only if DHCP is not used)

DNS servers (record only if DHCP is not used)

Host Name (computer name + DNS suffix)

DNS servers (record only if DHCPis not used)

Adapter MAC address

Default gateway (record only if DHCP is not used)

DHCP server in use (provides IP address information for clients)

4. If DHCP is in use as shown here, all you need to record is the MAC address (adapter address) for the PC connected to the broadband Internet device.

5. Disconnect the computer from the broadband Internet device.

6. Connect the computer to one of the LAN ports on the router. *Don't* connect the router with the rest of the network yet. Make sure you use a standard network cable, not a crossover cable (some broadband devices use a crossover cable to connect to the PC).

7. Turn on the router.

8. Restart your computer.

9. Open your web browser and enter the IP address of your router (`http://xxx.xxx.xxx.xxx`). See Figure 5.26.

10. Enter the password provided with the router to log in.

11. Configure the router's WAN settings to use the same settings as the computer (Figure 5.26).

USING DSL? DON'T FORGET THE PPPOE INFORMATION!

If you use a DSL connection to the Internet and you need to log in with a username and password to connect, your provider uses PPPoE. Be sure to record this information (not visible with IPConfig or WinIPCfg) as well so you can configure your router.

FIGURE 5.26

Configuring a Linksys router.

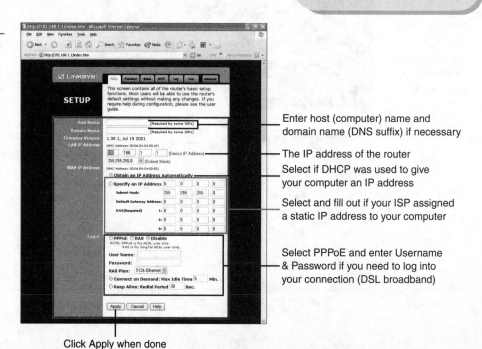

Enter host (computer) name and domain name (DNS suffix) if necessary

The IP address of the router

Select if DHCP was used to give your computer an IP address

Select and fill out if your ISP assigned a static IP address to your computer

Select PPPoE and enter Username & Password if you need to log into your connection (DSL broadband)

Click Apply when done

12. Configure the router's DHCP settings to provide a dynamic IP address to each computer on the network (Figure 5.27). Don't forget to include computers that are connected through bridges or external switches or hubs.

13. Clone the MAC address of the computer originally connected to the Internet to the router (Figure 5.28).

14. Run a cable from the router's WAN port to the ethernet port on the broadband Internet access device. To continue the process, see "Using the Windows XP Network Setup Wizard" below.

15. Connect each computer's network cable to a LAN port on the router. If you need additional ports, connect a switch to the Uplink port on the router. If you use the Uplink port, it takes over the connection used by the LAN port next to it. Thus, you can use all the LAN ports or all but the last LAN port and the Uplink port.

tip

CONNECTING TO YOUR ROUTER

If you get an error message in step 10 instead of the router sign-on screen, your computer is probably using an IP address that is not in the same range as the IP address used by the router. For example, if your router has an IP address of 192.168.1.1, your computer must use an IP address of 192.168.1.x (x = 0, 2-254) to connect to it. Run IPConfig or Winipcfg again to see the current IP address of your computer. If your computer's IP address starts with 169., or is otherwise not in the same range of numbers, set the IP address manually. See "Manual IP Address Configuration," p. 322, Chapter 11.

Using the Windows XP Network Setup Wizard

After the router has been configured to provide IP addresses for the computer, it's time to configure each computer to use the network. The easiest way to do this is with the Windows XP Network Setup Wizard. To start the wizard on a system running Windows XP, click Start, All Programs, Accessories, Communications, Network Setup Wizard.

You can also use the Windows XP CD to run the wizard on other systems running Windows 98/98SE or Windows Me. To do so, insert the Windows XP CD. If the Windows XP Welcome screen is not displayed after you insert the Windows XP CD, open the Setup.exe file in Windows Explorer. From the Windows XP Welcome screen, click Perform Additional Tasks. Click Set up a home or small office network to start the wizard.

Enter the number of PCs you will connect to the router

You can adjust the starting IP address if desired

FIGURE 5.27

Configuring
DHCP settings.

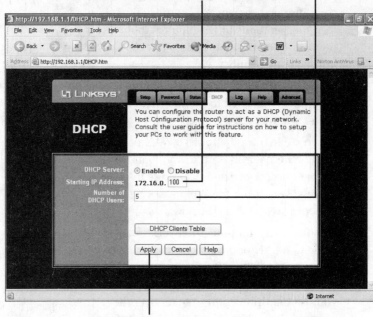

Click Apply when done

Enter the MAC address from your computer here

FIGURE 5.28

Cloning the
MAC address.

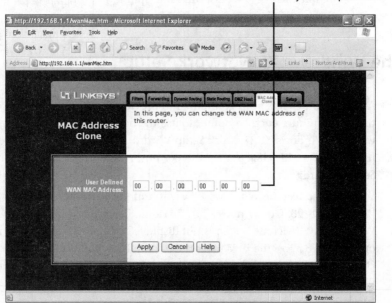

If you use a preinstalled version of Windows XP, you can also start the wizard this way: Click Start, All Programs, Accessories, Communications, Network Setup Wizard.

When you complete the Setup Wizard, you can make a floppy disk to run the Setup Wizard on systems that use other versions of Windows.

Before starting this process, connect each PC to a LAN port on the router or a port on a switch connected to the router:

1. Click Next at the opening screen, and click Next at the checklist screen.

2. If you see a warning that some of your network hardware is disconnected, look at the network connection listed (Figure 5.29). If your ethernet port is listed, double-check your cable connections (including any dongles). Fix any loose or disconnected cables and click Next to continue. Windows XP considers IEEE-1394 (FireWire) ports to be network adapters. If your 1394 adapter is listed, click Ignore disconnected hardware and click Next to continue.

3. Click This computer connects to the Internet through another computer on my network or through a residential gateway (Figure 5.30). Click Next to continue.

4. Click Let me choose my connections to the network (if prompted). Click Next to continue.

5. Clear all check marks except for the network interface card or port you are using (Figure 5.31). Click Next to continue.

tip

WHY CLONE?

Many broadband ISPs require you to provide the MAC address of your network adapter when you connect for the first time. By cloning your computer's MAC address to the router, you don't need to reregister your hardware with your ISP.

note

DON'T LIKE WIZARDS? D-I-Y SETUP IS ALSO AVAILABLE

If you don't like Windows wizards, or you're using a version of Windows (or another operating system) that doesn't work with the Windows XP wizard, see "Configuring a Shared Connection Without a Network Wizard," p. 137, this chapter.

Disconnected network adapter

FIGURE 5.29

Diagnosing
disconnected
network
hardware.

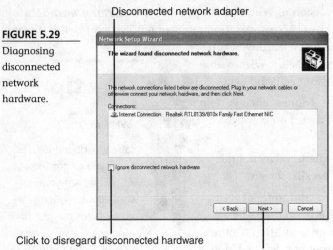

Click to disregard disconnected hardware

Click to continue after reconnecting network adapter or clicking Ignore

Selects a connection made with a router or Internet Connection Sharing

FIGURE 5.30

Selecting your
Internet
connection type.

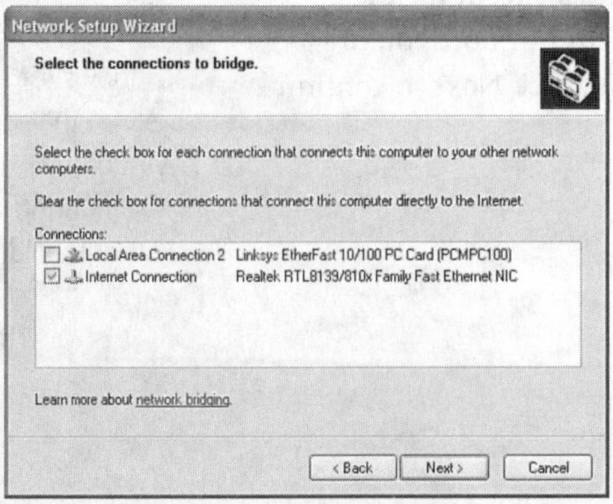

Click to continue

FIGURE 5.31

Selecting your
network
connection.

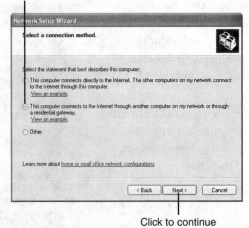

6. Enter a description for the computer. Enter a unique name if the computer is not already named (Figure 5.32). Click Next to continue.

Computer description (optional)

FIGURE 5.32
Entering your computer's name and description.

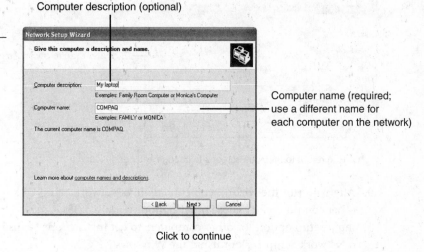

Computer name (required; use a different name for each computer on the network)

Click to continue

7. Enter the workgroup name you want to use (Figure 5.33); *don't* use the default (MSHOME). Make sure you use the same workgroup name for all computers. Click Next to continue.

FIGURE 5.33
Entering your home network name (work-group name).

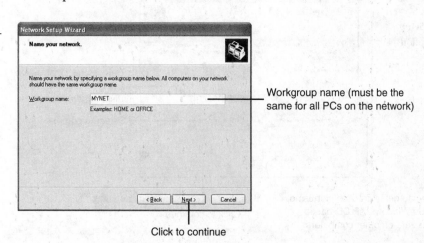

Workgroup name (must be the same for all PCs on the network)

Click to continue

8. Scroll through the settings. Use Back to retrace your steps and make any corrections (Figure 5.34). Click Next to apply the settings and complete the process.

FIGURE 5.34

Reviewing
Network Setup
Wizard settings.

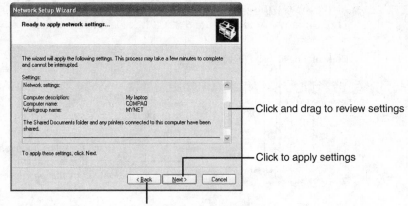

Click and drag to review settings

Click to apply settings

Click to return to previous screens to change settings

9. After you run the wizard, you can create a Network Setup Disk for use on other computers or choose other options (Figure 5.35). Click Next after selecting a setup option for other computers to get instructions for using or making a Network Setup Disk or using the Windows XP CD.

Select to create a Network Setup disk and display instructions for use

FIGURE 5.35

Selecting
Network Setup
Wizard options.

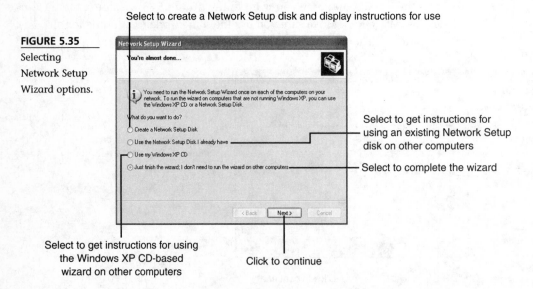

Select to get instructions for using an existing Network Setup disk on other computers

Select to complete the wizard

Select to get instructions for using the Windows XP CD-based wizard on other computers

Click to continue

10. Click Finish to close the wizard, or click Back to change settings. Click the underlined links for more help with your network (Figure 5.36).

FIGURE 5.36

Finishing the
Network Setup
Wizard.

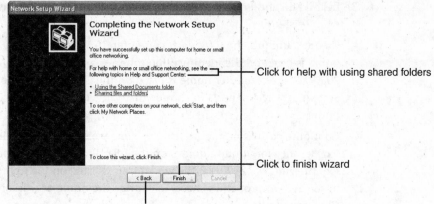

Click for help with using shared folders

Click to finish wizard

Click to return to previous screens to make adjustments to network settings

11. Remove the Windows XP CD or Network Setup Disk and reboot the computer. You should be able to access the Internet and use shared folders and printers after the computer restarts. See Chapter 8, "Home Networks at Work and School," to learn how to use shared folders and printers.

Run the networking wizard on each computer, using a unique name for each computer, but the same network (workgroup) and connection options you used previously.

Configuring a Shared Connection Without a Network Wizard

What if you're not using Windows XP or just don't like to use wizards? You can configure a network connection manually following this basic outline. Most steps are performed through the Network icon in the Control Panel:

1. Install the TCP/IP protocol if it is not already installed.

2. Configure the TCP/IP protocol to use a server-assigned IP address (the "server" is the router).

note

SHARE AND SHARE ALIKE

By default, the Windows XP Network Setup Wizard shares the Shared Documents folder and any printers connected to the computer with the rest of the network. To share additional folders or printers installed after the wizard was run, or to stop sharing folders or printers, see Chapter 8.

3. Install File and Printer Sharing on each computer with a printer or folder you want to share.

4. Create a unique name for each computer. In Windows 9x/Me, the computer name is listed on the Identification tab in the Network dialog. In Windows 2000/XP, the computer name is listed on the Computer Name tab in the System properties sheet. To change the name or workgroup, click the Change button.

5. Configure each computer to use the same workgroup name. In Windows 9x/Me, the workgroup name is on the Identification tab in the Network dialog. In Windows 2000/XP, the workgroup is listed on the Computer Name tab in the System properties sheet. To change the name or workgroup, click the Change button.

6. Connect each computer to the router.

7. Reboot each computer to achieve Internet access.

Creating a Strictly Local Network with APIPA

Windows 98 (but not Windows 95), Windows Me, Windows 2000, and Windows XP are designed to use IP addresses obtained in one of three ways:

- Manually
- From a DHCP server (such as a router)
- Automatically using APIPA

SHARING FOLDERS AND PRINTERS

To learn how to share printers and folders, see Chapter 8.

Windows 98, Me, and 2000 also support an older network protocol called NetBEUI. Before Windows XP was introduced, I would have told you to use NetBEUI to create a home network that didn't include Internet access. However, Windows XP doesn't install NetBEUI automatically, doesn't support it, and provides a complicated installation procedure if you want to use the NetBEUI drivers included "for troubleshooting" on the Windows XP CD. However, the biggest strikes against NetBEUI are that it doesn't provide Internet access if you add a broadband connection *and* it's very vulnerable to online attacks after you connect to the Internet.

So, if you're looking for a Windows-only, local network today, say goodbye NetBEUI and hello APIPA. What is APIPA? APIPA is a way to create a TCP/IP network that supports local connections today and enables you to move easily to sharing a broadband Internet connection tomorrow. The only difference is that you can use a switch with an APIPA-based network instead of a router, because each computer creates its own IP address, instead of receiving it from a router or another device. Here's the procedure:

1. Open the Network icon in Control Panel on each computer.

2. Install the TCP/IP protocol (if not already installed).

3. Configure the TCP/IP protocol to obtain an IP address automatically.

4. Configure each computer to use the workgroup name.

5. Create a unique name for each computer.

6. Install File and Printer Sharing on each computer with a printer or folder you want to share.

7. Connect the computer to the switch.

8. Reboot each computer. A message will indicate that automatic IP addressing is being used because a DHCP server is not available.

9. Select which resources you want to share (see Chapter 8 for details).

The beauty of an APIPA-based network is that you can easily swap the switch for a router with a built-in switch (or connect a separate router) later to share an Internet connection.

However, APIPA is not supported by all operating systems. Linux doesn't support APIPA, nor do versions of MacOS prior to version 8.5. If you want to put computers using these operating systems on your home network, use a router even if you don't have a broadband Internet connection yet. Use the router's DHCP server to provide IP addresses to all devices configured to obtain an IP address automatically.

Similarly, some non-PC devices (print servers, media adapters, and so on) might not support APIPA either. If the device doesn't support APIPA, it can't generate its own IP addresses and must depend on a DHCP server to obtain an IP address. See the documentation for the device to determine whether APIPA is listed as a supported TCP/IP protocol.

THE ABSOLUTE MINIMUM

10/100 Ethernet network hardware runs at 100Mbps unless 10BASE-T (10Mbps) network hardware is present on the network.

Desktop computers can use USB or PCI ethernet adapters.

Portable computers can use USB, PC Card, or CardBus Ethernet adapters.

You should install the drivers for a USB ethernet adapter before you connect the adapter to your computer.

The Microsoft Xbox video game system and ReplayTV PVR include built-in ethernet ports.

Other types of video game and PVR devices need add-on ethernet ports before they can be connected to a home network.

A hub is the slowest method of distributing signals to an ethernet network.

A switch is faster than a hub and usually supports full duplex for even faster performance.

A router links a home network to another network such as the Internet. Most routers made for home networks include an ethernet switch.

A WAN port on a router connects the router to a broadband Internet access device.

Ethernet cables you make yourself are less expensive per foot than pre-built cables, but you need special tools to do the job right.

You can hide your ethernet cables in the wall and use a wall plate with a keystone jack or snap-in coupler for a more professional look to your network.

The EIA 568B standard is the most common wiring standard for ethernet cable.

Wire-management systems make it easier to run your network cable through walls or conceal runs along baseboards or ceiling joints.

You can connect a wireless ethernet, HomePlug, or HomePNA network to your ethernet network as an alternative to building long ethernet cables.

Use an ethernet bridge to connect HomePlug or HomePNA networks to your ethernet network.

Routers use a feature called dynamic host configuration protocol (DHCP) to assign IP addresses to network clients.

You can use the Windows XP Network Setup wizard with Windows 98, Me, and XP to set up your home network.

If your home network will not be used to share an Internet connection, you can use APIPA to allow Windows 98, Me, 2000, and XP computers to assign their own IP addresses automatically. APIPA works with switches or hubs; no router is needed.

6

INSTALLING AND CONFIGURING A Wi-Fi NETWORK

Wireless ethernet networking, commonly referred to as *Wi-Fi*, is the hottest home network technology around. When you install a wireless ethernet network, you can put away your wire crimpers and stop worrying about hiding network cables because radio waves carry your signals between PCs and other devices.

Although you no longer need to worry about running cables all over your home when you install a wireless ethernet/Wi-Fi home network, you still need to be concerned about selecting the right types of hardware for your home network. You also need to protect your network from intruders and configure your network for maximum speed. In this chapter, you learn how to deal with these challenges.

What Is Wireless Ethernet?

A wireless ethernet network consists of the following:

- A wireless ethernet adapter for each PC or device on the network
- A wireless access point (WAP) to enable Internet sharing or connections to other networks (optional)
- A router connection to a broadband Internet device to enable Internet sharing (often combined with the WAP)

How does a device with a wireless network adapter connect to a network? By default, WAPs broadcast an identification known as a *service set identifier (SSID)*. Essentially, the SSID is the wireless network's name. Each WAP has a default SSID, usually derived from the vendor's name. For example, WAPs made by Linksys use the default SSID Linksys. The default SSID can (and should) be changed through the WAP's configuration utility. A properly equipped computer running Windows XP's built-in wireless ethernet support automatically scans for SSIDs and displays the wireless networks it detects. Select one, and you connect to that network. With other versions of Windows, you might need to enter the SSID to make the connection. The maximum range of a WAP extends for several hundred feet, although brick or concrete walls can greatly reduce range.

Wireless ethernet is also known as Wi-Fi. The Wi-Fi Alliance (www.wi-fi.org) is the trade group responsible for developing standards that help different brands of wireless ethernet hardware to work together. Wireless ethernet devices that pass the certification tests put forth by the Wi-Fi Alliance are known as Wi-Fi Certified devices. Although most wireless ethernet devices that are not Wi-Fi Certified also work with Wi-Fi Certified devices, it's generally safest and easiest for you to select devices for your home network that are Wi-Fi Certified.

The Three Flavors of Wi-Fi

Originally, wireless ethernet was based on just one network standard, IEEE 802.11b. However, today there are *three* different 802.11 network standards and several proprietary extensions. Mix and match some standards, and your network can still function. Mix and match others, and your network becomes a "notwork." The following sections bring you up to speed on each technology.

802.11b

IEEE 802.11b (also known as Wireless-B) is the original flavor of Wi-Fi. Initially, most Wi-Fi home networking products used this version. However, home networks are rapidly shifting to the faster 802.11g version of Wi-Fi. 802.11b hardware has a maximum speed of 11Mbps and uses the 2.4GHz frequency.

802.11a

802.11a (also known as Wireless-A) was developed to provide better performance and less interference than 802.11b. 802.11a runs at a maximum speed of 54Mbps, but uses the 5GHz frequency band. Consequently, it is not directly compatible with 802.11b-compatible hardware, which runs at 2.4GHz.

802.11g

802.11g (also known as Wireless-G) is the current champion of wireless ethernet home networks. It's directly compatible with existing 802.11b hardware because it uses the same 2.4GHz frequency, but it runs at up to 54Mbps, making it comparable in speed to 802.11a.

Comparing 802.11 Standards

Wi-Fi Certification covers all three types of 802.11 wireless networks, but they differ in many ways. Table 6.1 compares the major features of each network type.

Table 6.1 Wi-Fi/Wireless Ethernet Network Types

Wireless Ethernet (Wi-Fi) Standard	Radio Frequency Used	Maximum Speed	Also Known As	Connects With
802.11b	2.4GHz	11Mbps	Wireless-B	802.11g
802.11a	5GHz	54Mbps	Wireless-A	—*
802.11g	2.4GHz	54Mbps	Wireless-G	802.11b

*Requires dual-frequency hardware to connect to other standards.

Proprietary Extensions (22Mbps, 100Mbps, 108Mbps)

It's a story as old as the computer industry: a trade group develops a standard, and a few vendors say, "we can do better." A number of vendors have developed proprietary speedups to 802.11b and 802.11g networks, including

- *D-Link AirPlus Enhanced*—22Mbps extension to 802.11b (11Mbps)
- *D-Link AirPlus Xtreme G, Netgear Super G*—108Mbps extension to 802.11g (54Mbps) using Atheros Super G chipsets.
- *US Robotics Wireless Turbo*—100/125Mbps extension to 802.11g (54Mbps)

Although all of these proprietary extensions promise better performance than standard 802.11b or 802.11g networks, you should keep the following in mind:

- The speed increases provided by most proprietary technologies are more modest than the names suggest.

- To enable your network to run at proprietary speeds, all network devices need to support the *same* proprietary technology.

- If you mix and match standard and proprietary network devices, your network speed will be reduced, in some cases to the highest standard speed supported by your network. This can be a major issue if you want to use media adapters, print servers, or video games on your wireless network. Most proprietary speedups are for WAPs, routers, and PC network adapters only.

- Integrated wireless ethernet adapters built in to notebook or desktop computers support only standard speeds (11Mbps or 54Mbps).

- Some vendors claim that WAPs or network adapters using proprietary extensions can interfere with standard 802.11b or 802.11g networks.

> **tip**
>
> My advice? Don't spend extra money on proprietary "better-than" standard gear, especially if you're going to add game systems and other non-PC devices to your home network. Stick with 802.11g.

Dealing with Different Flavors at Home and at Work

If your corporate office already has a wireless network and you plan to use the same notebook computer at home and at work, you could have a problem: a lot of corporate networks use 802.11a wireless ethernet. As you have already learned, 802.11a uses a different frequency than 802.11g or 802.11b. Fortunately, you can get dual-frequency network adapters for your notebook computer that handle both 802.11a and 802.11b or 802.11g networks. Figure 6.1 shows a typical dual-frequency CardBus network adapter from Cisco that supports all three Wi-Fi Certified standards.

FIGURE 6.1

A typical dual-band CardBus network adapter that supports 802.11a, 802.11b, and 802.11g wireless ethernet (Wi-Fi) networks.

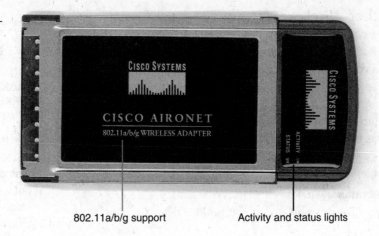

802.11a/b/g support   Activity and status lights

Wi-Fi–Ready Computers

You might not need to install a wireless ethernet (Wi-Fi) adapter in your notebook computer, particularly if it was built from mid-2003 on. Many vendors have started to incorporate wireless ethernet network adapters into most of the product lines. However, even if your notebook already has wireless ethernet on board, you might need to add a CardBus or USB adapter if you want support for the fastest wireless ethernet standards.

Intel Centrino Family

Originally, notebook computers with Intel's Centrino technology incorporated an 802.11b-compatible Wi-Fi network adapter made by Intel, the Intel PRO/Wireless 2100 network adapter or the dual-mode (802.11a/b 2100A). However, recent Centrino notebooks now include one of two other adapters:

- Intel PRO/Wireless 2200BG (supports 802.11g natively; interoperates with 802.11b networks)
- Intel PRO/Wireless 2915ABG (supports 802.11a/b/g natively)

Consequently, any Centrino notebook can connect with an 802.11b or 802.11g wireless home network. However, only Centrino notebooks that use the Intel PRO/Wireless 2200BG or 2915ABG network adapter can work at maximum speed with either network type. As you learned earlier in this chapter, 802.11b adapters can connect to an 802.11g-based network. However, depending upon your WAP or router, your entire network might run more slowly when 802.11b and 802.11g hardware is on the same network.

Other Wireless Solutions

You don't need Centrino to have wireless ethernet on board. Many notebook computer vendors use various third-party network adapters to provide wireless ethernet support. See the tips in Chapter 3, "Planning Your Home Network," to determine whether your computer has wireless ethernet already installed.

If you have a PDA or smart phone, it might have built-in wireless ethernet features or offer an optional wireless ethernet/Wi-Fi card. See your PDA or smart phone manual for details.

Building Your Wireless Ethernet Network

You can add wireless ethernet hardware to an existing network or build a wireless home network from scratch. In the following sections you learn how to select and install network adapters, set up and configure a WAP or router, and configure your network adapters and WAP to communicate with each other.

tip

FOR MAXIMUM HOME NETWORK SPEED, CHECK BEFORE YOU BUY!

If you're in the market for a Centrino-technology notebook computer, be sure to find out which network adapter is included. Look for Centrino notebooks with the Intel PRO/Wireless 2200BG for use on home networks or public hot spots. However, if you need to connect to corporate networks that use 802.11a and don't want to use a separate adapter, opt for Centrino notebooks that use the Intel PRO/Wireless 2100A network adapter.

Adding Wireless Ethernet Adapters to Your PCs

Unless your computers already include wireless ethernet adapters, you will need to add them to your PCs. Table 6.2 compares the choices you have.

Table 6.2   Wireless Ethernet Adapters for PCs

Computer Type	Adapter Type	How Added	Benefits	Drawbacks
Desktop	PCI	Installed into open PCI slot	Can't be lost; doesn't use up desk space; movable antenna helps improve reception	Requires opening PC; difficult to move between systems

Computer Type	Adapter Type	How Added	Benefits	Drawbacks
Notebook	CardBus	Installed into open CardBus Type II slot	Easy to install and remove; easy to store when not in use	Can't be used with desktop PCs; fixed antenna can cause slower connection
Desktop or Notebook	USB	Connects to open USB 2.0 or 1.1 port	Easy to install or move; works in any system with a USB port; moveable antenna and extension cord on some models help improve performance	Requires Hi-Speed USB port for best performance; more expensive than PCI card

Figure 6.2 compares these adapter types to each other.

Removable antenna on PCI card   Built-in antenna on CardBus adapter

FIGURE 6.2

Typical USB, PCI card, and CardBus adapters for 802.11g wireless networks.

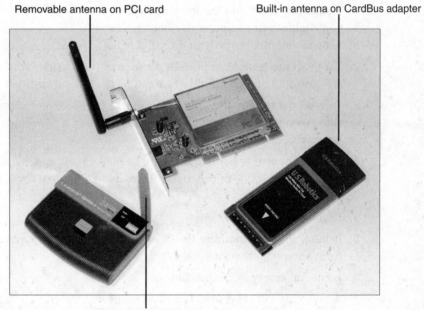

Folding antenna on USB adapter

Installing Wi-Fi Adapters in Your PC

The process of installing a wireless ethernet adapter is similar in many ways to the process of installing an ethernet adapter.

If you need to install a wireless ethernet adapter on your PC's USB port, see "Installing a USB Adapter," Chapter 5, "Installing and Configuring a Wired Ethernet Network," p. 103 for details. If you need to install a wireless ethernet adapter into your notebook computer's CardBus slot, see "Installing a PC Card or CardBus Adapter," Chapter 5, p. 105.

If you need to install a wireless ethernet adapter into a desktop computer's PCI card slot, follow this procedure:

1. Install the software supplied with the adapter. By installing the software first, you enable your computer to recognize the network adapter properly and configure it.

2. Take ESD precautions to prevent damage to your system or network adapter. See "Installing a PCI Adapter," Chapter 5, p. 106, for details.

3. Turn off the system and unplug it. Run the Windows Shutdown procedure to shut down your system. If your power supply has a power switch, turn it off before you unplug the power cord.

4. Remove the screws holding the cover in place. Some systems use separate panels for each side of the cover; others use a one-piece cover for the entire system.

5. Remove the cover.

6. Remove the antenna from the PCI adapter if necessary. Some adapters use a fixed antenna; others use a cable that connects to an external antenna.

7. Locate an empty PCI expansion slot.

8. Remove the slot cover corresponding to the expansion slot. In most cases, the slot cover is held in place by a screw. However, some systems use a snap-out slot cover that might be disposable. Some compact systems use a single screw on the outside of the case to hold all cards and slot covers in place (see Figure 6.3).

9. Line up the PCI card with the PCI slot and push it into place (see Figure 6.4).

> **tip**
>
> **RAISE THE ANTENNA FOR BEST CONNECTION SPEED**
>
> If your wireless ethernet USB adapter uses a folding antenna (refer to Figure 6.2), don't forget to unfold it after you install the adapter. Leaving it in the storage position will cause slow connections or might prevent you from making any connection to your WAP or router.

Fastening screw in place   Mounting screw

FIGURE 6.3

Fastening the
slot cover into
place and reat-
taching the
antenna.

Fastening
antenna in place

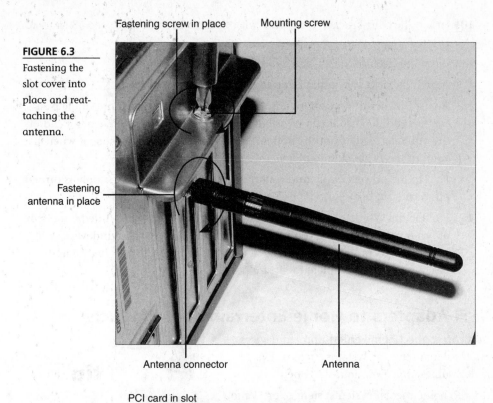

Antenna connector   Antenna

PCI card in slot

FIGURE 6.4

Installing the
wireless network
adapter into an
empty PCI slot.

Empty PCI slot   Wireless ethernet card lined up with slot

10. Fasten the card bracket to the case with the screw removed in step #8 (refer to Figure 6.3).

11. Close the case.

12. Attach the antenna to the PCI adapter (refer to Figure 6.3).

13. Adjust the antenna position. Lift the antenna to its normal right-angle position and adjust it so its tip is visible from the front of the PC. Keep the end of the antenna away from the bottom of the PC; you might damage it when you put the PC back into place.

14. Plug in the power supply and restart the system. If the power supply is turned off, turn it on before attempting to restart the system.

15. Provide the Windows CD if prompted. If you have already installed a modem or other network device, you might not need to provide the Windows CD. If Windows was preinstalled, Windows uses the installation files on the hard disk if needed to complete the installation.

Adding Wi-Fi Adapters to Home Entertainment Products

You can connect home entertainment devices such as home theater systems, stereos, TVs, video games, and PVRs to a Wi-Fi network.

To add home theater systems, stereos, or TVs to your network, connect them to a media adapter designed for use with wireless ethernet/Wi-Fi. These devices include software that enables the device to connect with a PC that contains the photo, video, or music files you want to play and a remote control for selecting and playing the files.

If you already have a media adapter connected to a wired ethernet network, you can continue to use it with your wireless ethernet network. Most media adapters have connections for both wired and wireless ethernet networks. If yours supports wired (10/100) ethernet only, you can connect it to the ethernet switch found in most wireless ethernet routers or WAPs or use an ethernet/wireless ethernet bridge.

tip

FOR MAXIMUM NETWORK SPEED, LOOK FOR 802.11G MEDIA ADAPTERS

Some media adapters, primarily those that do not support video, support 802.11b wireless ethernet. If you use 802.11g wireless ethernet network hardware for the rest of your network, mixing 802.11b and 802.11g hardware can slow your 802.11g hardware. For best network performance, look for media adapters made especially for 802.11g networks.

The Microsoft Xbox is ready to connect to a 10/100 ethernet network as soon as you take it out of the box. You can connect its ethernet port to an ethernet/wireless ethernet bridge to add it to a wireless ethernet network. Before you can add a Sony PlayStation2 or Nintendo GameCube to a wireless ethernet network, you must install each unit's ethernet adapter, and then connect each unit to an ethernet/wireless ethernet bridge.

ReplayTV PVRs have built-in 10/100 ethernet adapters. To add these units to a wireless ethernet network, use an ethernet/wireless ethernet bridge. TiVo Series 2 PVRs have built-in USB ports that can be used to connect wireless ethernet adapters.

For more details about adding home entertainment hardware to any type of home network, see Chapter 7, "Home Networks at Play."

Wireless Access Points and Routers

Stations on a wireless ethernet network can connect to each other in two ways. In *ad-hoc* mode, they connect directly with each other. This mode is the cheaper mode to set up, because you need only a wireless ethernet adapter for each station. However, ad-hoc mode doesn't support sharing an Internet connection or connecting to other networks. Ad-hoc mode is best suited for uses such as

- Connecting a media adapter to a PC containing media files for playback
- Connecting a wireless print server to a PC needing remote printer access

In these cases, the PC might already be connected to a wired network and uses wireless ethernet/Wi-Fi just for a particular specialized task. However, if you need to share an Internet connection or build a mixed network, such as wireless ethernet plus ethernet, or wireless ethernet plus HomePlug or HomePNA, you need to use *infrastructure* mode, which requires you to add a wireless access point, or WAP, to your wireless ethernet network.

A WAP provides the same function to a wireless ethernet network that a switch does to a 10/100 ethernet network: It sends and receives data between stations and provides a way to connect the network to other networks via a router or bridge. Some WAPs include a router. Figure 6.5 compares typical ad-hoc and infrastructure home network configurations.

If you are adding wireless ethernet access to an existing 10/100 ethernet network, the easiest way to do it is to plug a WAP into your existing ethernet switch or router. Figure 6.6 shows front and rear views of a typical WAP.

FIGURE 6.5

Ad-hoc (left) and infrastructure (right) Wi-Fi networks compared.

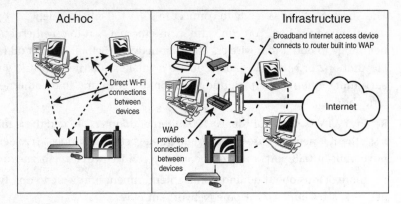

FIGURE 6.6

A typical WAP, the Linksys WAP54G.

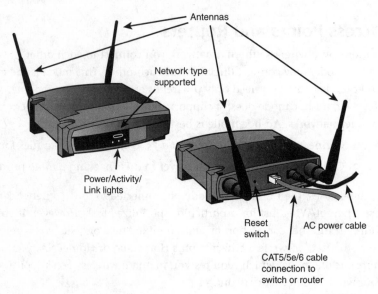

However, if you are building a home network from scratch and want to use wireless ethernet, I recommend that you buy a WAP that includes a router and an ethernet switch. You can connect the WAP's WAN port directly to a broadband Internet access device (such as a cable or DSL modem) to provide shared Internet access, and you can connect 10/100 ethernet network adapters to the integrated LAN ports. Figure 6.7 shows you the features of a typical wireless ethernet WAP with integrated router and 10/100 ethernet switch. Note that some of these devices have only one antenna.

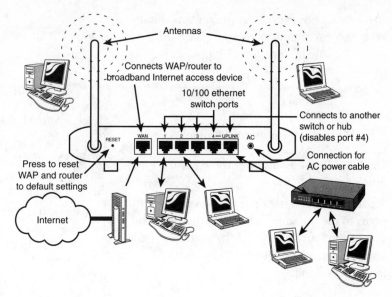

FIGURE 6.7

Features of a typical WAP with integrated router and ethernet switch.

Configuring Your Wireless Network

After you install wireless ethernet adapters and add a WAP to your existing 10/100 ethernet network or install a WAP with router, it's time to configure your network. In the following sections, we'll look at wireless configuration settings common to both WAPs and WAPs that have integrated routers.

To configure the WAP, you might use one of the following methods:

- Some WAPs include a wizard for basic configuration steps.

- Virtually all WAPs include a browser-based configuration utility for controlling basic and advanced WAP features and router features (on models with integrated routers).

To configure PCs with wireless network adapters, use one of the following methods:

- Use the Windows XP wireless configuration utility.

- Install and run the configuration utility provided by the adapter maker. This is the only way to configure a wireless adapter with versions of Windows that predate Windows XP.

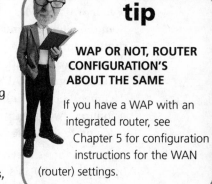

tip

WAP OR NOT, ROUTER CONFIGURATION'S ABOUT THE SAME

If you have a WAP with an integrated router, see Chapter 5 for configuration instructions for the WAN (router) settings.

To create an unsecured connection between a WAP and the stations on a wireless network, you need to set the following basic options on both devices:

- SSID
- Channel
- Encryption standards (disabled)

The following sections cover these basic configuration options.

Because each adapter on a wireless network needs to use the same settings as the WAP, you should configure the WAP first, record the settings, and then configure each device to use matching settings.

Configuring Your WAP

Although a WAP is a wireless device, it's easier (and in some cases, required) to connect it to a PC with an ethernet port or to a wired ethernet network for configuration. After you connect the WAP to your PC or to your network, plug it into a working AC power source.

If your WAP includes a wizard, start the wizard from the setup CD and select the option to change settings when prompted. If you use a web-based configuration program to set up the WAP, look up the WAP's default IP address in its documentation. In either case, look up the default password because you need to provide it to log on to the WAP.

Figure 6.8 shows the default configuration used by a Linksys WAP54G.

To make the changes using a wizard, follow the onscreen instructions to start the setup process. In the example shown in Figure 6.8, click Yes and provide the setup password.

tip

HANDLING MULTIPLE 802.11 VERSIONS WITH A SINGLE WAP

Just as 802.11g wireless network adapters can connect to 802.11g or 802.11b WAPs, an 802.11g WAP (including those that integrated a router and a switch) can connect with 802.11g or 802.11b network adapters.

You can buy 802.11b/a or 802.11g/a dual-mode WAPs for your home network. Choose dual-mode g/a WAPs if you need to support 802.11a network clients. As an alternative, you could connect a CardBus or USB adapter supporting your home network type (Wireless-B or Wireless-G) to those computers.

Dual-band A+G routers and network adapters from Linksys (www.linksys.com) enable high-bandwidth multimedia content to travel over the 5GHz 802.11a frequency at the same time the 802.11g/b 2.4GHz frequency handles normal web-surfing and network traffic.

FIGURE 6.8

Default configuration of a Linksys WAP54G wireless access point.

Default channel

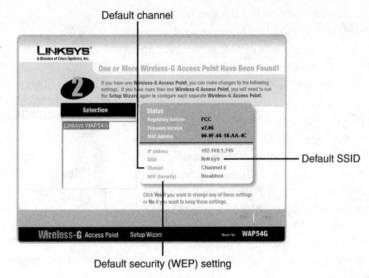

Default SSID

Default security (WEP) setting

Configuring the WAP's SSID

Wireless ethernet networks are identified by their SSIDs. By default, each different brand of wireless ethernet WAP has a different default SSID. For example, Linksys WAPs use linksys for the default SSID, Netgear WAPs use netgear, and so on. Also by default, WAPs broadcast the SSID, making it easy for wireless clients to detect the network.

To change the SSID when using a setup wizard, type the value desired when prompted. You should change the SSID from the default to something else, even during initial setup. If network intruders detect a default SSID, they can look up the documentation for your WAP, see the default password, log on to your network and start sneaking around. By using a nonstandard SSID (such as your last name, your dog's name, your favorite sports team, or whatever), you make it just a little bit harder to break into your network.

If your setup wizard permits it, you should also disable SSID broadcast. Leaving SSID broadcast enabled instructs your WAP to transmit the SSID to any wireless adapters within range. By disabling this option, you make it more difficult for casual snoopers to find your network.

caution

DON'T LEAVE YOUR NETWORK OPEN (FOR LONG)!

To make sure your wireless network is configured correctly, you can leave the encryption settings disabled (as they are in most brands of WAPs and wireless ethernet adapters by default). However, as soon as you determine that your network is working, you should *immediately* enable wireless security. See "Wireless Security 101," p. 165, this chapter, and Chapter 10, "Securing Your Home Network," for details.

Be sure to write down the SSID you use. If you disable SSID broadcast as I recommend, you will need to enter the WAP's SSID into the configuration for each wireless adapter on the network. No SSID = no connection.

Configuring the WAP's Channel

Wireless ethernet networks use radio signals to communicate. As with any other radio device, you need to select a matching channel at both ends of the network to make a connection. Although 802.11b and 802.11g networks offer channels from 1 to 11, this is a bit misleading. Only Channels 1, 6, and 11 are completely separate from each other. The remainder of the channels' frequencies partly overlap other frequencies.

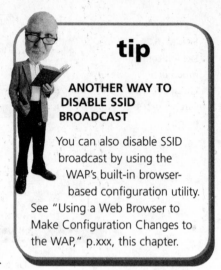

tip

ANOTHER WAY TO DISABLE SSID BROADCAST

You can also disable SSID broadcast by using the WAP's built-in browser-based configuration utility. See "Using a Web Browser to Make Configuration Changes to the WAP," p.xxx, this chapter.

By default, most WAPs are configured to use Channel 6. As a result, Channel 6 is the most crowded wireless ethernet channel, causing performance drops when many wireless networks using that channel are near enough to each other to cause signal overlap. I recommend using Channel 11 instead.

To change the channel, select a channel from the drop-down menu when prompted by the setup wizard. Figure 6.9 shows the wizard used by the Linksys WAP54G after the default SSID and channel settings have been changed.

FIGURE 6.9

Configuration of a Linksys WAP54G wireless access point after editing the SSID and channel settings.

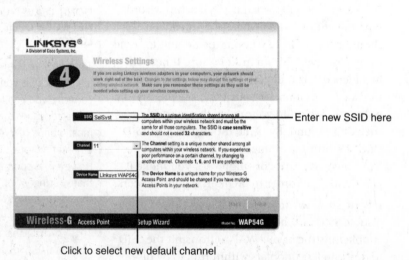

Enter new SSID here

Click to select new default channel

Be sure to record the channel you selected for the WAP. You might need to configure the channel used by your WAP in the configuration for each wireless adapter on the network with some network adapters' configuration utilities.

Adjusting Security Settings on the WAP

I'm a big believer in wireless security. In fact, I use two methods to protect my wireless networks. Much of Chapter 10 of this book is devoted to the various methods you can (and should) use to secure your wireless (and wired) networks. However, when you start to set up your wireless network, you should disable security settings. That might seem like a contradiction, but there's a method to my madness:

- If you mix and match brands of WAPs and network adapters, you could have problems caused by the differences in how various brands configure their security settings. Mismatched settings could cause your network to fail.

- Even if you use the same brand of WAP and network adapter, differences in wireless security features could cause problems in initial setup if security is enabled initially.

So, the best strategy is to

1. Get your wireless network running properly without security settings enabled.
2. Enable wireless security settings as soon as you know your network is working.
3. Configure folder and printer sharing (Chapter 8, "Home Networks at Work and School") *after* security settings have been enabled and tested.

To disable wireless security settings with the setup wizard, select Disabled when prompted for security settings.

Configuring IP Address Settings and Wrapping Up the Process

If you are using a WAP that connects to a router, you should configure the WAP to get an IP address from the router's DHCP server instead of using the WAP's default IP address. This is necessary because your home network might use a different range of IP addresses than the WAP's default, preventing the WAP and the wireless computers it hosts from connecting to the rest of the network. Select DHCP when prompted by the Wizard.

When you have made these changes with the setup wizard, save the changes when prompted and exit. The nonvolatile RAM in the WAP stores these settings for future use.

Using a Web Browser to Make Configuration Changes to the WAP

Some WAPs don't use a setup wizard for initial configuration. Instead, you use a web-based configuration tool for both basic and advanced settings. To configure the WAP using a web-based configuration tool, follow this procedure:

1. Look up the IP address and default username or password for configuration in the WAP's documentation.
2. Connect the WAP to your PC using its ethernet port.
3. Open your web browser and enter the IP address of the WAP.
4. Enter the default username or password to start the configuration utility.
5. Move through the menus and make the following changes:

   - Change the default SSID.
   - Disable SSID broadcast.
   - Change the default channel to 11 if it is set to 6.
   - Disable security (if it is enabled).
   - Use DHCP to obtain an IP address.

6. Record the settings used for SSID and default channel.
7. Save the changes and exit the utility.
8. Close the browser.

Figure 6.10 shows you an example of a browser-based configuration screen used by a U.S. Robotics WAP with integrated router and switch, the USR8054.

Enter new SSID here   Click to disable SSID broadcast

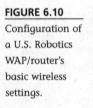

FIGURE 6.10

Configuration of a U.S. Robotics WAP/router's basic wireless settings.

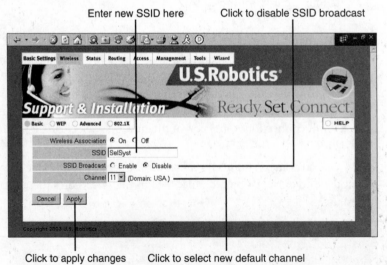

Click to apply changes   Click to select new default channel

Configuring Router Features

A WAP with a built-in router can be connected to a cable or DSL modem or other broadband Internet access device, enabling your wireless network to share Internet access (refer to Figure 6.7). When a WAP has an integrated router, you configure its router features the same way you would for a router on a 10/100 ethernet network. See "Configuring a Router for Broadband Internet Sharing," Chapter 5, for details.

Configuring Your Wireless Adapters

After the WAP has been configured, it's time to configure the wireless adapters on your network. In the following sections, I'll show you how to use the Windows XP wireless network configuration utility as well as a typical vendor-supplied configuration utility to get your wireless network up and running. If you don't use Windows XP, you *must* use the vendor-provided configuration utility.

Using the Windows XP Wireless Configuration Utility

After you install your network adapter (see "Installing Wi-Fi Adapters in Your PC," p. 148, this chapter) on a computer running Windows XP, you see a network icon appear in the system tray. Right-click on the icon, and a wireless network connections menu appears (see Figure 6.11).

To select a wireless network, click View Available Wireless Networks. The Connect to Wireless Network dialog appears, showing you the wireless network(s) visible to your PC's wireless ethernet adapter. Don't be surprised if you see more than one wireless network listed (see Figure 6.12).

tip

USING SAVE AS TO RECORD YOUR WAP CONFIGURATION

One of my favorite tricks for recording whatever's in my browser window (including WAP configuration) is to use the browser's Save As function. With Internet Explorer, you can select Web Archive to create a single file (.MHT) containing all the graphics, HTML code, text, and other features of the currently displayed page. Unlike screen captures, Save As grabs the entire page, no matter how long it is. If you use other browsers, use Save As Complete, but keep in mind that the graphics and other non-HTML elements are stored in a folder one level below where your page's HTML file is stored. I have used these methods to build an extensive list of online articles as well as my routers' and WAPs' configuration settings.

FIGURE 6.11

Opening the
Wireless
Networks menu
in Windows XP.

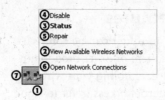

1. Wireless network icon in system tray
2. Displays available wireless networks
3. Displays wireless connection status
4. Disables connection
5. Repairs connection
6. Opens network connections menu
7. 10/100 Ethernet network icon
   (X indicates cable is unplugged)

Indicates selected wireless network

FIGURE 6.12

Selecting a wire-
less network
with the
Windows XP
wireless connec-
tion dialog.

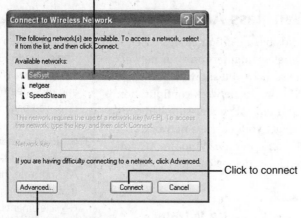

Click to connect

Click to open network connection
properties sheet (Figure 6.13)

To make the connection, click on the network you want to use and click Connect.
Some versions of Windows XP will display a prompt if the network is not secured,
asking you whether you want to connect anyway. Check the box Allow Me to
Connect to the Selected Wireless Network, even though it is not secured, then click
Connect.

In most cases, you won't need to open the Wireless Network Connection dialog
shown in Figure 6.13. However, in some circumstances you might need to, including

■ Your computer keeps connecting to a different wireless network than yours
and you want to force your system to use yours (Windows XP looks for the
strongest signal and uses it by default).

■ You add security settings to your wireless network and need to adjust the configuration settings for your client.

■ You want to disable Windows XP's built-in wireless client and use the wireless client supplied with your wireless network adapter.

If you need to configure these and other network settings, click Advanced to display the dialog box shown in Figure 6.13.

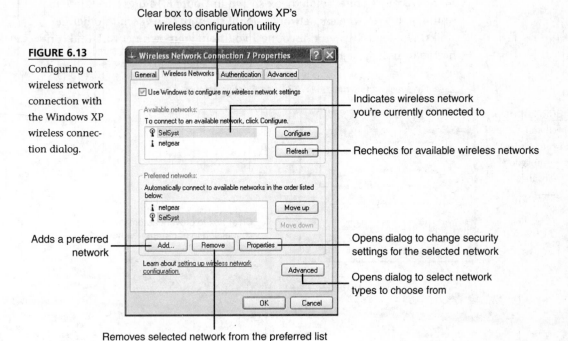

FIGURE 6.13

Configuring a wireless network connection with the Windows XP wireless connection dialog.

Clear box to disable Windows XP's wireless configuration utility

Indicates wireless network you're currently connected to

Rechecks for available wireless networks

Adds a preferred network

Opens dialog to change security settings for the selected network

Opens dialog to select network types to choose from

Removes selected network from the preferred list

Use the following checklist to adjust your connection:

■ To remove other networks from the Preferred list (non-preferred networks must be added manually), select the network in the Preferred Networks window and click Remove.

■ To change the order of preferred networks (for example, if you use wireless networks at home, at the office, and away from home), click the network you want to use first in the Preferred Networks window and click Move Up. Repeat until it is the top network in the list.

■ To adjust the properties (such as security settings) for a network, select it in the Preferred list and click Properties. For an example of using this dialog, see "Wireless Security 101," p. 165, this chapter, and also Chapter 10.

■ Windows XP can look for both ad-hoc and infrastructure (WAP-based) wireless networks. To control which type(s) of networks Windows XP uses, click Advanced and select the network type you want to use (see Figure 6.14). Click Close to continue.

■ To prevent Windows XP from logging on to non-preferred networks, clear the Automatically Connect dialog box shown in Figure 6.14 and click Close to continue. If your wireless network's signal strength is lower than other networks, Windows XP might disconnect you from your own network and connect to a stronger signal if this box is not cleared.

Select to specify infrastructure (WAP-based) networks only

FIGURE 6.14

Specifying advanced wireless connection options in Windows XP.

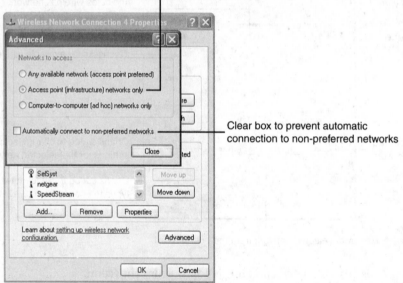

Clear box to prevent automatic connection to non-preferred networks

After making changes to the Wireless Networks or Properties tabs, click OK. The changes take effect immediately.

Using a Vendor-Supplied Wireless Network Configuration Tool

If you don't use Windows XP, you must use the wireless network configuration tool provided by your wireless adapter vendor.

If you installed the vendor-supplied configuration tool when you installed the network adapter, you should find a shortcut to it on your Start menu—click (All) Programs to see it—or on your Windows desktop. If you didn't install the configuration tool previously, install it from the CD provided with the network adapter, or visit the vendor's website for the latest version.

After you start the configuration utility, one of the options provided is typically a site survey. This is a more elaborate version of the Windows XP network selection screen shown earlier in Figure 6.12. Vendor-supplied configuration utilities usually provide much more information about the wireless networks available. To determine the mode, channel, and other information for any wireless network listed, click it to see a display similar to the one shown in Figure 6.15.

To connect to a secured network, provide the WEP key type, WEP key, and other information requested by the utility. You can usually store this information in a profile, which stores the connection information for reuse. To reconnect using a profile, open the profile dialog and select the profile you want to use.

After you connect to your wireless network, you can usually get even more information about your connection. In this example, the Link Information tab displays confirmation of your connection. Click More Information to see more detailed information, including TCP/IP network information, as shown in Figure 6.16.

tip

USING THE SITE SURVEY TO FIND THE BEST CHANNEL TO USE

Although Channel 6 is used most often by wireless networks' default settings, many users have switched to alternative channels to avoid interference. If you find that the channel you are using is also used by other wireless networks displayed by the Site Survey tool, reconfigure your WAP to use another channel. Keep in mind that Channels 1, 6, and 11 are the best channels to use to avoid interference from other 2.4GHz devices, such as telephones and Bluetooth networks.

FIGURE 6.15
Using the Linksys Site Survey feature to connect to a wireless network.

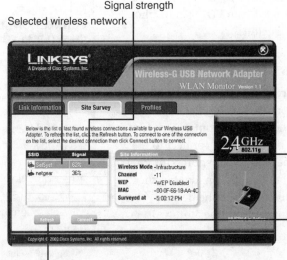

Signal strength

Selected wireless network

Detailed information about selected wireless network

Click to connect to selected wireless network

Click to perform new search for wireless networks in range

FIGURE 6.16

Using the
Linksys Link
Information tab
to view detailed
connection
information.

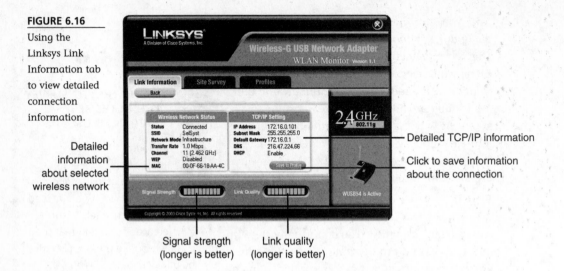

Detailed
information
about selected
wireless network

Detailed TCP/IP information

Click to save information
about the connection

Signal strength
(longer is better)

Link quality
(longer is better)

Configuring a PDA or Smart Phone's Wireless Connection

If your PDA or smart phone has a built-in wireless ethernet adapter, use the configuration utility included in your PDA or smart phone's operating system to configure it. If your PDA or smart phone uses an add-on card for wireless ethernet, install and run the configuration utility provided with the card to configure your connection. When prompted by the configuration utility, provide the mode (infrastructure or ad-hoc), the SSID of your WAP (infrastructure mode only), the channel (ad-hoc mode only), and the WEP or WPA encryption key used by your network. See the documentation for your PDA, smart phone, or add-on card for details.

Testing Your Wireless Network

Even before you complete the configuration of your home network (see "Using the Windows XP Network Setup Wizard," in Chapter 5, p. 131, for details), you should be able to connect to the Internet if your network offers shared Internet access. To start your connection, double-click on the Internet Explorer icon on the desktop, or open your preferred browser from the Start, (All) Programs dialog.

caution

NO INTERNET CONNECTION? GO TO CHAPTER 11 FOR HELP!

If you can't connect to the Internet, your wireless network adapter probably didn't receive a valid IP address from the DHCP server built in to your router. For typical causes and solutions, see "The Home Networker's Guide to TCP/IP," p. 316, Chapter 11, "Troubleshooting Your Home Network."

Completing Wireless Network Setup

To complete wireless network setup, you should enable basic wireless security and configure your PCs to be part of the same network. See the following sections for details.

Wireless Security 101

You should enable basic wireless security as soon as you know your wireless network is working correctly. Every moment you delay is another moment that somebody down the hallway or in the street could spy on your home network. Grabbing bandwidth to connect to the Internet is the least of your worries—you could be vulnerable to the following:

■ Information in shared folders can be copied, or even erased.

■ Your identity could be stolen if you keep bank or credit-card information in shared folders.

■ You could run out of IP addresses for your own network devices because moochers are borrowing your home network, preventing you from getting on the Internet yourself.

There are many ways to lock down your wireless network (see Chapter 10 for more advanced methods), but for right now let's discuss how to use WEP, the basic wireless security feature supported by every wireless ethernet WAP and network adapter.

WEP stands for Wireless Equivalent Privacy, but despite the name, it isn't perfect. Think of it as one of several locks to put on the digital "doorway" into your home network.

WEP uses one of three encryption levels:

■ 64-bit

■ 128-bit

■ 256-bit

The names refer to the length of the password you use; the longer the password, the harder it is for an intruder to break into your home network. In this example, I show you how to set up 64-bit WEP encryption. Why not a stronger encryption example? There are two reasons:

■ 256-bit encryption is supported only by network hardware built for corporate uses; 128-bit is the strongest encryption generally available on home networks.

■ Enabling encryption can slow down your network, and 128-bit encryption has a bigger impact than 64-bit encryption.

In the long term, other security measures discussed in Chapter 10 will provide even better security with less impact on your network's performance.

To enable 64-bit WEP encryption, follow this procedure:

1. Open the configuration wizard or web-based tool for your WAP.

2. After logging in, select the security or encryption menu.

3. Select 64-bit WEP security.

4. Enter the WEP key you want to use, or use the Passphrase option (if available) to generate one for you. Although some WAPs support plain-text WEP keys—they convert to hexadecimal for you—all wireless ethernet devices can use hexadecimal WEP keys. A 64-bit WEP key uses 10 digits (see Figure 6.17).

FIGURE 6.17

Using the Linksys WAP setup wizard to configure 64-bit WEP encryption security.

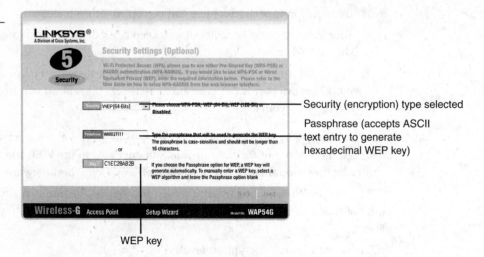

5. After you set up encryption, be sure to write down the WEP key and encryption type so you can use it on each network adapter.

6. Save your changes to the WAP's configuration.

To connect to the WAP with Windows XP, follow this procedure:

1. Right-click the wireless network icon in the Windows system tray.

2. Select View Available Wireless Networks. Although you are prompted to type a network key, I find it's better to configure the connection manually.

3. Click Advanced (Figure 6.18) to configure the connection.

4. Check the box next to Use Windows to Configure if it is not checked.

FIGURE 6.18

Selecting a wireless network that requires an encryption key.

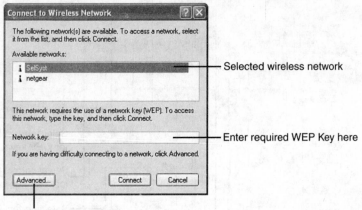

Selected wireless network

Enter required WEP Key here

Click to configure network encryption

5. Select the network you want to connect to from the Preferred Networks windows and click Properties. The properties sheet opens.

6. Check Data Encryption (WEP enabled).

7. Clear the check box next to The Key Is Provided for Me Automatically.

8. Enter the Hex key code in the Network key box. Make sure you have written down the WEP key!

9. Select Hexadecimal digits for the Key format if necessary.

10. Select key length as 40 bits (10 digits, the equivalent of 64-bit encryption).

11. Make sure the key index is set to the first key index available; in some versions of Windows XP, the key index is 0–3, in others it is 1–4. See Figure 6.19 for an example of the completed properties sheet.

12. Click OK.

13. Click OK to exit the Wireless Networks dialog.

14. Right-click the wireless network icon in the system tray and select View Available Wireless Networks.

note

MULTIPLE KEYS ARE A-OK!

If you use the browser-based configuration utility for your WAP, you might generate multiple WEP keys. Key 1 is the default key Windows XP's configuration utility looks for, so use that key for wireless adapter configuration. Select Key 1 as the default transmit key in the WAP's configuration.

Must be checked

FIGURE 6.19
Configuring a
wireless network
that requires an
encryption key.

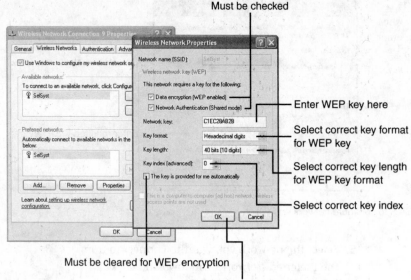

FIGURE 6.19

Configuring a
wireless network
that requires an
encryption key.

Enter WEP key here

Select correct key format
for WEP key

Select correct key length
for WEP key format

Select correct key index

Must be cleared for WEP encryption

Click when all settings completed or confirmed

15. Click the network you configured and click Connect.

16. To check your connection, double-click the wireless network icon.

17. The General tab shows your connection status, speed, signal strength, and
    activity (Figure 6.20).

Click to see
TCP/IP settings

Connection status

FIGURE 6.20

Checking the
status of a wire-
less connec-
tion with Win-
dows XP.

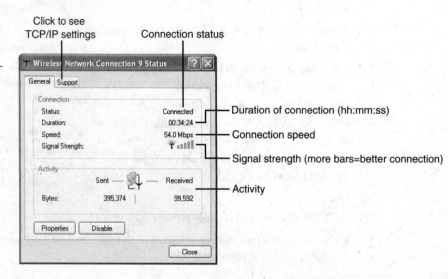

Duration of connection (hh:mm:ss)

Connection speed

Signal strength (more bars=better connection)

Activity

18. Click the Support tab to see information about your connection's IP address and other TCP/IP settings (Figure 6.21). Click Close when done.

FIGURE 6.21

Checking the TCP/IP settings for a wireless connection with Windows XP.

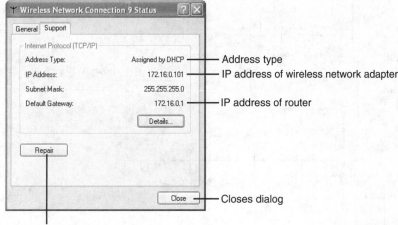

Click to attempt to repair a defective connection

If your network uses a router to provide shared Internet access, the router usually provides IP addresses used on the network through DHCP. However, if you see Private IP Address instead of Assigned by DHCP, this means that this adapter did not receive an IP address from the router or other DHCP server. For help dealing with this and other IP address problems, see Chapter 11.

Home Networking Wizard

To enable you to share printers and folders, you need to wrap up the configuration of your home network by running the Windows XP Networking Wizard or configuring shared folders and computer and workgroup names manually. See "Using the Windows XP Network Setup Wizard," Chapter 5, for details.

When you run the Windows XP Network Setup Wizard, it detects the network adapters installed in your PC and determines whether the network adapters are connected to a network. The wizard might not display your wireless adapter (Figure 6.22), or might determine it is disconnected. To continue running the network wizard, click the box marked "Ignore disconnected network hardware."

Disconnected wired ethernet network adapter

FIGURE 6.22

Bypassing the detection of disconnected networking hardware with the Windows XP Network Setup Wizard.

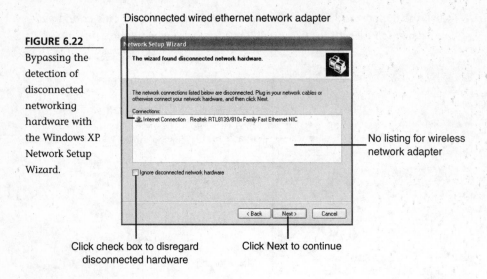

No listing for wireless network adapter

Click check box to disregard disconnected hardware

Click Next to continue

Increasing the Range and Speed of Your Connection

After you have created a working wireless network, take some time and relax! You've earned it. But, if you're not satisfied with the speed of your wireless network, or some distant computers are picking up a very weak signal (resulting in low speed) or can hardly connect at all, it may be time to consider how to improve the range and speed of your wireless network.

Improving Speed

You can improve the speed of your wireless network with the following changes:

- Reduce interference from other devices with wireless adapters.
- If you use only Wireless-G (802.11g) devices on your network, configure your router to support G-type devices only.
- Use alternatives to WEP encryption.

Get more information about these strategies in the following sections.

Reducing Interference with Wireless Adapters

Interference from wireless phones, AC adapters, and other EMI sources can cause a 54Mbps wireless network to nosedive to barely functional 1Mbps performance. What can you do to improve the situation? Check the following:

- Try a different channel for your WAP. Although Channel 6 is the traditional default used by most WAPs, many users have switched their WAPs to other channels. Channel 11 is becoming the most common alternative.

- Look at interference sources near the PC with the slow connection. For example, if you can plug a USB wireless adapter into a different USB port, try it. You might find that a USB port on the front of the PC is a better choice than the ones on the rear of the PC. Adjust the antenna on a PCI card to a different position, or move a USB device on a cord away from PC or AC power sources.

- Use cordless phones that run on different frequencies than your wireless network. Both 802.11b and 802.11g use the 2.4GHz frequency band. Consequently, popular 2.4GHz wireless phones pose a major potential for interference. Adjust them to use different channels, or move up to 5.8GHz cordless phones, which use a completely different frequency than 2.4GHz home networks, so they can't interfere with your home network signals.

All G? Use the G Only Setting

By default, almost all 802.11g WAPs and routers are configured to support a mixture of 802.11g and 802.11b devices. The additional overhead needed to support both types of devices can slow down your network, even if you use only 802.11g devices. Change your router configuration to use only 802.11g devices if your network doesn't use 802.11b devices. Figure 6.23 illustrates this option on a U.S. Robotics 802.11g WAP/router.

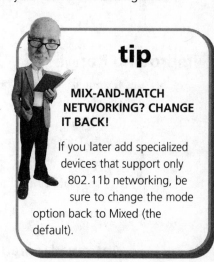

tip

MIX-AND-MATCH NETWORKING? CHANGE IT BACK!

If you later add specialized devices that support only 802.11b networking, be sure to change the mode option back to Mixed (the default).

Alternatives to WEP Encryption

Instead of WEP encryption, which can slow down your wireless network, you might be able to use WPA, a newer and better encryption scheme. Or, you can configure your WAP or router to work with only the network adapters and devices on your network by enabling MAC address filtering. For details, see Chapter 10.

FIGURE 6.23

Switching to G
Only mode with
a U.S. Robotics
WAP/router.

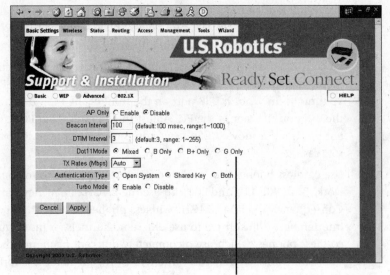

Use G Only if you have only 802.11g devices on the network

Improving Range

If some of your network stations get a very poor signal or an erratic signal, slow
speed connections or dropped connections are the result. You can fight back with the
following:

- Larger, more powerful antennas
- Signal Repeaters
- Using HomePlug instead of wireless ethernet for some locations

To learn more, check out the following sections.

Antenna Upgrades

The single or twin antennas on the top or rear of typical WAPs and routers work well
in residential wood-framed homes or over relatively short distances. However, if your
wireless network is trying to connect your home and a detached garage or workshop,
or if brick, stone, masonry, or concrete walls or floors interfere with signals, consider
antenna upgrades.

If you suspect that you need better antennas, start by selecting a brand and model
of WAP or WAP/router that supports replacement antennas. Although you can
remove the antenna(s) from most models, you should not attach an unapproved

antenna as a replacement. To find out whether more powerful or directional antennas are available for the WAP or wireless router you have or are considering purchasing, check the vendor's website. The following are some of the WAP and wireless router vendors that offer antenna upgrades for certain models:

- Linksys (High Gain Antenna kit); http://www.linksys.com
- Buffalo Technology (indoor and outdoor omnidirectional and directional antennas); http://www.buffalotech.com
- D-Link (indoor and outdoor omnidirectional and directional antennas); http://www.dlink.com
- Netgear (indoor and outdoor omnidirectional antennas); http://www.netgear.com

If you have two or more antennas to choose from, which should you select?

- Select a directional antenna if all your stations are located in the same general direction relative to your WAP or router.
- Select an omnidirectional antenna to improve the range and quality of connections for stations located in many different directions relative to your WAP or router.
- Select an outdoor antenna to improve connections for users outside (patio, pool, garage, workshop). Be sure to look for models that include a lightning arrester.

Repeaters

Even with an antenna upgrade, you might not be able to reach all the users in a very large area with a single WAP or wireless router. In such cases, consider using a repeater to increase range. Some WAPs can be configured as repeaters, or you can buy specialized devices from some vendors that perform this function.

Although you can mix and match WAPs and network adapters, repeaters usually need to be the same brand as the WAP or wireless router they work with. Be sure to check the compatibility listings for a repeater or WAP with repeater functions before you buy.

If you use a WAP or wireless router that has a repeater option, you configure repeater options through the WAP or wireless router's web-based configuration utility, as shown in Figure 6.24.

FIGURE 6.24
Configuring a
Linksys WAP to
act as a wireless
repeater.

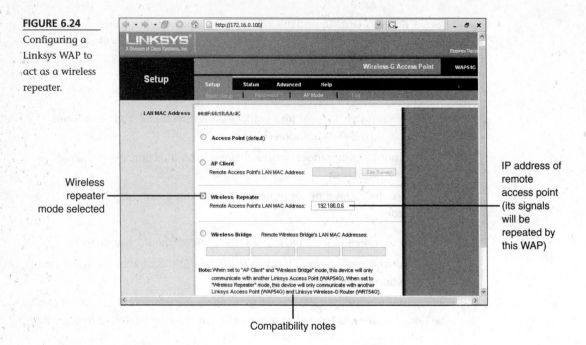

Wireless
repeater
mode selected

IP address of
remote
access point
(its signals
will be
repeated by
this WAP)

Compatibility notes

Covering Blind Spots with HomePlug Networking

HomePlug networks use the AC power lines in your home as the network.
Consequently, this type of network can be used when range or construction makes
other types of networks, including wireless ethernet, impossible or impractical. You
can connect a HomePlug network to an ethernet network with a HomePlug-ethernet
bridge. The bridge device can plug into the ethernet switch built in to most wireless
routers or into an ethernet switch that also hosts a WAP, making it possible for
HomePlug and wireless ethernet networks to communicate with each other.

For more information about using HomePlug, see "Using HomePlug or HomePNA as
an Alternative to Rewiring," p. 126, and "Bridging Ethernet to Other Network
Types," p. 127, Chapter 5. In Chapter 2, see "HomePlug Home Networking," p. 42,
and "Building a Mix-and-Match Network," p. 44.

Building Up Your Wireless Network

In this chapter, you've learned how to build a wireless network with PCs. But that's
just the beginning of what a wireless network can do for you. If you want to add
home entertainment devices to your wireless network, join me in Chapter 7. To learn
how to use your wireless network to share printers, share folders, and get more work
done at home, join me in Chapter 8.

THE ABSOLUTE MINIMUM

Wireless networking connects PCs and other devices to each other with radio waves.

A wireless access point (WAP) enables a wireless network to connect to other networks. A WAP can include a router and an ethernet switch.

Many, but not all, wireless ethernet adapters and other devices have Wi-Fi Certification.

Wi-Fi Certification indicates that different brands of devices have been tested to work properly with each other.

802.11b and 802.11g can connect with each other, although 802.11b runs at up to 11Mbps and 802.11g runs at up to 54Mbps.

802.11a also runs at up to 54Mbps, but it uses a different frequency (5GHz) than 802.11b/g (2.4GHz), so it cannot connect to those networks.

Some computers, such as portables that use Intel's Centrino technology, as well as others, have built-in wireless ethernet.

You can use PCI or USB adapters to add wireless ethernet to a desktop PC, or USB or CardBus adapters to add wireless ethernet to a laptop or portable computer.

You can add entertainment devices such as home theater systems, personal video recorders, and video games to a wireless ethernet network.

Networks running in ad-hoc mode provide direct connections between PCs and devices. Networks running in infrastructure mode use a WAP, but can connect to other networks or the Internet.

To configure a wireless connection, all stations (and the WAP) must use the same settings for SSID, channel, and encryption.

If you change encryption or other settings on the WAP, network adapters must make the same changes or their connections will stop working.

WAPs can be configured with a special wizard or by logging in to the WAP's IP address with a web browser.

Windows XP's wireless configuration utility works with any wireless adapter that works with Windows XP.

You can use 64-bit or 128-bit encryption with virtually all wireless network devices made for home use.

You can improve the speed and range of your connection by replacing standard antennas on WAPs and wireless routers with more powerful models.

PART III

Enjoying Your Home Network

7

HOME NETWORKS AT PLAY

After the work you dragged home from the office is done and after the last bit of homework is ready for tomorrow's class, your home network is just getting warmed up. You can use your home network to share all kinds of online entertainment sources, and to share video, music, and photos you create yourself. In this chapter, you discover the many ways you can make your home network make your home theater, TV, and game systems more fun and more exciting.

Playing Photos, Video, and Music on Your Home Theater System

Although you can view your digital photos and videos on your computer monitor and listen to digital music tracks with your PC's speakers, it's a lot less enjoyable if you're trying to share your digital favorites with others. Even the largest computer monitor is small compared to a typical TV, and most computers' speakers are tiny and don't have much oomph. The solution? Pipe that content over to your home theater system. Dolby Digital surround sound will make your favorite digital music tracks sound great, and your big-screen television will banish the bad memories of boring slide shows in dark rooms forever.

Whether you prefer a wired or wireless network solution, vendors offer a growing number of solutions that can help you enjoy your digital media through TVs, stereo systems, or home theater systems. Depending on the vendor, these devices might be called *media adapters*, *media players*, or similar terms. What's more important is choosing the right media adapter for your needs.

Selecting a Home Media Adapter

With many models to choose from, each with different features and price tags, the process of selecting a home media adapter can be overwhelming at first glance. However, if you use the following process, it will become clear to you which models make the cut:

1. Determine what type(s) of digital content you want to play through your home entertainment system. Some media servers handle only music, and others handle music and still photos. A few can also play back certain types of video files. Refer to Table 7.1 for media file types.

2. Determine the type(s) of connections to your home entertainment system that a media adapter needs to have. For example, if your home theater system has component video jacks as well as S-video, you'll see the best video quality if you can connect your media server to the component video jacks.

> **caution**
>
> **WATCH OUT FOR WMA PITFALLS!**
>
> Although almost all digital media adapters can play back some types of WMA files, many do not support files created with *digital rights management* (*DRM*; also known as *copy protection*) enabled (the default setting used by Windows Media Player). Other WMA options such as lossless compression can also cause problems, so find out what a particular device's limitations in handling WMAs are before you buy.

3. Determine which media adapters support the media types and connections you need. Keep in mind that most wireless media adapters also support wired ethernet networks. See Table 7.2 for examples.

Table 7.1 Typical Media Types Supported by Digital Media Servers

	Photo	Audio	Video
Media Types*	JPG	MP3	MPEG-1
	BMP	WMA	MPEG-2
	PNG	WAV	MPEG-4
	TIF	Internet radio	QuickTime
	GIF		AVI

Check the specifications for a particular media server to determine which media types it supports.

Table 7.2 Selected Digital Media Adapters Feature Comparison

Vendor	Model #	Photo Playback	Audio Playback	Video Playback	PC Software App Req	Supported Networks
Creative Labs	Sound Blaster Wireless Music	—	Yes	—	Yes	802.11g; 802.11b
D-Link	DSM-320 Wireless Media Player	Yes	Yes	Yes	Yes	802.11g; 10/100 Ethernet
Gateway	Connected DVD Player	Yes	Yes	Yes*	Yes	802.11g or 10/100 Ethernet
GoVideo	D2730	Yes	Yes	Yes*	Yes	10/100 Ethernet; optional 802.11b
HP	EN5000	Yes	Yes	—	Yes	10Mbps Ethernet
HP	EW5000	Yes	Yes	—	Yes	802.11b(g); 10Mbps Ethernet
Linksys	WMLS11B	—	Yes	—	Yes	802.11b(g); 10/100 Ethernet
Linksys	WMA11B	Yes	Yes	—	Yes	802.11b(g);

Table 7.2 (continued)

Vendor	Model #	Photo Playback	Audio Playback	Video Playback	PC Software App Req	Supported Networks
Netgear	MP-101	—	Yes	—	Yes	10/100 Ethernet; 802.11b(g); 10/100 Ethernet
Turtle Beach	Audiotron-100	—	Yes	—	No	10/100 Ethernet; 10/100 Ethernet

*Device also includes a DVD player.

As you can see from Table 7.2, most media adapters require that a PC on the network run server software. Some media adapters can work with multiple PCs running server software, but others require that only one PC on the network run server software. In either case, only the PC(s) running server software can be accessed by the media player.

If your media player works with only one PC, copy the media files from other PCs on the home network into the media folders on the server PC.

You should also consider the type(s) of audio and video connectors you want to use. Many media adapters support only stereo jacks for audio and composite or S-video output for video. However, a few models support component video and digital audio output for better video and sound quality. If your home theater system and big-screen TV are equipped to handle these inputs, consider home media adapters that support those outputs.

tip

GOT A SPARE PC? MAKE IT A MEDIA SERVER!

If you find yourself with an older Pentium II, Pentium III, or AMD Athlon or Duron-based system that isn't fast enough for gaming or modern office suites, give it new life by making it your media server. Install your favorite network adapter, install the server software for your media adapter, copy all the media files you want to use with your media adapter to folders on its hard disk, and use it strictly to host media files. If the hard disk on the old PC is too small for your collection of media files, upgrade to an 80GB or larger hard disk or use a network storage device. See "Using Network Storage," in Chapter 8, "Home Networks at Work and School," p. 239, for details.

Installing and Configuring a Home Media Adapter

To connect a typical media adapter, follow these basic steps:

1. Install the media server software on the PC containing the media files you want to play.

2. Connect the media adapter to the network or to the PC for configuration.

3. Select the folders where your media is stored.

4. Select the network type if your media adapter supports more than one network type.

5. Configure your media adapter to use the network. Figure 7.1 shows a typical configuration screen using a server-assigned (dynamic) IP address. Figure 7.2 shows a typical configuration screen for a Wi-Fi (Wireless ethernet) network.

6. If your Wi-Fi network uses encryption, you need to select an encryption level and supply the WEP key or the WPA passphrase your network is configured to use (Figure 7.3).

tip

GOT A PLAYSTATION2? MAKE IT A MEDIA PLAYER!

If you have a PlayStation2 with the Sony Network adapter installed, you can use it as a networked media player for music, movies, and photos on your PC. Just add the GameShark Media Player program (about $30). For more information or to order, see the developer's website at http://www.broadq.com.

note

USE THE WIRE, EVEN FOR WIRELESS NETS

Most media adapters can be connected to a 10/100 Ethernet port on your PC or network switch (or router). Even if the media adapter will eventually be connected to a wireless network, it's usually faster and easier to configure the media adapter via its ethernet port for configuration. Check your media adapter's manual for details.

Select Static IP only if you want to enter a specific IP address for the device

Device name (identifies devices on the network)

FIGURE 7.1

*Configuring a
Linksys Wireless-B
Media Adapter
with a dynamic
(server-assigned)
IP address.*

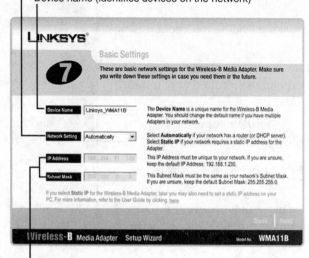

Enter these options only if Static IP is selected

Enter the SSID used by your wireless network

Infrastructure mode connects to other wireless devices via a WAP

FIGURE 7.2

*Configuring a
Linksys Wireless-B
Media Adapter to
use a secured
Wi-Fi (wireless
ethernet)
connection.*

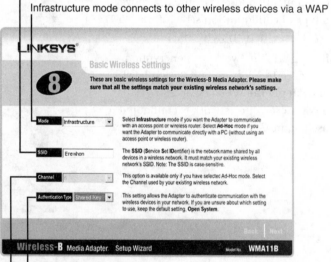

Select Shared Key if your network uses WEP or WPA encryption

Select the channel only if Ad-Hoc (direct connection to another PC) is chosen

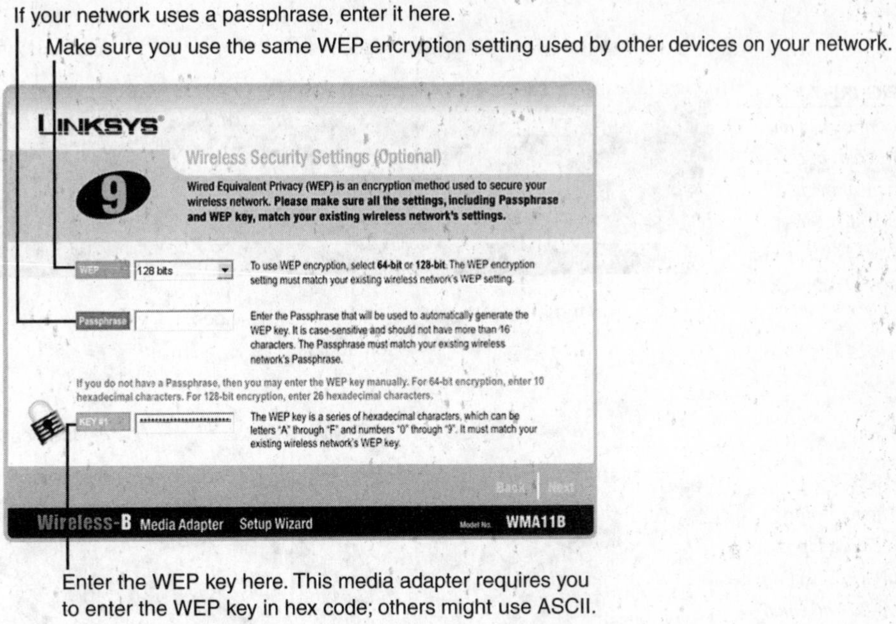

If your network uses a passphrase, enter it here.

Make sure you use the same WEP encryption setting used by other devices on your network.

FIGURE 7.3

Selecting a Wi-Fi encryption level and supplying the key used by a wireless network.

Enter the WEP key here. This media adapter requires you to enter the WEP key in hex code; others might use ASCII.

If you use an ASCII-to-hex converter, keep in mind that many of them output hex code using a spacer symbol (such as a percent sign) between hex characters. For example, if your WEP code (in ASCII) is LAN80211WIF54, an ASCII-to-hex converter might output %4C%41%4E%38%30%32%31%31%57%49%46%35%34. Enter only the hex characters when you enter the hex equivalent of your ASCII WEP key. See Table 7.3.

Table 7.3 ASCII to Hex Translation Example

ASCII	L	A	N	8	0	2	1	1	W	I	F	5	4
HEX	4C	41	4E	38	30	32	31	31	57	49	46	35	34

7. After the media adapter is configured, attach its antenna (if necessary).

8. Connect cables to the appropriate jacks on the media adapter. Refer to Figures 7.4 and 7.5.

FIGURE 7.4

Connections on the rear of a typical media adapter, the Linksys Wireless-B Media Adapter.

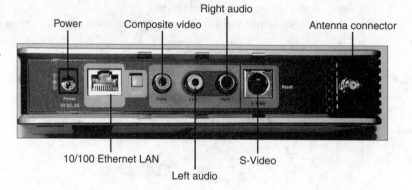

Power   Composite video   Right audio   Antenna connector

10/100 Ethernet LAN   Left audio   S-Video

FIGURE 7.5

The rear of the media adapter after connecting audio and video cables and the antenna. The inset shows the use of an S-video cable instead of a composite video cable.

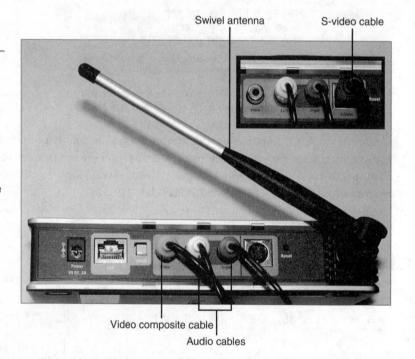

Swivel antenna   S-video cable

Video composite cable   Audio cables

9. Connect the audio cables from the media adapter to your home theater or stereo system's audio input jacks. See Figure 7.6.

10. Connect the video cable from the media adapter to your TV or monitor's video input jack. See Figure 7.7.

FIGURE 7.6

The rear of a home theater system after connecting audio jacks from the media adapter.

FIGURE 7.7

Connecting the composite video cable to the composite video input jack on a TV.

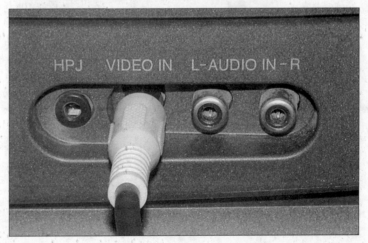

Playing Your Media Files with Your Media Adapter

After connecting your media adapter to your TV and home theater system, it's time to enjoy the digital goodness that's been trapped on your PC until now. Most media adapters include a remote control that can be used to

- Turn the media adapter on and off.
- Select the type(s) of media content to play.
- Select specific folders, artists, genres, or specific files to play.
- Check or change adapter configuration.

To start the fun, follow this basic procedure for media players that connect to your TV:

1. Turn on your home theater system.
2. Select the mode appropriate for the connection between your home theater system and the media adapter. For example, Figure 7.6 shows the audio cables from the media adapter plugged into the jacks marked "video" on the home theater system. In this example, Video mode should be selected on the home theater system.
3. Turn on your TV.
4. Select the connection you used between the TV and the media adapter. For example, if you used the video-in jack, select Video.
5. Turn on your media adapter.
6. After the media adapter displays its startup menu, select the media you'd like to play from the menu.
7. Sit back and enjoy the fun!

tip

EASY ASCII-TO-HEX CONVERSIONS

If you entered the WEP key in your wireless network's WAP or router configuration using ASCII (plain text), but your media adapter or other Wi-Fi devices require you to enter code in hexadecimal, try these solutions:

- Open your WAP or router's configuration screen to see whether the router can be switched from ASCII to hex display of the WEP key. If so, note the hex characters and enter them when needed.

- Use an ASCII-to-Hex conversion utility or website, such as the one available at the Mikezilla website:http://www.mikezilla.com/exp0012.html.

Troubleshooting Playback Problems with Your Media Adapter

Media adapters, like any other computer-related device, are wonderful when they work, but frustrating when they don't work. Use this checklist of typical problems and solutions to help you enjoy your media.

The Media Adapter Can't Connect to Server PC(s)

Make sure the server PC is turned on and that the server program is running. Most media adapters' server programs display an icon in the system tray.

If you have just installed the media adapter's server program on your PC, you should reboot the PC. The program will load after the reboot.

If the server PC was started in Safe Mode or another mode that does not load startup programs, the media server application is not running. Restart the server PC in normal mode.

Check the network configuration on the media adapter. The network type or wireless network configuration settings might be set incorrectly on the media adapter. The router's configuration might not be set to permit the MAC address for the media adapter to access the network, or it might not be configured to provide enough IP addresses via DHCP. For more information about these and other network-specific problems and solutions, see Chapter 11, "Troubleshooting Your Home Network."

> **caution**
>
> **DON'T LOSE THE REMOTE!**
>
> Depending on the media adapter, losing the remote can prevent you from selecting the media files you want to play and can also prevent you from configuring the media adapter. Make sure you keep the remote for your media adapter in a safe place!

> **tip**
>
> **MUSIC WITH A SIDE OF PHOTOS? YES, YOU CAN!**
>
> Some media players enable you to play music and view digital photos at the same time. Typically, you need to select the music you want to play, start playing it, and then select the photos you want to view. See your media adapter's instructions for more information.

Check the network configuration of the PC running the media adapter's server software. If the PC is unable to connect with other network resources (the Internet, shared folders, shared printers), the media adapter will not be able to connect to it. See Chapter 11 for solutions.

If the media adapter or server PC is connected to a wired network, check the cable connections. If the cable is disconnected or loose, shut down the media adapter or the PC, reconnect the cable, wait about 30 seconds, and restart the media adapter or the PC.

The Media Adapter Doesn't Respond When I Use the Remote Control

If you can't turn on the media adapter with the remote control, make sure the media adapter is plugged in to a working AC power source. If you can't turn on the media adapter with its on/off switch after verifying that it's plugged into a working power source, contact the vendor for help.

If you can't move the onscreen selector with the remote control, make sure there is nothing blocking the infrared (IR) transmitter on the remote control or the IR receiver on the media adapter. If the transmitter or receiver windows are free of obstructions, remove and replace the batteries in the remote control with fresh alkaline batteries. If the remote control continues to fail, contact the vendor for help.

> **note**
>
> **VIEWING ALL THE ICONS WITH WINDOWS XP**
>
> To see all the icons with Windows XP, click the left arrow next to visible icons in the system tray (the icons next to the clock). To display only active icons, click the right arrow.

I Can't Select the Media Files I Want to Play or View

Open the folder maintenance program on the PC(s) running the media server program and verify that the folders selected for use contain the media files you want to play. If incorrect folders are selected, select the correct folders (Figure 7.8) and retry selecting the files you want to play with your media adapter's remote control.

Make sure the files you want to play or view are compatible. Files stored in formats that are not supported by your media adapter are ignored by your media adapter. For example, if you want to play audio files in .WAV format, but your media adapter is not compatible with .WAV files, .WAV files stored in the folders used by your media adapter will not be displayed in your media adapter's selection menu.

FIGURE 7.8

*Managing folders
on a PC running
the server
program for a
Linksys Wireless-B
media adapter.*

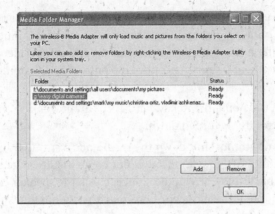

I Selected Files, but They Don't Play

If your media adapter displays a file name but doesn't play it, chances are the file or
files you selected for playback have features not supported by the media adapter.

For example, WMA files created with Digital Rights Management (copy protection)
are not supported by most media adapters. MP3 files with quality settings below a
certain quality standard or above a certain quality standard are not supported by
some media adapters. Certain types of photo files (such as CMYK TIF files) are not
supported by most media adapters. Video files created with codecs not supported by
your media adapter won't play.

To solve the problem, rerecord DRM (copy-protected) music files with the DRM or
copy-protection setting disabled in Windows Media Player or other ripping programs. Rerecord digital music files into MP3 files using a quality setting supported
by your media adapter. Convert graphics files with unsupported features with a
photo editor or graphics file-conversion program. Convert video files using an
unsupported codec into files using the correct codec with a video-editing or creation
program.

The Music File Appears to Play, but I Can't Hear It

Make sure your home theater system is turned on. If it is turned off, turn it on.

Make sure the audio cables are connected tightly between the home theater system
and the media adapter.

Check the audio setting on your home theater system. Make sure you have selected the correct source for audio. For example, if your media adapter is plugged into the Video connectors on the home theater system, you need to select Video as the audio source using the home theater's remote control or controls on the home theater receiver.

Adjust the volume on the home theater system. Turn up the volume on your music adapter's remote control if it is turned down.

If you still don't hear anything, shut down the media adapter and try playing some other audio source (radio, CD, movie) through the home theater system. If the home theater system is unable to play any audio source, check the speaker connections, audio source and volume. If these appear to be set correctly but you still can't hear anything, contact the vendor of your home theater system for help.

If your home theater system is working correctly with other audio sources, your media adapter might need servicing. Contact the vendor for help.

Adding Network and Online Gaming to Your Home Network

If you play action or strategy games on your PC, chances are you've enjoyed some type of network or online play for awhile, either by using a dial-up modem or a broadband Internet connection. With a home network, multiple PC gamers can play, and console game players can also join the action.

A home network makes the following gaming scenarios possible:

- Host your own LAN party. Get friends with PCs together for pizza, snacks, beverages, and friendly deathmatches.
- Sibling rivalry takes on a whole new meaning with head-to-head combat over the home network between the game consoles in the den and the spare bedroom.
- If you have broadband Internet access connected to your home network, the gamers in your household can take on the (gaming) world.

All three of the premiere game consoles on the market, the Sony PlayStation 2, the Microsoft Xbox, and the Nintendo GameCube, can be added to a home network. Depending on the console, it might be ready out of the box for some types of home networks or it might require add-on hardware.

Table 7.4 compares the network features of each of these game systems.

Table 7.4 LAN and Online Gaming Compatibility by Game System

Game System	Online Gaming	LAN (Network) Gaming	Network Ready	Additional Hardware Required
Microsoft Xbox	Yes	Yes	10/100 Ethernet	Xbox Live Starter Kit (for online play)[1,2]
Nintendo GameCube	Yes	Yes	No	Nintendo GameCube Broadband Adapter[3]
Sony PlayStation 2	Yes	Yes	No	Sony PlayStation2 Network adapter[4,5,6]

[1] *The Xbox Live Starter Kit includes a subscription service for online play with supported titles, a special headset with microphone, and integration with MSN Messenger to provide chat, buddy list, and other features.*

[2] *Optional adapters from Microsoft or third-party vendors can be used to add the Xbox to other types of networks.*

[3] *Optional adapters from third-party vendors can be used to add the GameCube to other types of networks after the Nintendo GameCube Broadband (10/100 Ethernet) adapter is installed.*

[4] *Optional adapters from third-party vendors can be used to add the PlayStation2 to other types of networks after the Sony Network (10/100 Ethernet and 56Kbps dial-up modem) adapter is installed.*

[5] *Some PlayStation2 retail bundles include the Sony Network Adapter.*

[6] *A few early PlayStation2 online games—such as Tony Hawk ProSkater 3, and ProSkater 4—can be played using various third-party USB-to-ethernet adapters plugged into the USB port on the PlayStation2. However, most recent online games require the official Sony Network adapter.*

Using the Xbox for Network and Online Gaming

To play LAN-enabled games through a 10/100 Ethernet network with the Xbox, select LAN or Network when prompted by the game. No configuration is necessary.

If you want to play online games on a 10/100 Ethernet network, you need the following hardware:

- Xbox Live Starter Kit
- An approved router

The Xbox Live Starter Kit contains the Xbox Communicator (headset and microphone), Xbox Live starter disc (CD modifies the Xbox Dashboard for online play), an Xbox Live subscription code good for 12 months, and instruction manuals.

Selecting a Router Compatible with the Xbox

Although the Xbox can be used with any 10/100 Ethernet switch for LAN play, Microsoft has approved only a few routers for use with Xbox Live online gaming. These are listed in Table 7.5.

Table 7.5 Xbox Live Approved Routers

Brand	Model	Firmware Versions	Network Type(s) Supported	Vendor Website
D-Link	DI-604	2.18, 3.2, 3.36	10/100 Ethernet	www.dlink.com
	DI-614+	2.18[1], 3.2, 3.35	10/100 Ethernet; 802.11b; 802.11b+[2]	
	DI-624	2.25, 2.28, 2.42	10/100 Ethernet; 802.11b; 802.11g; 108G[3]	
Linksys	BEFSR41 (v3)[4]	1.04.8	10/100 Ethernet	www.linksys.com
	BEFW11S4 (v4)[5]	1.45.3	10/100 Ethernet; 802.11b	
	WRT54G	2.02.7[6]	10/100 Ethernet; 802.11g; 802.11b	
Microsoft	MN-100	1.08[7], 1.11.017	10/100 Ethernet	www.microsoft.com
	MN-500	1.08[7], 1.11.017	10/100 Ethernet; 802.11b	
	MN-700	02.00.07.0331, 02.00.08.0333	10/100 Ethernet; 802.11g; 802.11b	

[1] *Router might disconnect multiple Xbox consoles after nearly 24 hours of operation; upgrade to newer firmware to resolve this issue.*

[2] *D-Link's proprietary high-speed (22Mbps) extension to 802.11b. This mode is not supported by the Microsoft MN-740 Wireless Xbox adapter. Configure the router to run in standard 802.11b mode if the MN-740 is used on the Xbox.*

[3] *D-Link's proprietary high-speed (108Mbps) extension to 802.11g. This mode is not supported by the Microsoft MN-740 Wireless Xbox adapter. Configure the router to run in standard 802.11g or 802.11b modes if the MN-740 is used on the Xbox.*

[4] *Version 3 of this router has six signal lights. See http://www.linksys.com/products/imagelib2/befsr41_v3.jpg. Compare to older versions, which have additional signal lights. See http://www.linksys.com/products/imagelib2/befsr41.jpg.*

[5] *Version 4 of this router has seven signal lights. See http://www.linksys.com/products/imagelib2/befw11s4_v4.jpg. Compare to older versions, which have additional signal lights. See http://www.linksys.com/products/imagelib2/befw11s4.jpg and http://www.linksys.com/products/imagelib2/befw11s4v2.jpg.*

[6] *This firmware version's implementation of Universal Plug and Play (UPnP) prevents users from connecting to Xbox Live. Disable UPnP in the router's configuration until an upgrade version of the firmware is available.*

[7] *Router might disconnect all but the first Xbox console after a few minutes of operation; upgrade to the other firmware listed.*

Some popular models of routers have been tested but have been found not to work with Xbox Live. These routers are listed in Table 7.6.

Table 7.6 Routers Incompatible with Xbox Live

Brand	Model	Network Type(s) Supported	Notes	Vendor Website
D-Link	DI-754	10/100 Ethernet; 802.11a (optional upgrade to 802.11b)		www.dlink.com
	DI-764	10/100 Ethernet; 802.11b; 802.11b+[1]; 802.11a		
Linksys	BEFSR11	10/100 Ethernet	Firmware versions 1.43, 1.44.2 tested; must use external switch to support network	www.linksys.com
	BEFW11S4 (v2)	10/100 Ethernet; 802.11b	Firmware versions 1.43, 1.45 tested	
Netgear	MR314	10/100 Ethernet; 802.11b	Firmware version 3.29 tested	www.netgear.com
	RP114	10/100 Ethernet	Firmware version 3.26 tested	
	RP334	HomePNA; 10/100 ethernet	Firmware version 3.26 tested	
	RT311	10/100 Ethernet	Firmware version 3.25 tested; must use external switch to support network	
	RT314	10/100 Ethernet	Firmware version 3.25 tested	
Network Everywhere	NR041[2]	10/100 Ethernet	Firmware version 1.2 tested	www.network everywhere.com

Table 7.6 (continued)

Brand	Model	Network Type(s) Supported	Notes	Vendor Website
SMC	7004VBR	10/100 Ethernet	Firmware version 1.20 tested	www.smc.com
	7004WFW[1]	10/100 Ethernet; 802.11b	Firmware version 1.00	

[1] *When multiple Xbox consoles are used with this router, consoles might be disconnected after random periods of time.*

[2] *The Xbox Live website identifies this router as a Linksys product; however, it is sold under Linksys' Network Everywhere brand.*

What if you already have a home network and your router is not listed or has been tested and found not to work with Xbox Live? A router not listed as Compatible or Not Compatible *might* work; try it and see whether you can play a game. If you have a router listed as Not Compatible, try upgrading the firmware to a newer version than those tested by Microsoft. If you need to replace your router, use Table 7.6 to determine which features a replacement router (see the models listed in Table 7.5) should have.

Selecting an Xbox-compatible Broadband Service

Xbox Live can work with a wide variety of broadband services. However, a number of major broadband cable and DSL ISPs have provided specific support information to Microsoft. If you're having problems getting Xbox Live to work with your current broadband ISP, check out the list available at http://www.xbox.com/en-US/live/connect/providers.htm. Some providers list specific cable modems and other equipment tested to work with Xbox, and all provide setup information.

tip

GETTING THE LATEST NEWS ON WHAT WORKS—OR DOESN'T

To stay on top of the latest test results for Xbox Live-compatible routers, go to http://www.xbox.com/en-US/live/connect/routerlanding.htm.

caution

AOL BROADBAND AND XBOX? YES, AND NO

AOL High-Speed Broadband DSL works with Xbox, but AOL High-Speed Broadband cable does not.

Setting Up the Xbox for Online Gaming

To configure the Xbox for online gaming using a 10/100 Ethernet network:

1. Install the Xbox Live Starter Kit's hardware and software.

2. Shut down the Xbox.

3. Connect the Xbox to your router's LAN port.

4. Turn on the Xbox.

5. Select Xbox Live from the Xbox Dashboard.

6. Follow the instructions to create your account (a 12-month account is included with the Starter Kit).

The Xbox is configured by default to receive an IP address from the DHCP server built in to your router. However, you might need to use the Xbox Dashboard to adjust PPPoE configuration. The Xbox, unlike some other console games, uses the router's PPPoE configuration to connect with broadband services that use PPPoE. If you see a PPPoE error with the Xbox, but computers on the network can connect to the Internet, turn off PPPoE in the Network Settings section of the Xbox dashboard.

Using the PlayStation2 for Network and Online Gaming

PlayStation2 users need to connect the Sony Network adapter to the expansion bus on the rear of the PlayStation2. An 8MB memory card is necessary to store the network configuration you select. PlayStation2 offers a very large collection of online and LAN-enabled games.

To install the Sony network adapter for use with a 10/100 Ethernet network:

1. Turn off your PlayStation2 console.

2. Unplug it.

3. Remove the expansion bay cover on the back of the console.

tip

CHECK YOUR SERIAL NUMBER BEFORE YOU BUY!

If your PlayStation2 was not bundled with the Sony Network adapter, you should verify that it will work with the Sony Network adapter. The online version of the Sony Network adapter's instruction manual lists PlayStation2 serial number series that do not work with the Sony Network adapter, along with a toll-free number for more information.

To download the manual, set your browser to http://www.playstation.com.

Select your region, click Hardware, click Network Adaptor, and click Product Manual. The manual requires Adobe Acrobat Reader 5.x or Adobe Reader 6.x or above.

4. Push the Network adapter into place, making sure the connectors on the rear of the unit mate properly with the connectors inside the unit.

5. Tighten the mounting screws (Figure 7.9).

6. Connect a CAT5/5e/6 network cable to the network adapter and to the network's router.

FIGURE 7.9

*The Sony
PlayStation2
Network adapter
after installation.*

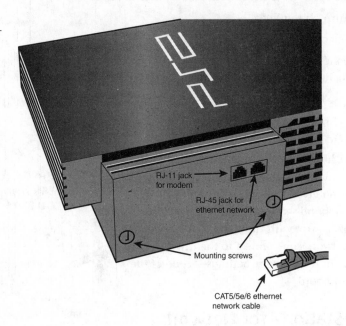

7. Be sure an 8MB memory card with at least 137KB of empty space is inserted into the PlayStation2. The memory card is used to store your network configuration.

8. Plug the console into an AC power source.

9. Turn on the console and verify that the power light is green.

To configure the Sony network adapter, use the CD included with the Network adapter. Enter the following information when prompted:

▓ Name of network configuration (your choice)

▓ Behind a firewall: Yes (basic firewall protection is built in to all routers)

▓ Subscribe to an ISP: No

▓ High Speed Connection: Yes

▓ Enter username and password if your connection uses PPPoE (required by many DSL service providers)

Follow the prompts onscreen to complete your configuration.

For more information on network settings, see Chapter 11.

Using the Nintendo GameCube for Network and Online Gaming

Nintendo GameCube users need to install the Broadband Adapter to play games online through a broadband Internet connection or through a 10/100 Ethernet LAN. Unlike PlayStation2, the library of GameCube games that support online play is very small, and only a few games support LAN play.

To install the Nintendo GameCube Broadband Adapter for use with a 10/100 Ethernet network:

1. Turn off your GameCube console.

2. Unplug it from AC power.

3. Disconnect the controllers.

4. Turn the unit over.

5. Remove the cover labeled Serial Port 1.

6. Insert the Broadband Adapter (Figure 7.10).

tip

NEED HELP? SONY HAS YOU COVERED

For more information on the PlayStation2 Network adapter configuration process, use the Network Adaptor Installation and Troubleshooting Wizard, by setting your browser to http://www.playstation.com.

Select your region, click Hardware, click Network Adaptor, and click Network Adaptor Installation and Troubleshooting Wizard.

FIGURE 7.10

Inserting the Broadband Adapter into a Nintendo GameCube.

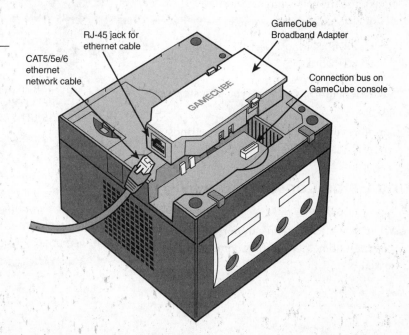

CAT5/5e/6 ethernet network cable

RJ-45 jack for ethernet cable

GameCube Broadband Adapter

Connection bus on GameCube console

7. Turn the unit upright.

8. Connect a CAT5/5e/6 network cable to the Broadband Adapter and to the network's switch.

9. Reconnect the controllers.

To play LAN-enabled games through the Broadband Adapter, select LAN when prompted by the game. No configuration is necessary.

To configure the Broadband Adapter for use with online games, configure the adapter within each game's option menu. In the first online game for GameCube, Phantasy Star Online, this option is located in the Options menu, Network Options submenu, Provider Option submenu. With a network that uses DHCP (IP addresses provided by a router), use the following settings:

- ethernet Settings: Automatic
- IP Address Auto Settings (DNS and DHCP): these are provided automatically by the DHCP server in the router

If your ISP uses PPPoE (used by many DSL connections), use the following settings:

- ethernet Settings: PPPoE
- PPPoE Settings: User ID (username) and password

Save the settings, and then you can start your game.

For more information on network settings, see Chapter 11.

Connecting Game Consoles to a Wi-Fi Network

When it comes to *official* support of Wi-Fi (wireless ethernet) home networking, game consoles are a mixed bag:

tip

NEED HELP? NINTENDO HAS YOU COVERED

For more information on the GameCube Broadband Adapter configuration process, go to http://www.nintendo.com/online/index.jsp.

note

BUILDING A BRIDGE BETWEEN WIRED AND WIRELESS ETHERNET

A bridge is a network device that converts one type of network signal to another, enabling devices using different types of adapters to become part of the same network. An ethernet/Wi-Fi bridge converts ethernet signals into Wi-Fi signals.

- Microsoft sells a Wi-Fi adapter (actually an ethernet/Wi-Fi bridge), the MN-740, for Xbox.
- Sony officially supports using the PlayStation2 Network adapter to connect to a Wi-Fi/ethernet bridge but doesn't sell one.
- Nintendo doesn't provide support for any wireless network solution.

Fortunately, there are plenty of third-party ethernet/Wi-Fi bridges that will enable you to connect your consoles to a Wi-Fi network. Table 7.7 lists some of the most popular products.

Table 7.7 Wi-Fi/Ethernet Bridges Compatible with Console Games

Brand	Model	Compatible With	Networks Supported	Vendor Website
Belkin	FSD7330[1]	PlayStation2, Xbox, GameCube	802.11g (b)	www.belkin.com
D-Link	DWL-G810[1]	PlayStation2, Xbox, GameCube	802.11g (b)[2]	www.dlink.com
	DWL-810+[1]	PlayStation2, Xbox, GameCube	802.11b[3]	
Linksys	WGA54G	PlayStation2, Xbox, GameCube	802.11g (b)	www.linksys.com
	WGA11B	PlayStation2, Xbox, GameCube	802.11b	
Motorola	WE800G[1]	PlayStation2, Xbox	802.11g (b)	broadband.motorola.com
Netgear	WGE101[1,4]	PlayStation2, Xbox, GameCube	802.11g (b)	www.netgear.com
	ME101[1]	PlayStation2, Xbox, GameCube	802.11b	

[1] *This bridge can be used with any wired ethernet device, including set-top boxes and printers.*

[2] *Also supports D-Link's proprietary Xtreme G (108Mbps) extension to 802.11g.*

[3] *Also supports D-Link's proprietary AirPlus (22Mbps) extension to 802.11b.*

[4] *Supports multiple-device bridging; connect an ethernet switch to this bridge and you can bridge two or more consoles or other ethernet devices to Wi-Fi.*

An ethernet/Wi-Fi bridge connects to your game console's ethernet port with a standard CAT5/5e/6 cable (usually included with the bridge). Figure 7.11 shows a home network with a console connected via ethernet and another console connected via a wireless bridge.

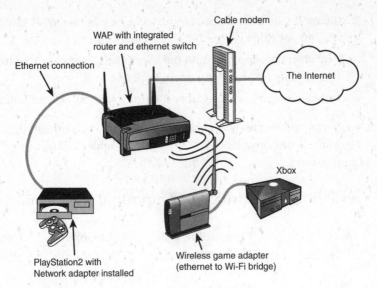

FIGURE 7.11

Game consoles with ethernet (left) and wireless bridge (right) connections to a home network with broadband Internet access.

Configuring Your Game Console to Connect to a Wi-Fi Network

Depending on the exact configuration of your network and your ethernet/Wi-Fi bridge, you might perform the configuration work with the bridge's own controls by connecting the bridge to a PC's ethernet port and configuring it through a utility supplied with the bridge or by logging into the bridge's built-in web-based utility. In most cases, you need to connect the bridge to your PC for configuration before you can connect it to your game console.

Configuration options for an ethernet/Wi-Fi bridge are the same as for any other Wi-Fi device (refer to Chapter 6, "Installing and Configuring a Wi-Fi Network," for details). To connect through a router or WAP (infrastructure mode), you need to configure options such as

- Mode: Infrastructure (router or WAP)

- SSID: Wireless network identification for infrastructure-mode networks (same for all computers)

caution

READY TO WORK? NOT WITH A ROUTER OR WAP

Bridges built especially for use with console games are usually preconfigured for ad hoc mode, so expect to reconfigure almost any bridge you use with a console game for use with a router-based network (which uses infrastructure mode). Even if the bridge is designed to connect to a router, you will need to configure it manually if your wireless network uses WEP encryption or other security options.

- Channel: (same for all computers)
- WEP encryption: select disabled, 64-bit, or 128-bit (must be same for all computers)
- WEP key: used only if WEP encryption is enabled (must be same for all computers)
- DHCP: Enabled (router or WAP provides an IP address for the bridge)
- Transmission rate: Auto (auto-negotiates the best possible data rate; choose a specific speed only if Auto doesn't work well)
- Mode (802.11g-based bridges only): Use Mixed if 802.11b and g devices are both found on the network; use 802.11g, G-only, or similar options to increase speed if network does not have 802.11b devices

After you have configured the bridge to work with your wireless network, disconnect it from your PC's ethernet port, plug it into your console game, and play your favorite LAN or online game.

LOG ON FOR MAXIMUM CONTROL

Even if the bridge is equipped with a PC-based configuration program, you might need to log into the web-based configuration program built in to the bridge to configure some options. Check your bridge's instruction manual for the IP address to specify and the login name to use to gain access.

Troubleshooting Your Game Console's Network Connection

If you've connected your game console to your home network, but you can't play your favorite LAN or online games, you won't be happy until it works. And, if you're not the game player, but your kids, spouse, or friends are the gamepad mavens, you're going to hear about it until you ride to the rescue and make it work. Here are some of the most common problems and solutions.

My Console Doesn't Know It Has a Network Connection

The PlayStation2 and GameCube network adapters must be installed correctly before these systems are network-aware. Double-check the installation: Turn off the system, remove the adapter, and reinstall. If the console still cannot detect the adapter, try the adapter on a friend's console. If the adapter doesn't work on any console, the adapter has a problem and should be serviced. If working adapters don't work when plugged into your console, your console has a problem and should be serviced.

The Xbox's ethernet port is built in to the system. If this system doesn't detect a network connection, contact the vendor for help.

My Console Can't Connect to the Network

If you can't connect to an ethernet network, double-check the following:

- Is the network cable plugged in correctly to both the network port on the console and the switch or router? If not, turn off the console, reconnect the cable, and turn it on again.

- Is the network cable a straight-through cable or a crossover cable? Use a straight-through cable between your console and the switch or router. Standard ethernet cables are straight-through (same wire pairs on both ends).

- Have you configured the console? Review the configuration notes earlier in this chapter, and see the vendor websites for additional information.

For ethernet or wireless networks, check the following:

- Have you updated the security settings used by your router? These settings include the number of IP addresses provided by the DHCP server (increase the number by one to provide an IP address for your console), and MAC address filtering (add the MAC address of your console or its network adapter to the MAC address listing in your router). See Chapter 11 for more details.

- Is your console securely connected to the ethernet/Wi-Fi bridge? If the cable is loose or damaged, the console won't be able to connect to the Wi-Fi network via the bridge.

- Has the ethernet/Wi-Fi bridge been configured for the network? Most bridges, especially those made for game consoles, are configured by default for ad hoc

tip

CASE STUDIES FOR SUCCESS

Check out these online resources for more help in getting your console on a Wi-Fi network:

Microsoft Xbox—The official Xbox guide for wireless connections is located at http://www.xbox.com/ en-us/live/connect/ wireless_connect.htm.

A user relates his experience at http://www.xbox.com/en-US/ community/lifestyle/lifestyle-going-wireless.htm.

All Consoles—A guide to networking console games with an ethernet/Wi-Fi bridge (referred to as a "converter") http://www. transparent.uk.com/acatalog/ Wireless_Gaming.html.

PC Magazine's ExtremeTech site provides a good overview of wireless networking for console games at http://www.pcmag.com/ print_article/0,1761,a=109717,00. asp.

networks or open (unsecured) infrastructure networks. Configure the bridge with the necessary security settings (WEP encryption level, WEP key) used by your network. See Chapters 6 and 11 for more details.

Adding Set-Top Digital Video Recorders to Your Home Network

Recall from Chapter 2, "Building Blocks of the Home Network," that digital video recorders (DVRs) such as TiVo and ReplayTV are replacing VCRs as the method of choice for time-shifting TV shows and recording personal libraries of favorite programs. They can also pause live TV broadcasts while you answer the door, take a phone call, or grab a snack between commercials. Those features already put them miles beyond the VCR. But, you can get much more out of your DVR by adding a home network equipped with broadband Internet access.

When you connect TiVo to your home network, you can

- Schedule recordings remotely through a web browser much more quickly than via a dial-up connection.

- Use your TiVo as a media adapter, playing MP3 music and TIFF, JPG, and other common photo and graphics formats through your TV and home theater system.

- Transfer programs between TiVos or PCs on the home network for multiroom viewing.

ReplayTV DVRs 5500-series DVRs (the latest version as of mid-2004) have the following network features built in:

- Network recording automatically switches to an available ReplayTV unit on the home network to prevent recording conflicts.

- Pause and resume enables you to pause playback on one unit and continue viewing on another unit.

- Room-to-room live video streaming between ReplayTV units on the home network.

- Remote scheduling of recordings via the Internet.

tip

NETWORK CHANGES MEAN CONSOLE CONFIGURATION CHANGES

If you originally connected your consoles directly to each other, but are now using a switch or router, you will need to change the network configuration for your console.

- ▪ JPEG photo transfer between any PC on the network and a ReplayTV DVR.
- ▪ Upload of *non-copyrighted* content via the Internet to other ReplayTV DVRs.

As you can see, although TiVo and ReplayTV units differ somewhat in their network capabilities, both benefit from being connected to your home network. If you already have two or more TiVo or ReplayTV DVRs, adding them to a home network makes them even more entertaining.

Connecting TiVo to Your Home Network

TiVo Series 2 DVRs can be added to your home network through purchase of your choice of network hardware; TiVo service now includes home network support. TiVo connects to your home network via a USB network adapter, using one of the two USB ports on the rear of the unit. Table 7.8 lists network adapters recommended by TiVo.

Table 7.8   TiVo-Recommended Network Adapters

Brand	Model	Network Types Supported	TiVo Service Numbers Supported	Vendor Website
Linksys	WUSB11 v 2.6, v2.8*	802.11b (g)	All	www.linksys.com
	WUSB11 v3.0*			
	WUSB12*	802.11b (g)	Service numbers starting with 230, 240, 264, 275	
	USB100TX	10/100 Ethernet	All	
	USB200M	10/100 Ethernet	All	

*Requires upgrade to latest TiVo DVR software. See http://customersupport.tivo.com/tivoknowbase/root/public/tv2006.htm for more details.

However, if you already have a different brand or model of USB network adapter, you might be able to use it with your TiVo. Table 7.9 lists USB adapters that TiVo customers report work properly with their TiVo units.

Table 7.9   TiVo Customer-Suggested Network Adapters

Brand	Model	Network Types Supported	TiVo Service Numbers Supported	Vendor Website
3Com	3C460B	10BASE-T Ethernet	All	www.3com.com
Belkin	F5D6050, F5D6050 ver 2000	802.11b (g)	All	www.belkin.com
	F5D5050	10/100 Ethernet	All	

Table 7.9 (continued)

Brand	Model	Network Types Supported	TiVo Service Numbers Supported	Vendor Website
D-Link	DWL-120 Ver E	802.11b (g)	All	www.dlink.com
	D-Link DWL-120 Ver A	802.11b (g)	Service numbers starting with 110, 130, 140	
	D-Link DWL-120 Ver D	802.11b (g)	Service numbers starting with 230, 240, 264, 275	
	D-Link DWL-122	802.11b (g)	Service numbers starting with 230, 240, 264, 275	
	D-Link DSB-650TX	10/100 Ethernet	All	
	D-Link DUB-E100	10/100 Ethernet	All	
Dell	True Mobile 1180 USB	802.11b (g)	Service numbers starting with 230, 240, 264, 275	www.dell.com
Hawking	WU250	802.11b (g)	All	www.hawkingtech.com
	UF200	10/100 Ethernet	All	
	UF100	10/100 Ethernet	All	
Linksys	USB100M	10/100 Ethernet	All	www.linksys.com
Microsoft	MN-510	802.11b (g)	Service numbers starting with 230, 240, 264, 275	www.microsoft.com
	MN-110	10/100 Ethernet	All	
Netgear	MA101 Ver A	802.11b (g)	Service numbers starting with 110, 130, 140	www.netgear.com
	MA111	802.11b (g)	Service numbers starting with 230, 240, 264, 275	
	FA101	10/100 Ethernet	All	
	FA120	10/100 Ethernet	All	
Siemens	SS1001	10/100 Ethernet	All	www.siemens.com
SMC	SMC2662W ver 2	802.11b (g)	All	www.smc.com
	SMC2208	10/100 Ethernet	All	

If you have a USB network adapter other than those shown, give it a try. The worst that can happen is that you'd need to buy a TiVo-approved or customer-suggested model if your TiVo doesn't like your adapter.

Figure 7.12 illustrates typical wireless ethernet (Wi-Fi) and wired (10/100) ethernet adapters and how they connect to a TiVo Series 2.

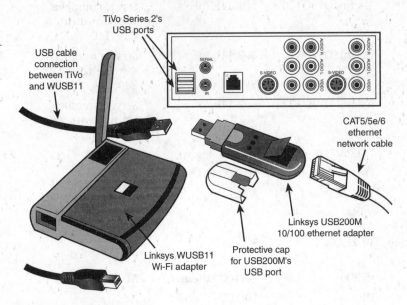

FIGURE 7.12

Wireless (left) and wired ethernet (right) connections to a TiVo Series 2 DVR.

After you connect your TiVo Series 2 to a wired or wireless network adapter, turn it on to complete the configuration process.

To configure a wireless adapter on a network that uses DHCP to provide IP addresses automatically, follow this procedure:

1. Allow TiVo to provide a firmware update for your wireless adapter if prompted.

2. Review the Important Message onscreen.

3. Press SELECT to go to TiVo Central.

4. From TiVo Central, select Messages and Setup, Settings, Phone and Network Setup, Edit settings, and Wireless Settings.

5. Review the Wireless Checklist, and then press SELECT to continue.

6. Select your network's SSID if listed. If not listed, select Connect to a closed wireless network.

7. Use the onscreen keyboard to enter the name of your wireless network.

8. If your network uses WEP encryption, enter the password as you entered it in the router or WAP's configuration (TiVo can use either ASCII text or hex).

9. Select an encryption level (up to 128-bit; this must match the encryption level used by your WAP or router).

10. Select Yes to change your connection type from phoneline to broadband Internet if you have a broadband Internet connection on your home network.

11. Go to the TCP/IP settings screen and select Obtain the IP address automatically.

12. Enter a DHCP Client ID if your ISP requires this option.

13. Confirm the settings.

14. Use the Test Connection option to check your new connection.

If you connected TiVo to a wired ethernet network, follow this procedure:

1. Review the Important Message onscreen.

2. Press SELECT to go to TiVo Central.

3. Wait for a few minutes for TiVo to receive an IP address from the DHCP server in the router.

4. To confirm the settings, select Messages and Setup, Settings, Phone and Network Setup, Edit settings, and TCP/IP Settings.

5. Go to the TCP/IP settings screen and select Obtain the IP address automatically.

6. Enter a DHCP Client ID if your ISP requires this option.

7. Confirm your settings.

8. Select Yes to change your connection type from phoneline to broadband Internet if you have a broadband Internet connection on your home network.

9. Use the Test Connection option to check your new connection.

tip

STUDYING TIVO NETWORKING

Before you take the plunge into TiVo networking, download and read the Home Media Features instruction manual (requires Adobe Acrobat Reader/Adobe Reader) from the TiVo website: http://www.tivo.com/pdfs/HMF_guide.pdf.

Connecting ReplayTV to Your Home Network

ReplayTV units include a 10/100 Ethernet port, so they're ready to connect to an ethernet network. You can use an ethernet/Wi-Fi bridge to connect a ReplayTV unit to your Wi-Fi network.

ReplayTV states that any ethernet router should work with its DVRs. However, ReplayTV recommends using one of the routers listed in Table 7.10 *if* your current router does not work properly.

Table 7.10   Ethernet Routers Recommended by ReplayTV

Brand	Model	Network Types Supported	Vendor Website
Linksys	BEFW11S4	10/100 Ethernet; 802.11b	www.linksys.com
Netgear	RT311	10/100 Ethernet	www.netgear.com
	RP114	10/100 Ethernet	
SMC	Barricade SMC7004BR	10/100 Ethernet	www.smc.com

After you connect your ReplayTV unit to a router on your network, follow this procedure to configure it on a network using a DHCP server (usually built in to your router) to provide IP addresses:

1. Turn on the unit.
2. Provide your Zip Code when prompted.

To connect using an ethernet/Wi-Fi bridge connecting to a router or WAP:

1. Configure the bridge with the correct settings for the network as discussed in Chapter 6.
2. Connect the bridge to the ReplayTV unit's ethernet port.
3. Turn on the unit.
4. Provide your Zip Code when prompted.

If you plan to use MAC address filtering to secure your wireless or wired/wireless network (see Chapter 10, "Securing Your Home Network," for details), you should set up your ReplayTV unit to use a static IP address. To enter a static IP address:

1. Press Menu on the remote control.
2. Select Setup from the menu listing.
3. Select Network and Input Settings.
4. Select Change Network.

5. Select Change from Automated to Manual.

6. Enter the desired IP address, subnet mask, default gateway, and other information required.

For details, see "Manual IP Address Configuration," Chapter 11, p. 322 or your ReplayTV unit's manual.

If you need to set up your ReplayTV unit to connect through different types of networks, see the official ReplayTV website or third-party websites for help.

Using Multimedia PCs on Your Home Network

If you prefer to use a PC as a DVR, you can purchase a new Media Center PC with Microsoft Windows XP Media Center Edition or add a graphics card with integrated DVR and TV-viewing features such as the ATI All-in-Wonder series or the NVIDIA Personal Cinema series to an existing PC.

You can add any of these computers to a home network (see Chapters 5, "Installing and Configuring a Wired Ethernet Network," and 6,"Installing and Configuring a Wi-Fi Network," for details); but the real question is, how easily can you enjoy the digital goodness you record on one PC on the rest of your home network? Keep reading to discover what you can do.

tip

BONING UP ON REPLAYTV NETWORKING

Before you take the plunge into ReplayTV networking, read the manual for your ReplayTV unit. If yours has gone missing, you can download it from the ReplayTV website (requires Adobe Acrobat Reader/Abobe Reader).

Get your manuals from http://www.digitalnetworksna.com/support/replaytv/manuals_downloads.asp. Select your unit's series to see the user manual, quick setup guide, and other documents.

Don't have Adobe Reader yet? Get it from http://www.adobe.com/products/acrobat/readermain.html.

ATI All-in-Wonder and EAZYSHARE

Starting with ATI's Multimedia Center software version 8.8, you can share recorded content created on your ATI All-in-Wonder card with other systems through the EAZYSHARE feature.

EAZYSHARE sets up one All-in-Wonder card as the server, and other computers running ATI graphics cards or All-in-Wonder cards based on the Radeon 7000 graphics processor (GPU) or newer as clients.

Client PCs can select the following options:

- Timeshare (record now, view later) with rewind, fast forward, pause, store on disk, closed caption, and still-image capture.
- Schedule a recording.
- Separate channel, volume, screen appearance, and other options for each client.
- Optional use of ATI's radio-control REMOTE WONDER. REMOTE WONDER units can be set to separate IDs to reduce interference.

For more information about EAZYSHARE and other features of ATI's Multimedia Center application, see http://www.ati.com/products/multimediacenter/. Upgrades to Multimedia Center 8.8 are free for owners of 8.1 and later versions; users of older versions can purchase the MMC 8.1 CD for about $10.

tip

REPLAYTV NETWORKING HELP

If you run into trouble getting your ReplayTV unit to work with your network configuration, see the Modem and Networking FAQ page at the ReplayTV website http://www.digitalnetworksna.com/support/replaytv/find_answer.asp.

Select Modem and Network from the appropriate category, then select your ReplayTV series for model-specific help.

For user-to-user help on all aspects of using ReplayTV, including home networking, check out ReplayTV FAQ at http://www.replayfaqs.com and the Planet Replay forums at http://www.planetreplay.com.

NVIDIA Personal Cinema and ForceWare Multimedia

NVIDIA's Personal Cinema cards enable you to share live TV or recorded programs over your home network through the use of the optional ForceWare Multimedia program. Unlike ATI's EAZYSHARE, which works only with ATI-built graphics cards, ForceWare Multmedia works with graphics cards using recent NVIDIA or ATI RADEON chips.

Fore more information, including a free trial version and pricing, see http://www.nvidia.com/page/multimedia.html.

Media Center PCs and Windows XP Media Center Edition

You can enjoy content created on a Windows Media Center PC over your home network by sharing its My Pictures, My Videos, and My Music folders. Use Windows Media Player version 9 on other Windows-based PCs to play the content from the shared folders. Other media players might also be able to play the content, depending on what format it was recorded in and with what options. To learn more about sharing folders, see Chapter 8.

If you want to view TV programs recorded with Windows XP Media Center Edition on other PCs running Windows XP, you need to install the following on each client PC:

- Windows XP Service Pack 1 (includes Windows Media Player 9)
- DirectShow Playback Support Update (Knowledge Base article 810243)

To download Windows XP Service Pack 1, you can use Windows Update (http://windowsupdate.microsoft.com) or go to http://www.microsoft.com/windowsxp/downloads/updates/default.mspx.

To locate the update to the DirectShow components, go to http://support.microsoft.com, click Knowledge Base Article ID Number Search, and search for 810243.

Media Center Extenders devices and software, which enable home network clients, TVs, and Xbox consoles to access TV, photo, video, and music content from PCs running Windows XP Media Center Edition 2005, are now available from Hewlett-Packard, Linksys, and Microsoft. To learn more about Media Center PCs and Windows XP Media Center Edition, see http://www.microsoft.com/windowsxp/mediacenter/default.mspx. To learn more about Media Center Extenders in general, see http://www.microsoft.com/windowsxp/mediacenter/evaluation/devices/default.mspx.

To learn more about HP's Media Center Extender X5400, see www.hp.com. To learn more about the Linksys Media Center Extender, see www.linksys.com/extend. To learn more about the Microsoft Media Center Extender for Xbox, see http://www.microsoft.com/windowsxp/mediacenter/evaluation/devices/xboxextenderkit.mspx.

The Absolute Minimum

Devices known as media adapters can enable stereos, home theater systems, and TVs to play digital music, photo, and video files stored on your PC.

Media adapters vary in the file types they can play, their network connections, and the audio and video connections they use, so shop carefully for the best device for your needs.

Media adapters usually must be configured through a connection to a PC's network port, even if they will be used on a wireless network.

Media adapters that are not configured properly for the network cannot find or play your media files.

The Microsoft Xbox has a built-in 10/100 Ethernet port, but the Sony PlayStation2 and Nintendo GameCube require you to add an optional ethernet port before they can connect to a home network.

Xbox Live is required for online gaming with Xbox.

Microsoft has tested a variety of network hardware for use with Xbox. For best results, use tested hardware.

The Xbox Dashboard is used to configure the Xbox's network settings.

The PlayStation2's network (ethernet/modem) adapter includes a CD that is used for configuration.

The GameCube's broadband adapter is configured through each compatible game's option menu.

Although only Microsoft makes an official Wi-Fi adapter for its game (Xbox), all three major consoles can use ethernet/Wi-Fi bridges to connect to a Wi-Fi network.

If you have two or more networked TiVo or networked ReplayTV units, you can share recorded programs between units.

To connect TiVo to a home network, you need a USB ethernet or Wi-Fi adapter and the Home Media Features service.

ReplayTV is network-ready (it has a 10/100 Ethernet port).

ATI and NVIDIA offer software that can be used to share video recordings and live TV captured with All-in-Wonder (ATI) or Personal Cinema (NVIDIA) with other computers on a home network.

Windows Media Center version 9 can be used to play some content captured by a Media Center PC, but updates are needed by many PCs for video.

8

HOME NETWORKS AT WORK AND SCHOOL

Your home network is more than a way to enjoy media files and play games. If you need to work from home or take classes online, a home network helps you work as hard as you play. In this chapter, you learn how to configure your home network to share files, printers, and scanners, how to select network-ready all-in-one devices, how to expand your home network with direct connections to printers and additional storage, and how to create secure connections between your home network and office or school networks.

Sharing Network Resources

Your home network isn't just for fun. Chances are you use it to work from home, run a home-based business, or continue your education. In the following sections, you learn how to share printers, drives, folders, and other resources so you can get your work done and get back to playing.

Sharing Printers

From the beginning of home networking, one of the biggest benefits a home network offers has been the ability to share a printer. Instead of walking documents to the computer with a printer, you can print from any computer on the network to the shared printer. Whether your network is wired or wireless, you now have more ways than ever to share a printer, but you have some pitfalls to watch out for. This section helps you avoid the traps on the road to easy network printer access.

Shared and Remote Printers

If you used the Windows XP Networking Wizard to set up your home network (see "Using the Windows XP Network Setup Wizard," p. 131, Chapter 5, "Installing and Configuring a Wired Ethernet Network," for details) and selected the option to share installed printers, any printer that was connected to a PC on your home network is now a shared printer. When you open the Printers and Faxes or Printers folder in Windows, a shared printer connected to your computer is displayed with a hand icon. A remote printer (a printer accessed over the network) is displayed with a cable icon. See Figure 8.1 for typical examples.

If you didn't select the option to share your printers when you set up your home network or you want to share a printer you just added to your system, you can set up printer sharing manually. See "Sharing a Newly Installed Printer," p. 220, this chapter, for details.

Accessing a Remote Printer

To set up access to a shared printer from another PC on your home network, use this method with Windows XP (the process is similar with other versions of Windows):

1. Open the Printers and Faxes or Printers folder from the Start button or from Control Panel.
2. Click Add a printer (refer to Figure 8.1).
3. Click Next on the introductory screen to continue.

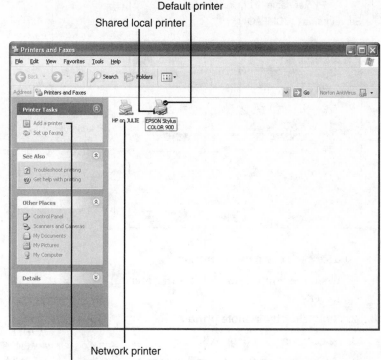

FIGURE 8.1

A network printer and a shared printer as seen in the Windows XP Printers and Faxes folder.

4. Select A Network Printer and click Next.

5. Select Browse for a Printer and click Next.

6. Select the printer you want to use from the list of printers on your home network (Figure 8.2) and click Next. There's a brief wait while printer drivers are copied to your system from the remote computer. If the remote computer doesn't have the printer driver you need for your system, you can also install the drivers from your Windows CD. The wizard will prompt you for the CD if necessary.

7. If you are prompted to insert your Windows CD, do so. This will be the case if the remote computer doesn't have the right printer driver for your version of Windows.

8. Specify whether you want the selected printer to be the default printer and click Next.

9. Click Finish to close the wizard.

Printer name (\HP LaserJet 5P – test)

Server name (\\COMPAQ)

FIGURE 8.2

Selecting a network printer with the Windows XP Add Printer Wizard.

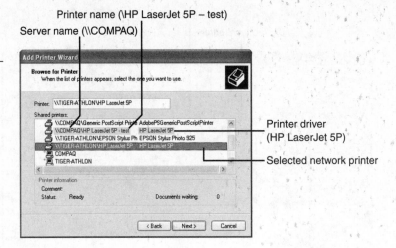

Printer driver (HP LaserJet 5P)

Selected network printer

To test access to your network printer:

1. Open the Printers and Faxes or Printers folder.

2. Right-click the remote printer.

3. Select Properties (Figure 8.3).

4. Click Print Test Page to send a page to the printer (Figure 8.4).

5. A dialog box appears in some versions of Windows. Click OK if the page printed correctly, or Troubleshoot to start a print troubleshooter.

6. Click OK to close the network printer's properties sheet.

tip

WHEN TO SAY YES AND WHEN TO SAY NO TO A DEFAULT PRINTER

If your computer stays at home and doesn't have a printer connected to it, go ahead and say "yes" to making the network printer the default printer. Keep in mind that you can switch to a different default printer, or choose a printer for particular print jobs, anytime you like. However, if this is a notebook or portable computer that does most of its printing at the office, or this computer has a local printer attached to it, keep your previous default.

FIGURE 8.3

Preparing to view properties for a network printer in Windows XP.

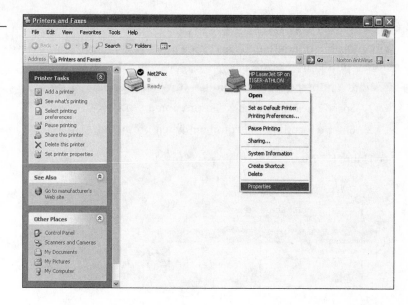

Computer hosting remote printer

Remote printer

FIGURE 8.4

Printing a test page in Windows XP.

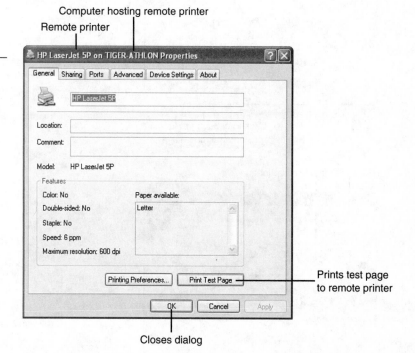

Prints test page to remote printer

Closes dialog

Sharing a Newly Installed Printer

Windows does not automatically share a newly installed printer. However, you can share a printer in two ways.

To share a printer during installation in Windows XP:

1. Specify a share name when prompted.

2. Enter a location and comment when prompted.

See Figure 8.5 for example dialogs.

FIGURE 8.5

Setting up printer sharing during new printer installation in Windows XP.

Select to enable printer sharing

Enter share name here

Click to continue to location & description dialog

Enter printer location (optional)

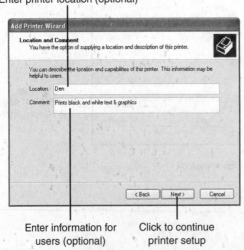

Enter information for users (optional)

Click to continue printer setup

To share a printer after installation:

1. Open the Printers and Faxes or Printers folder from the Start button or from Control Panel.

2. Right-click Sharing. This opens the Sharing tab on the printer's properties sheet.

3. Click Share This Printer.

4. Specify a share name (Figure 8.6) and click OK. The printer icon changes to indicate it is a shared printer (refer to Figure 8.1).

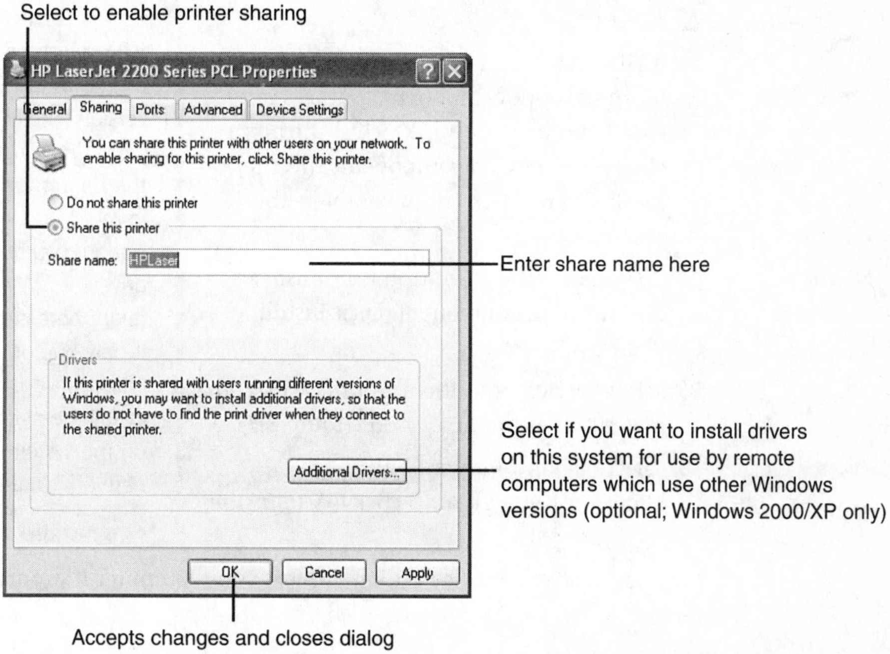

Select to enable printer sharing

FIGURE 8.6

Sharing a printer after installation in Windows XP.

Enter share name here

Select if you want to install drivers on this system for use by remote computers which use other Windows versions (optional; Windows 2000/XP only)

Accepts changes and closes dialog

Fixing "Broken" File and Printer Sharing in Windows XP/2000

Windows 2000 and XP, unlike older versions of Windows, installs the File and Printer service automatically; normally, you don't need to install it before you can share printers or folders. However, it's possible to delete this service from Windows (not that you should...) or disable it.

If you use the procedures in the previous section for Windows XP (similar procedures work with Windows 2000) and you don't have a shared printer when you're finished (you might or might not get an error message), it's likely that somebody's been fiddling with the network configuration and it needs to be fixed.

To reinstall or re-enable File and Print Sharing in Windows XP or 2000:

1. Click Start.

2. Click Control Panel.

3. Click Network and Internet Connections if you use Category View (Windows XP only).

4. Click Network Connections.

5. Right-click a network connection and select Properties.

6. If File and Printer Sharing is visible in the list of network components but it is not enabled (no check mark), click the box to enable it (enabled components are check marked) and click OK to complete the process.

7. If File and Printer Sharing is not listed as a network component, click Install (Figure 8.7).

8. Select Service from the list of network component types and click Add (Figure 8.8).

9. Select File and Printer Sharing for Microsoft Networks and click OK to install it (Figure 8.8).

10. Click Close to exit the dialog. Restart your computer if prompted.

tip

ADDITIONAL DRIVERS? A CONVENIENCE, NOT A NECESSITY

Windows 2000 and Windows XP provide an option called Additional Drivers (refer to Figure 8.6), which enables the shared printer to provide drivers for other versions of Windows over the network when network users set up the printer for the first time. Keep in mind that if you choose this option, *you* must provide these drivers for Windows to use. It might be easier for you, especially if only one or two computers use older versions of Windows, to install the needed drivers manually on the system that will access the network printer.

Installing File and Print Sharing in Windows 9x/Me

If you're using Windows 9x or Me on some of the computers in your home network, File and Print Sharing is *not* installed by default. If you didn't use the Network Wizard, or you decided not to share folders and printers when you first set up your network, you need to install File and Print Sharing support before you can share a printer connected to a Windows 9x/Me system.

Click to re-enable File and Printer Sharing if not enabled

FIGURE 8.7

Enabling File
and Printer
Sharing in
Windows XP.

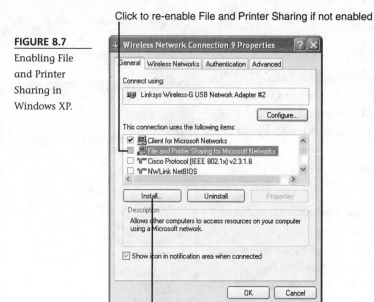

Click to install File and Printer Sharing if not listed

Select Service

Select this service

FIGURE 8.8

Installing the
File and Printer
Sharing service
in Windows XP.

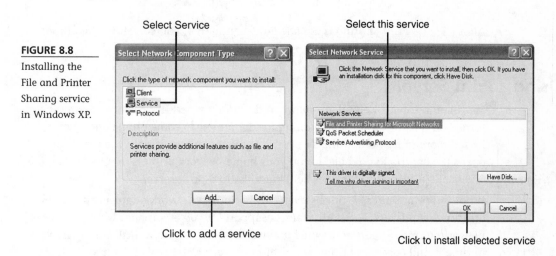

Click to add a service

Click to install selected service

To install and configure File and Print Sharing in Windows 9x/Me:

1. Click Start, Settings, Control Panel.

2. Right-click Network and select Properties.

3. Scroll through the list of network components to see whether File and Print Sharing is installed. If it is listed, skip to step 6.

4. Click Add, Service, File and Print Sharing.

5. Click OK.

6. Click the File and Print Sharing button on the Configuration tab.

7. To share your printer(s), make sure I Want to Be Able to Allow Others to Print is checked. To share folders, make sure I Want to Be Able to Give Others Access is checked. Click OK.

8. Click OK. Restart the computer if prompted.

> **tip**
>
> **INSTALL FILE AND PRINT SHARING ONLY WHEN NECESSARY**
>
> Keep in mind that you don't need to install File and Print Sharing on a Windows 9x/Me system that doesn't have resources you want to share with other users. Install File and Print Sharing only on Windows 9x/Me systems that have printers or folders you want to share with other network users.

After File and Print Sharing is installed and configured, you can share the printer as discussed earlier in this chapter.

Using a Print Server

Sharing a printer is helpful, *except* when the computer with the shared printer is turned off (print jobs stack up waiting for the printer to come online again) or is in a locked room (your homework is in there, but you can't get it until Mom or Dad opens the door!). If you'd like to put your home network printers in a location that's accessible to everyone, consider hooking them to a print server.

What is a print server? A print server is a specialized network adapter that can host one or more printers. Most print servers support 10/100 ethernet or wireless ethernet networks (some support both wired and wireless ethernet networks). You manage print jobs and check on printer status through your web browser. Figure 8.9 shows typical features of a print server that supports both 10/100 ethernet and wireless ethernet networks.

Depending on the print server you choose, you can get a print server that supports only USB printers, only parallel printers, or, as in Figure 8.9, both types of printers.

FIGURE 8.9

A typical print server for wired and wireless ethernet networks with both USB and parallel printer support.

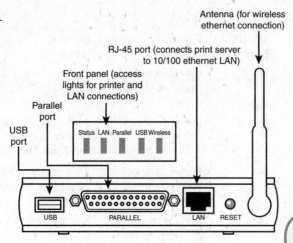

Antenna (for wireless ethernet connection)

RJ-45 port (connects print server to 10/100 ethernet LAN)

Front panel (access lights for printer and LAN connections)

Parallel port

USB port

Status LAN Parallel USB Wireless

USB PARALLEL LAN RESET

Before you configure the print server, connect the printer(s) you want to use to the server and install the printer drivers for these printers on each computer. You might need to modify the configuration later so that the printers use the correct logical printer ports for the server.

For initial configuration, the print server might use a setup wizard or a web-based configuration utility. If you use a web-based configuration utility, you must know the IP address of the print server (check the instruction manual for this information).

Even if you have a wireless network, connect the print server to an ethernet port on your PC or your network for initial configuration. If you have a wired/wireless print server, you may need to disconnect the network cable, unplug the server, wait about one minute or so, and plug it back in *after* you have configured it so it can recognize your wireless network.

Table 8.1 provides an overview of typical configuration options for wired or wireless ethernet print servers.

tip

USE THE RIGHT NETWORK LOGIN, OR NO SHARES FOR YOU!

Windows XP/2000 automatically logs users into the network as soon as they logs in to the system. However, Windows 9x/Me users must enable the Client for Microsoft Networks logon to be able to use shared resources, such as printers or folders.

To verify that the network login type is set correctly, open the Network icon in Control Panel. Look at the dialog for Primary Network Logon. If necessary, select Client for Microsoft Networks. Click OK, and restart the computer when prompted. Be sure to provide your username and password (if any) when the computer starts up. Don't press Esc or cancel logon to get past the logon dialog: if you do, you can't get to the network.

Table 8.1 Configuring a Print Server

Configuration Option	Wireless Ethernet	10/100 Ethernet	Recommended Setting	Notes
Device Name	Yes	Yes	(Use descriptive name of your choice.)	You might want to use the names of the printers connected to the server.
IP address^	Yes	Yes	DHCP	This enables the print server to obtain the IP address from the router on the network.
SSID*	Yes	No	(Enter SSID of your wireless network.)	This needs to match the SSID of your WAP or wireless router.
Channel*	Yes	No	(This is the same channel as other devices.)	Specify only for ad-hoc mode.
Network Type*	Yes	No	Infrastructure	Use ad-hoc only if you don't have a WAP or wireless router.
Wireless security*	Yes	No	(These are the same settings as WAP or wireless router.)	

^See Chapter 5, "Installing and Configuring a Wired Ethernet Network," for more information about this option.
*See Chapter 6, "Installing and Configuring a Wi-Fi Network," for more information about these options.

After the print server is configured, the driver must be installed on each computer that will use the print server. The print driver assigns a logical printer port to the print server so applications can send print jobs to the print driver and enables you to assign each printer connected to the print server to a separate logical printer port.

To adjust print server features after the print server is configured and running, use the web-based configuration utility built in to the print server. To log on, enter the IP address of the print server into the address bar of your web browser and provide the password when prompted.

Sharing Folders

Folder sharing has many benefits:

- You can use a large hard disk on a single PC for storing your files instead of upgrading all the computers on your home network with bigger hard disks.
- By placing important files on a single system, you make backups easier.

- If the kids need homework help, you can retrieve their files from their folders, take a look, and add some comments.

- You can use a large hard disk on a single PC to create a library of digital audio, photo, and video files you can enjoy with your home theater system (see Chapter 7, "Home Networks at Play," for details).

As with printer sharing, folder sharing uses the File and Print Sharing service. If you need to install or enable this service, see the following sections in this chapter: "Fixing 'Broken' File and Printer Sharing in Windows XP/2000," p. 221, or "Installing File and Print Sharing in Windows 9x/Me," p. 222.

Windows XP and Simple File Sharing

By default, Windows XP Home Edition uses Simple File Sharing, and Windows XP Professional uses Simple File Sharing by default on workgroup networks such as home networks. Simple File Sharing is designed to enable you to keep documents private, share them with other users on the same PC, or share them with other network users.

To select a folder for sharing with Windows XP when Simple File Sharing is enabled:

1. Right-click the folder you want to share.

2. Click Sharing and Security.

3. Click the box next to Share This Folder on the Network.

4. Enter a share name.

5. To permit read-only access, clear the check box next to Allow Users to Change My Files. To allow full access (other users can erase or alter files), leave this check box marked.

6. Click OK (see Figure 8.10).

> **caution**
>
> **PRINTER COMPATIBILITY IS FAR FROM UNIVERSAL!**
>
> With many inkjet (and even some laser printers) using the computer's processor and memory to help digitize the page, there are quite a few printers on the market that do not work with a print server. Unfortunately, some vendors list printer compatibility on their websites, but others do not. Typically, multifunction printers (print, fax, scan/copy) don't work at all with a print server or might work only for printing. Some photo printers, particularly the HP PhotoSmart series, work only with HP's own wireless print servers. Parallel printers often work better than USB printers. User reviews for particular print servers at Amazon.com and Epinions.com are valuable resources for determining what combinations of hardware work—and don't work! Check compatibility before you buy.

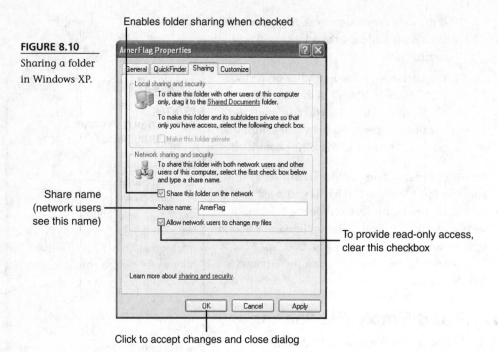

Enables folder sharing when checked

FIGURE 8.10

Sharing a folder
in Windows XP.

Share name
(network users
see this name)

To provide read-only access,
clear this checkbox

Click to accept changes and close dialog

If a folder isn't shared after you follow this procedure, the File and Printer Sharing service might be disabled or not installed. See "Fixing 'Broken' File and Printer Sharing in Windows XP/2000," p. 221, this chapter, to learn how to re-enable or reinstall it.

Simple File Sharing (SFS), as the name implies, is simple. In fact, if you're accustomed to the more complex sharing procedures used with previous Windows versions, you might prefer the simplicity of SFS. However, with simplicity comes potential dangers:

- SFS does not permit you to assign a password. Anybody who gets on the network can read files in a shared folder.

- With the default full access option enabled, anyone with network access can erase or alter files.

Whether you're concerned about mistake-prone family members or intruders on your home network, SFS's security limitations should give you pause.

SFS has one benefit over previous versions of Windows: it warns you if you try to share an entire drive, rather than just a folder (Figure 8.11). You must click the warning to display the dialog shown in Figure 8.10.

FIGURE 8.11

Sharing a drive
in Windows XP.

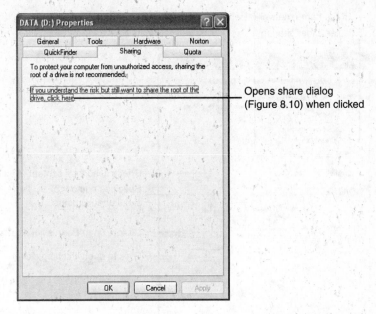

Opens share dialog
(Figure 8.10) when clicked

SFS is the only file-sharing option you have with Windows XP Home Edition.
However, if you have Windows XP Professional, you can disable SFS and use file and
folder permissions instead.

Permissions-Based File Sharing in Windows XP Professional and Windows 2000

If you disable SFS in Windows XP Professional and select a folder for sharing, you'll
see a dialog similar to the one shown in Figure 8.12. This is similar to the default
folder sharing feature in Windows 2000. You can

- Specify a comment as well as a share name.
- Limit the number of users who can access the share at the same time (10 maximum).
- Specify access permissions that permit different users and groups different lev-els of access.
- Use caching to enable work with folder contents when the server is offline.

As you can see from Figure 8.12, disabling SFS provides a lot of additional options
for shared folders. On a home network, do you really *need* this level of control? It
depends. You should consider disabling SFS if you

FIGURE 8.12

Sharing a folder in Windows XP when Simple File Sharing is disabled.

Share name (network users see this name)

Enables folder sharing

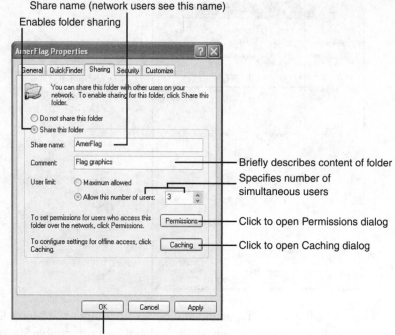

Briefly describes content of folder

Specifies number of simultaneous users

Click to open Permissions dialog

Click to open Caching dialog

Accepts settings and closes dialog when clicked

- Run a home business that has multiple employees performing different tasks with the same data.
- Use your home network to store company data temporarily while you work.
- Want to control access at different levels for children, teens, and adults.
- Are willing to spend the time and effort to learn how to specify access control and manage it.

Here's a brief overview of using Permissions to control access:

1. Create user accounts on each computer with shared resources and specify the password on each PC. For example, if your daughter, Jane, needs access to folders on a PC named Mom and another PC named Dad, there needs to be a user called Jane set up on both PCs with the same password. Use the Limited setting so that Jane can't do unauthorized things to other PCs.

2. Configure the user's own PC as a password-protected system. For example, Jane's PC must be set so that Jane has to log in using a password. This password should be the same password used on the other computers where Jane has an account.

3. You can create groups of users (for example, Jane and her brother Joe could be put in a group called Kids) to make assigning permissions easier.

4. After creating a shared folder, click the Permissions button and select the users you want to access the folder. For example, if the folder is Jane's Homework, you might select Jane, Mom, and Dad, but not Joe. If the folder is Kids Music, you could select the Kids group (Jane and Joe).

5. Delete the Everyone group so that only specific users have access.

6. Specify the type(s) of access for each user: full control (erase, change, read, save), change (alters files), or read (view but can't change files).

7. Be sure each user provides the correct username and password when logging into his or her system.

tip

FOR THE WHOLE STORY, SEE PRACTICALLY NETWORKED

The steps above provide a highly condensed view of this process. For a fully illustrated guide to this process including troubleshooting, see http://www. practicallynetworked.com/ sharing/xp_filesharing/index.htm.

Permissions-based access control is similar to how corporations running Windows Server protect data. As a consequence, it's a lot more involved than simple file sharing. Use it *only* if you need a high level of data security.

Creating Folder Shares in Windows 9x/Me

If you have Windows 9x/Me computers on your home network, folder sharing is different in several ways:

■ You can specify password-based access to any given share (including printers!).

■ Read-only access and full (read-write) access can have different passwords, or you can use a password for only full access if you prefer.

■ There is no warning given if you share an entire drive.

To share a folder or drive with Windows 9x/Me:

1. Install and configure File and Printer Sharing if you have not already done so. See "Installing File and Print Sharing in Windows 9x/Me," p.xxx, this chapter.

2. Open Windows Explorer or My Computer.

3. Right-click the folder you want to share and select Sharing.

4. Click the Sharing tab.

5. Click Shared As and specify a share name.

6. Enter a comment if desired.

7. Select an access type:

   ■ Full (anyone on the network can create, delete, or alter files)

   ■ Read-only (network users can read but not delete or alter files)

   ■ Depends on password (specify passwords to control access)

8. Enter password(s) as desired. Remember, if you don't specify a password, anyone can access the folder.

When a remote user tries to access a password-protected shared resource for the first time, he or she must provide the password when prompted. If Depends on Password was selected and a password was entered only for full access, providing no password allows the remote user to have read-only access. If Depends on Password was selected and passwords were entered for both full and read-only access, the remote user gets no access unless he or she provides one of the passwords.

Although password-protected folders might seem safer than SFS in Windows XP, there are some drawbacks:

■ Anyone with the password can access the shared folder.

■ If a password is compromised (the kids' friends find out the password for the family accounting folder, for example), a new password should be created and only the users who should have access should be given the new password.

■ Windows 9x/Me stores passwords for network resources it accesses, so anyone who gets on a system could access a "protected" network resource after it's been accessed the first time.

As you can see, security isn't easy, but there are some ways to make your home network more secure, as the next section discusses.

Safeguarding Your Data in Simple Ways

For most of us, the complexity of setting up users, groups, and permissions as a way to protect data isn't very appealing. And, if you don't use Windows XP Professional, this option isn't available. Fortunately, there are alternatives that can be used with

Windows XP's SFS or Windows 9x/Me's folder sharing to keep data safe in simple ways:

- *Don't share data you don't need to share.* The only reason to share a folder is if two or more users on the home network need access to it. There's no need to make every folder (or worse yet, every drive) a shared drive.

- *Don't put sensitive data in a shared folder, even with read-only access.* Bank account and credit card statements should **never** be stored in a shared folder.

- Never *share an entire hard drive letter.* If you share an entire drive, there's no way to "unshare" any portion of it. It's OK to share a CD-ROM or other optical drive, but I recommend doing it for temporary situations only (such as if you need to install a program to a system that lacks an optical drive or has a defective drive).

- *If you suspect unauthorized access to your home network, unshare any folders with important contents.* You can turn off sharing through the same dialog that enables sharing.

- *Create folder shares you can use for temporary data storage.* For example, on my home network, I have a shared folder called Shared Files. This folder is set for full access. I save data from other computers on the network to this folder. However, the data doesn't stay there long. I use drag and drop or cut and paste in Windows Explorer to move data files to their final destination as soon as possible.

- *Create a folder share for originals and another for changed files.* If you store homework on a shared folder, make the folder with the original files a read-only folder and create a separate folder for corrections, changes, and suggestions. Children who need help with an assignment can save a copy of their work to the Originals folder on their system (read-only), and then you can retrieve it over the network and save your suggestions into the Corrections folder (full access).

- *If you need to provide two levels of access for information but you use Windows XP, consider storing the data in two separate folders.* As you have learned, the only way to create multiple levels of access is to use Windows XP Professional and to wrestle with the complexities of access control lists, users, groups, and permissions. Instead, store files you want to keep intact in a read-only folder and files that can be changed in a folder with full access.

- *Keep unauthorized users out of your network.* If you have a wireless network, at a minimum you should use WEP encryption as described in Chapter 6. However, there are many additional ways to keep crackers and intruders from connecting to your network. See Chapter 10, "Securing Your Home Network," for details.

Accessing Shared Folders

After you create shared folders, how do you access them? They don't show up in My Computer or Windows Explorer. Instead, you need to open an icon on your desktop or Start button called My Network Places (Windows XP/2000/Me) or Network Neighborhood (Windows 9x). My Network Places/Network Neighborhood lists local network shared folders. Figure 8.13 shows a typical list of network shares as seen by Windows XP's My Network Places.

FIGURE 8.13

My Network Places displaying network shares in Windows XP.

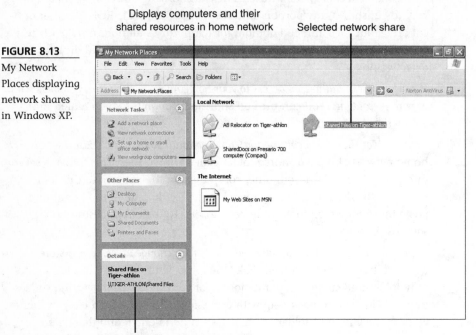

Displays computers and their shared resources in home network

Selected network share

\\Servername\sharename of selected share

To view the contents of a network share, double-click it. Figure 8.14 shows the contents of the network share selected in Figure 8.13.

As the right-click menu shown in Figure 8.14 suggests, when you read a file from a network share, you can perform the same types of actions on it as you can from a file stored on a local drive, including Edit, Copy, Print, and so on. The only exception is that if the share is read-only, you need to save changes to the file to a different location (a network share with full read-write access or a local drive).

If you prefer to open a network share within a Windows application, use the File, Open menu as you normally would. Open My Network Places or Network

Neighborhood, open the network share and open the file. To save the file to a network share with read/write (full) access: Click File, Save As; open My Network Places or Network Neighborhood; open the network share; and save the file as shown in Figure 8.15.

As this section shows, working with shared folders is almost as simple as working with local drives. However, there's a way to make it even simpler.

Drive Mapping

If you (or some family members) have never worked with network shares before, opening My Network Places instead of My Computer in Windows 2000/XP or scrolling way down in My Computer in older Windows versions to access them can be a little hard to deal with. If you find yourself explaining over and over, "The files aren't gone, they're on the network," it's time to introduce you to a trick that makes network shares look like local drives: *drive mapping*.

Drive mapping was originally developed to help the old MS-DOS operating system work with network resources. Drive mapping matches unused drive letters (chances are your systems have plenty of these) with network shares.

Here's how it works with Windows XP and Windows 2000:

1. Right-click My Network Places.
2. Click Map Network Drive.
3. Select a drive letter from the list of unused drives.
4. Click Browse to select a network share.
5. Select the network share you want to use and click OK.
6. Click Finish.

FIGURE 8.14

Contents of a
network share
folder as dis-
played by
Windows XP.

Share location (\\servername\sharename)

Selected file

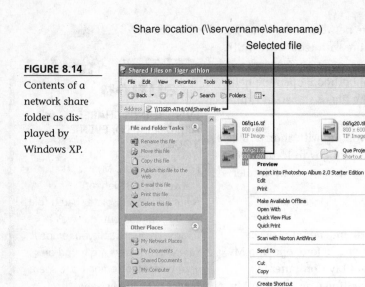

Preview showing contents of selected file

Right-click menu displaying possible actions for file

Edited file   Original file   Share location

FIGURE 8.15

Saving changes
to a network file
back to a net-
work share.

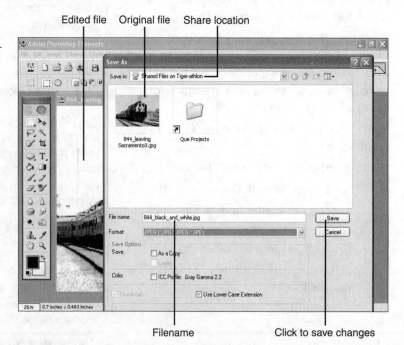

Filename

Click to save changes

Figure 8.16 shows the Map Network Drive dialog after a network share has been created.

If a mapped folder requires a password, a prompt appears asking for the password. Enter the correct password to continue. After you click Finish, your computer attempts to log on to the network share. If it is successful, it displays the contents of the mapped drive. By default, the drive mapping is used each time you turn on your computer. To create a temporary drive mapping that stops when you turn off or restart your computer, clear the check box next to Reconnect at logon (refer to Figure 8.16).

As long as the drive mapping exists, the network share is displayed in My Computer with a special drive icon. See Figure 8.17. Its contents can be viewed and opened without the need to switch to My Network Places.

You can also create mapped drives with Windows 9x and Me. Open My Computer, right-click the network share folder and select Map Network Drive. These versions of Windows display both already mapped and unused drive letters (Figure 8.18).

tip

NETWORK OR LOCAL, SAVING UNDER A DIFFERENT NAME IS GOOD PRACTICE

In the example shown in Figure 8.15, I changed the name of the photo before I saved it (the original was color; the edited version was changed to grayscale). Even for more modest changes to any type of document, I prefer to use Save As and specify a new filename rather than just use Save and replace the old version with a new version. By using Save As, the original stays intact, and I can always open it and edit it again if I decide my changed version was not an improvement.

Click to select drive letter

Selected drive letter

FIGURE 8.16

Creating a mapped drive using Windows XP.

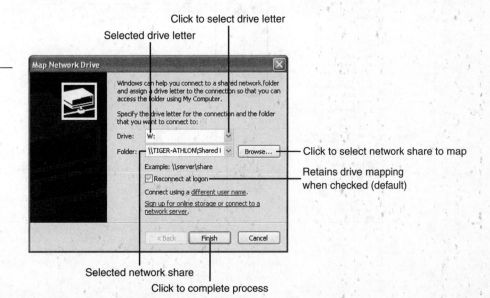

Click to select network share to map

Retains drive mapping when checked (default)

Selected network share

Click to complete process

Local hard disk drives   Mapped network drive

Local floppy drive   Local optical drive

FIGURE 8.17
Viewing mapped network and local drives in My Computer (Windows XP).

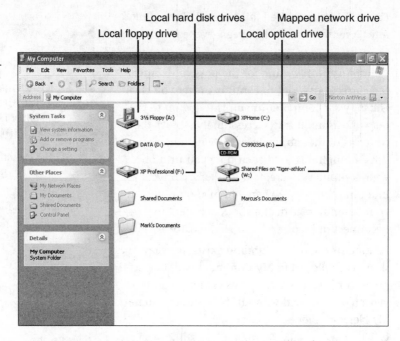

Already-mapped drive letter and path to share

Selected drive letter

FIGURE 8.18
Selecting a mapped drive letter in Windows 98.

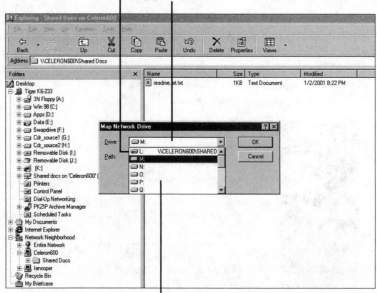

Available drive letters

As with Windows XP/2000, you can make the mapping persistent (available after the next restart) or temporary. Mapped drives are listed in My Computer, Windows Explorer or application File, Open dialogs with an icon similar to the one shown in Figure 8.17.

Using Network Storage

One of the limitations of shared folders is similar to that for shared printers: the computer with the shared resource must be running to enable other users to gain access to that resource. If you don't want to leave a computer on all the time to provide shared folders, you can now connect storage devices directly to your home network.

Network attached storage (NAS) arrays have been popular in corporate networking for several years. However, classic NAS technology is too expensive and complicated for home networking. Several companies have now developed NAS-like devices made especially for home networks.

These devices combine on-board or USB 2.0-based external storage (some have both options) integrated management tools. Some use special client software to manage connections, and others use standard network share access as discussed earlier in this chapter. Some network storage devices for home networks enable simultaneous read and write access. Others enable simultaneous read access, but only one user at a time can write to the device.

These devices have native support for 10/100 ethernet networks. They can also be connected to a wireless router with a built-in ethernet switch (see Chapter 6 for details). Figure 8.19 shows a typical network configuration using network storage.

Table 8.2 lists leading vendors of storage devices and adapters suitable for home networks and their products.

Which network storage device is the best for you? It depends on your needs and your comfort with configuring a storage device for network use.

Table 8.2 Network Storage Products for Home Networks

Vendor/Website	Product	Onboard Storage Capacities	External Drive Interfaces	Network Support	Other Features
Buffalo Technology www.buffalotech.com	LinkStation Network Storage Center	120GB 160GB 250GB 300GB	USB 2.0 (1)	10/100 ethernet	USB print server; Windows, MacOS, Linux
D-Link www.dlink.com	Media Lounge Central Home Drive	20GB 40GB	—	10/100 ethernet	Windows, MacOS, Linux
	Network Storage Adapter	—	USB 2.0 (2)	10/100 ethernet	Windows, MacOS, Linux
	Media Lounge Wireless Central Home Drive	20GB 40GB	USB 1.1 (1)	10/100 ethernet; 802.11g	Windows, MacOS
Iomega www.iomega.com	Network Hard Drive High-Speed Ethernet	160GB 250GB	—	10/100 ethernet*	Windows MacOS Linux
Linksys www.linksys.com	Network Storage Link	—	USB 2.0 (2)+	10/100 ethernet	Drivers for Windows
Ximeta www.ximeta.com	NetDisk	80GB 120GB 160GB 250GB	—	10/100 ethernet*	Drivers for Windows, MacOS X, Linux^
	NetDisk Mini	40GB	—	10/100 ethernet*	Drivers for Windows, MacOS X, Linux^
	NetDisk Office	120GB	—	10/100 ethernet; 8-port ethernet switch	Drivers for Windows, MacOS X, Linux^
	NetDisk Wireless	160GB	—	802.11g router; 3-port 10/100 ethernet switch	Drivers for Windows 2000/XP

*These drives also feature a USB port that enables these drives to connect to a PC and be used as local hard disks.

+One each for a USB 2.0 hard disk and USB 2.0 flash memory "keychain" drive.

^Provides simultaneous read/one-at-a-time write access; on networks using Windows XP/2000 only, you can use drivers that provide simultaneous read/write access.

FIGURE 8.19

A wireless ether-net/ethernet net-work that uses a network storage device with inte-grated print server.

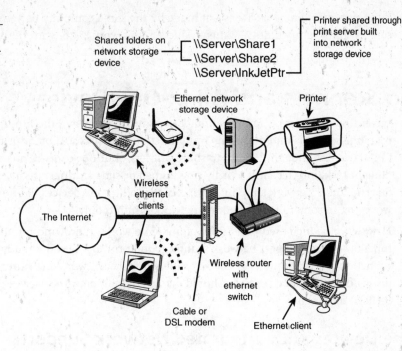

MY ADVICE

First, decide whether you need to replace or supplement share-level storage on your network. Don't buy one of these devices until you've created some network shares and used them awhile. If you decide you need direct network storage, take time to download the documentation for the devices that interest you (you need Adobe Reader or Acrobat Reader to view these files). Sit down at your PC and read through the device configuration process. At a minimum, you need to configure any of these devices to get an IP address from your network's router (DHCP) or set the IP address manually. Most require you to set up network shares, but some also require you to build lists of users and assign access rights. The device that's best for you is the device that

- Has enough built-in storage or supports external drives to meet your needs for at least a year
- Seems easy to manage
- Supports the operating systems on your home network
- Has good technical support

As you review Table 8.2, note that some network storage devices are primarily or exclusively for Windows XP/2000, but others support all recent versions of Windows or support Windows as well as MacOS X and Linux. If you have a diverse collection of PCs (and operating systems) on your home network, be sure your network storage device works with all of them.

If the network storage device is not made by the same company as your router, be sure to check compatibility. Some products might work better with the same brand of router.

Sharing Scanners and All-in-One Devices

Increasing numbers of home computer users have discovered the fun and usefulness of image scanners and all-in-one multifunction (print/scan/copy or print/scan/copy/fax) devices. Although it's easy to share printers, sharing scanners has been a more difficult task until recently. Hardly any flatbed or slide scanners at any price level feature native network support. Until recently, all-in-one devices did not support networks, or, in some cases, supported network printing only.

Now, with the increased popularity of home networks, a growing number of multifunction devices support network scanning and printing. If you already have a multifunction device, or prefer flatbed or slide scanners, software and hardware products also enable these devices to be shared across ethernet networks. See the following sections for details.

All-in-One Devices with Integrated Network Support

For a home computer user with limited space and limited budgets, all-in-one devices that support print/copy/scan or print/copy/scan/fax are excellent choices. They cost less than separate devices with comparable features and use little more space than a traditional flatbed scanner or inkjet printer.

If you're in the market for an all-in-one device for your home network, look for models that support scanning as well as printing on your home network. Typically, these devices feature built-in wired or wireless ethernet adapters, built-in web-based configuration, and special client software that enables you to perform network printing or scanning.

Expect to pay more for an ordinary all-in-one unit. Table 8.3 provides an overview of current all-in-one models selling for less than $700 (U.S. retail) that feature network support for scanning and printing.

Although the number of all-in-one models featuring built-in network support is relatively small, I expect this category to grow. Before you make your purchase, download and review the documentation for the models you're most interested in to learn how to configure and use these features.

Table 8.3 All-in-One Devices with Network Support

Brand	Model	Print Engine	Network Print	Network Scan	Networks Supported
Brother www.brother.com	MFC-3320CN	Inkjet	Yes	Yes^	10/100 ethernet*
	MFC-3820CN	Inkjet	Yes	Yes+	10/100 ethernet*
	MFC-8820DN	Laser	Yes	Yes+	10/100 ethernet*
	MFC-8840DN	Laser	Yes	Yes+	10/100 ethernet*
Hewlett-Packard www.hp.com	PhotoSmart PSC 2500	Inkjet	Yes	Yes+	10/100 ethernet 802.11b(g)
	PSC2500xi	Inkjet	Yes	Yes+	10/100 ethernet 802.11b(g)

^*Sheet-fed scan mechanism.*

*Connect to wireless router with ethernet switch to support 802.11/Wi-Fi networks.

+*Flatbed scan mechanism.*

RemoteScan

RemoteScan (www.remote-scan.com) is a software program that works with almost any scanner (including all-in-one devices) because it uses the scanner's own TWAIN drivers. RemoteScan includes a server program that is run on the computer hosting the scanner and a client program that is run on each PC that will access the scanner. RemoteScan supports up to four clients in its home version (around $40); business licenses starting at 10 clients are also available.

Figure 8.20 shows a preview scan performed using the free trial version of RemoteScan. The scanner being used is located at the RemoteScan offices and was controlled via the broadband Internet connection on my home network.

Many recent scanners and all-in-one devices have advanced features such as transparency adapters or sheet feeders. RemoteScan supports these features as well as basic scanning functions. RemoteScan is a low-cost yet highly useful way to share a scanner through your home network.

FIGURE 8.20
Controlling a
remote scanner
with the trial
version of
RemoteScan.

Area selected for final scan   Selected remote scanner

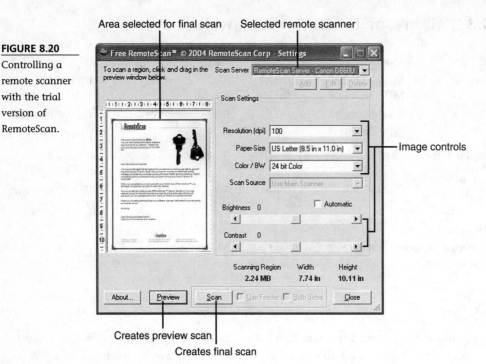

Image controls

Creates preview scan
Creates final scan

Keyspan USB Server

The Keyspan USB Server (about $130; www.keyspan.com) takes a hardware
approach to sharing USB printers, scanners, all-in-one units, and other types of USB
devices. The USB Server has four USB 1.1 ports for devices and a 10/100 ethernet
port. To use devices plugged into the USB Server, users must install the appropriate
drivers for each device on their PCs as well as the USB Server software. The USB
Server software requires Windows 2000, Windows XP, or MacOS X 10.2.8 or higher.

The USB Server software displays the devices connected to the server, which devices
are in use by what user, and which devices are available. To operate a device, the
user "subscribes" to a device, performs the tasks desired (such as printing or faxing),
and then "unsubscribes" to enable other users to access the device. An autoconnect
feature for Windows-based USB printers enables transparent printing without
the subscribe/unsubscribe process, and version 1.1 of both MacOS and Windows
software enable users to "repossess" a device that another user forgot to release
after use.

Connecting Securely to a Remote Network with Your Home Network

One of the benefits of a home network with broadband Internet access is your ability to work from home on a business, school, or university network while other family members also use the Internet.

There are three ways to achieve this:

■ Set up a VPN connection.

■ Use remote access software.

■ Use a remote access service.

Which one of these is right for you? Mainly, it depends on who is in charge of the remote network: they'll make the decisions for you. In the following sections, I show you what you need to know to connect to a VPN and what you can do with the remote access products and services available today.

VPN Connections and Home Networks

Many corporate networks use a technology known as *virtual private networking (VPN)* to provide secure connections between the corporate network and telecommuters.

VPN works by creating a secure "tunnel" within the public Internet for encrypted data to travel between the corporate network and a remote computer user. Unlike an ordinary Internet connection you make with a web browser, you log in to a remote server using VPN with a username and password.

VPN solutions were originally designed for dial-up modem users, but VPN also works over broadband Internet connections, particularly cable and DSL modems. Because the extra overhead involved in data encryption slows the effective speed of a VPN connection compared to a normal broadband connection, satellite broadband connections are not suitable for use with VPNs.

To create a VPN connection you can use through your home network, you need

■ VPN support on the remote network

■ A VPN client that supports the Internet connection type used on your home network and the VPN on your corporate network

■ Configuration settings for the remote network server

■ A router that supports pass-through of VPN traffic (also known as IPSec and PPTP pass-through support)

Get details about VPN support and approved VPN clients from the IT department in your company. Most routers made for home networks support IPSec and/or PPTP pass-through; check the specifications for your router and verify that the VPN solution used by your corporation is compatible with pass-through support provided by your router.

Depending on the VPN software used by your corporation, you might need to install third-party client software. However, in many cases the VPN client built in to recent versions of Windows can be used.

To configure a VPN connection using Windows XP (Windows 2000 is similar):

1. Click Start, Control Panel, Network and Internet Connections, Create a Connection to the Network at Your Workplace. If you don't see Network and Internet Connections, click the Switch to Category View option in the left-hand window.

2. Select Virtual Private Network connection (Figure 8.21) and click Next.

caution

WITH ORDINARY ROUTERS, ONE VPN CONNECTION AT A TIME, PLEASE!

If two or more people in your household need to make VPN connections at the same time, you need a better router than the typical $50–125 models sold in electronics superstores. Look for routers identified as VPN routers. They feature support for multiple VPN tunnels (enabling two or more users to use VPN at the same time) and other advanced VPN options. VPN routers are also useful if you want to create VPN connections from a remote location to your home office. VPN routers are available from D-Link (DI-808HV and DI-804HV), Linksys (BEFVP41 and WRV54G), NetGear (FMV318), and other vendors.

Select to make a VPN connection

FIGURE 8.21

Starting the configuration process for a VPN connection in Windows XP.

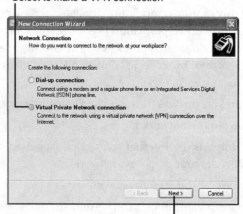

Click to continue

3. Enter a name for the connection, such as My Office or Accounting Server. Click Next.

4. Enter the hostname or IP address of the server (this information is provided by your company's IT department), such as 10.20.30.40 or erewhon.com.

5. Click Finish (Figure 8.22).

Click this checkbox if you want a shortcut
on your desktop for this connection

FIGURE 8.22

Completing the
configuration
process for a
VPN connection
in Windows XP.

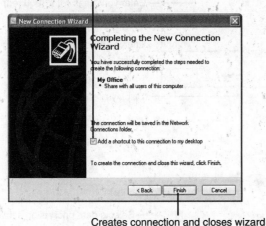

Creates connection and closes wizard

To use the connection, double-click the shortcut on the desktop or open the Network Connections folder and double-click the connection icon. The first time you open the connection, you are prompted to provide a username and password (Figure 8.23). If you don't want to enter this information each time, click the box next to Save this user name and password and specify which users of the PC can use this connection.

At this point, you're almost ready to open your connection. But, before you do, click the Properties button shown in Figure 8.23 to make any changes required by your remote server's configuration. Ask your network administrator for the correct settings and for assistance in making changes if necessary.

The General tab displays the hostname or IP address; this is the same information you entered during the connection creation process. Click Options only if you need to adjust login settings; most of the options on this page apply to dial-up connections only. The Security tab has an Advanced (custom settings) option. Select it and click the Settings button if you need to select a particular login protocol (Figure 8.24) or configure a protocol.

FIGURE 8.23
Providing login information for a VPN connection in Windows XP.

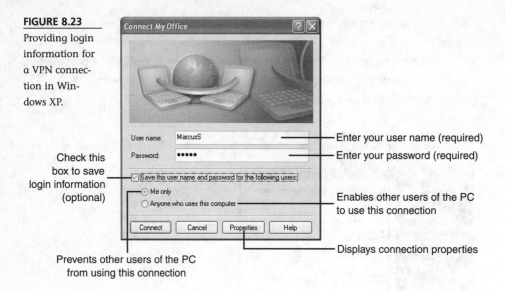

Enter your user name (required)

Enter your password (required)

Check this box to save login information (optional)

Enables other users of the PC to use this connection

Displays connection properties

Prevents other users of the PC from using this connection

Select if remote server uses EAP

FIGURE 8.24
The Advanced Security Settings dialog for a VPN connection in Windows XP.

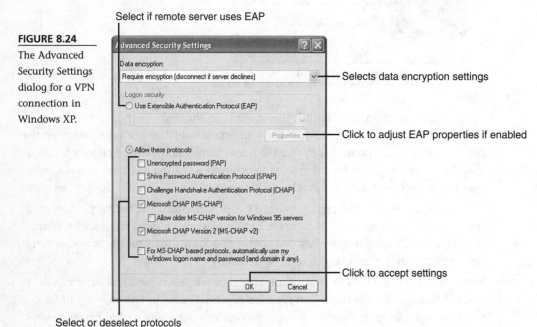

Selects data encryption settings

Click to adjust EAP properties if enabled

Click to accept settings

Select or deselect protocols supported by remote connection

Click the Networking tab if you need to select the type of VPN you connect to or if you need to install, uninstall, or configure network components to match the requirements of the remote server (Figure 8.25).

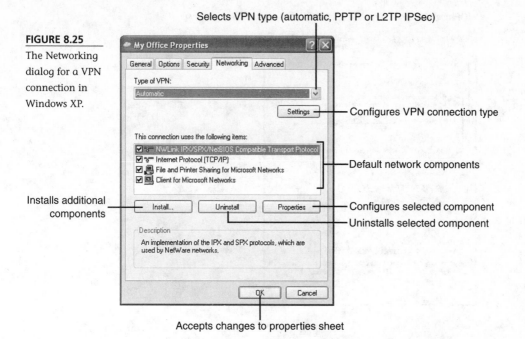

FIGURE 8.25

The Networking dialog for a VPN connection in Windows XP.

Selects VPN type (automatic, PPTP or L2TP IPSec)

Configures VPN connection type

Default network components

Installs additional components

Configures selected component

Uninstalls selected component

Accepts changes to properties sheet

Click the Advanced tab and make certain that Internet Connection Firewall (ICF) is *not* enabled. ICF interferes with VPN connections. Internet Connection Sharing (ICS), a type of networking that uses a PC as a gateway to another network, is not supported on VPN connections. Thus, both check boxes in Figure 8.26 should be cleared, as shown.

After reviewing the settings to verify that your connection is configured correctly, click OK to close the properties sheet.

Click Connect to make your connection. If you see an error message dialog, contact your network administrator for help.

Windows 9x and Me use the Dial-Up Networking wizard to create a VPN connection. For a step-by-step tutorial, see http://poptop.sourceforge.net/dox/pptp_win9x_me/.

note

THIRD-PARTY IS SOMETIMES FIRST CHOICE

In some cases, your network administrator might provide you a third-party client that requires less configuration than the Windows VPN client. Use whatever your company provides—or recommends—to avoid connection headaches.

ICF and ICS should not be selected; leave checkboxes empty

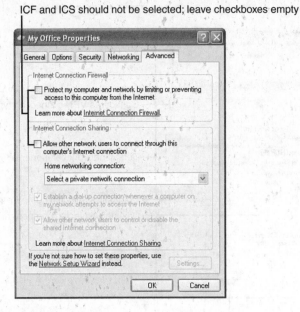

FIGURE 8.26

The Advanced dialog for a VPN connection in Windows XP.

Using Remote Access Solutions

As you learned in the previous section, a VPN connection can take some configuration, even at the client end, to work properly. It is far more difficult to configure an incoming VPN connection to provide secure access to your home PC or home network from a remote site. Another problem with VPN access is that you need to be at the computer with the VPN client to connect to your remote server.

As an alternative to VPNs, many companies and individuals are using secure remote access solutions that require little or no configuration. Two of the leading services are

- GoToMyPC (http://www.gotomypc.com)
- Laplink Everywhere (http://www.laplink.com)

Both companies offer free trials. In the following sections, you learn how these services can be used.

note

ASK THE IT DEPARTMENT BEFORE YOU INSTALL A REMOTE ACCESS SOLUTION

Some corporate networks don't permit the use of third-party remote-access solutions. To avoid problems, check with your company's IT department to see if you can use a third-party service and which ones they recommend or support.

Using GoToMyPC

GoToMyPC is a complete remote-control service. It is web-browser-based. You can use it from any PC that has an Internet connection to connect to the Windows-based PC running the GoToMyPC server application, as long as it is also connected to the Internet. I use it to connect to my office PC from home (both are on broadband networks) or from remote locations (hotels, client sites, vacations). Although GoToMyPC is a service, *you* control security: You choose the login password to use to access the service and the login passwords for your servers are stored on each server, not by GoToMyPC. You can change the passwords as needed.

GoToMyPC requires you to install a small client on the PC you use to access your remote computer. A universal viewer is also available if you are using a web browser on a PC that doesn't enable you to run programs.

A typical GoToMyPC session starts like this:

1. Open your web browser and navigate to http://www.gotomypc.com.
2. Enter your email address (username) and password to log in.
3. Click the Connect icon next to the server you are accessing.
4. Download and run or open the viewer application when prompted.
5. Click the computer you want to access.
6. Enter the access code and click OK.

Figure 8.27 shows a typical GoToMyPC session. The remote server's desktop is displayed inside the GoToMyPC window on the client PC. The client can use any software installed on the GoToMyPC server.

In addition to complete control of the remote PC, GoToMyPC also features file transfer, remote printing, and other tools in its top-level menu (Figure 8.28).

GoToMyPC enables you to check your email remotely, work remotely, and stay home if you forgot to get a file from the office. It beats driving!

note

MULTIPLE FLAVORS OF GOTOMYPC

GoToMyPC remote access is also available for multiple computers (GoToMyPC Pro) and for large companies (GoToMyPC Corporate). Visit the GoToMyPC website at http://www.gotomypc.com for more information and free trials.

GoToMyPC session

FIGURE 8.27

Using GoToMyPC to perform operations on a remote PC's hard disk.

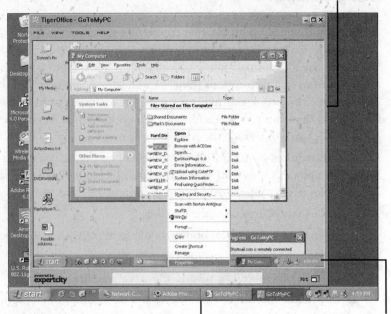

System tray and taskbar on client computer

System tray and taskbar on remote computer

Tools for conferencing, file transfer, remote printing

Closes connection to remote computer

FIGURE 8.28

GoToMyPC's remote access tools.

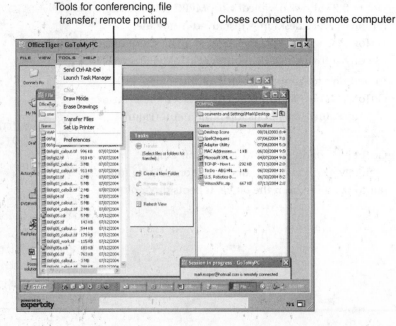

Using LapLink Everywhere

LapLink Everywhere (www.laplink.com) is designed primarily to provide remote access to your Microsoft Outlook or Outlook Express emails and for file management (including file transfer). To enable the service, you install a server program on up to three PCs you want to access remotely. You should have the settings for your email program handy (such as server name, account name, email address, and password) when you install LapLink Everywhere; without this information, you will not have email support.

LapLink Everywhere does not require you to install a client for basic remote access. Because LapLink Everywhere does not require a separate client program, it can be used by PDAs that have web-browsing capabilities as well as PCs. LapLink Everywhere includes one hour of LapLink Secure VNC, which enables any Java-enabled web browser with 128-bit encryption to control the Windows desktop and run programs. You can upgrade the LapLink Everywhere service to provide unlimited LapLink Secure VNC.

A typical LapLink Everywhere file-transfer session works like this:

1. Go to http://www.ll2go.com and log in.
2. A new web page opens with a welcome message. Click the icon for the computer you want to access.
3. Select the viewing type (PC or PDA) that matches your client type.
4. To transfer files, click the Files button. A list of your drives appears (Figure 8.29).
5. Click the drive and click the folder you want to view.
6. To transfer a file, click the file to select it and then click it again.
7. Specify a location on your PC for the file.

To transfer multiple files to a client PC, click the Multiple File Transfer button. This installs a special client on your PC.

Although LapLink Everywhere supports a wider range of clients than GoToMyPC and costs less per month, GoToMyPC works like your PC. LapLink Everywhere requires you to learn a new interface and to reproduce your email settings if you want to have email support.

As you can see from this chapter, some types of preparation for working from home might require you to understand more about home networking than you expected. If you're having problems or just want to know more about TCP/IP and network issues, join me in Chapter 11, "Troubleshooting Your Home Network."

Starts LapLink Secure VNC service

Optimizes screen display for PCs or PDAs

FIGURE 8.29

Using LapLink
Everywhere.

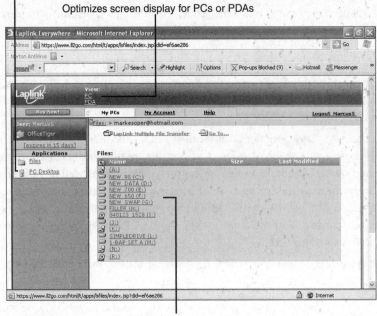

Drives on remote system

THE ABSOLUTE MINIMUM

A shared printer is a printer that can be used by other network clients.

A remote printer is a printer that you can use located elsewhere on the network.

You use the Add Printer wizard to add a remote printer to your system.

Windows 2000 and XP have File and Print Sharing installed and active by default; you just need to select the resources you want to share.

Windows 9x and Me require you to install and configure File and Print Sharing before you can share resources.

A print server is a device that connects directly to a wired or wireless network to host printers.

Print servers don't work with all printers.

Print servers need network configuration just as other network adapters do.

Windows XP Home uses Simple File Sharing (SFS), as does Windows XP Professional by default.

SFS does not use passwords, but does provide read-only and full access.

You can configure Windows XP Professional to use permissions-based file sharing, but this requires you to set up a list of users and groups.

Windows 9x/Me can use passwords to protect shared folders. However, each folder has its own password.

Creating shared folders especially for temporary storage and using read-only access are two simple ways to help protect network data.

You can access shared folders through My Network Places or Network Neighborhood.

To access shared folders with drive letters, use Drive Mapping.

Network storage devices enable you to use shared folders without leaving a PC running all the time.

A few scanners and all-in-one devices have built-in network support, but software and hardware solutions enable sharing of a wide range of these devices.

If your corporate network supports virtual private networking (VPN), you can use Windows or third-party clients to access the network remotely.

As an alternative to a VPN, you can use subscription services to create secure access from any PC with an Internet connection. These services can also be used to enable you to connect to your home network from other locations.

9

HOME, SWEET, CONTROLLED AND SECURE HOME

Home networks can do more than help you work harder and play harder. You can also use your home network to help make your home more comfortable, more energy-efficient, and more secure—even when you're away from home.

In this chapter, you learn how to

- Use your home network to control lighting and HVAC settings.
- Provide security when you're away from home.
- Notify you when there's trouble at home.

What You Can Do with Home Control

Home control means exactly what it says. If you want to, you can use home control to

- Turn on, turn off, and dim lights.
- Activate porch or interior lights in response to a motion detector.
- Turn on your stereo system.
- Adjust heating and cooling.
- Control your TV and home theater system.
- Open or close draperies.
- Turn on your spa.

...and that's just a few of the possibilities.

Some home control technologies were developed with home networking and Internet access in mind, but others have needed to adapt to the network and online world.

Technologies Available for DIY Home Control

If you want to control your home with a do-it-yourself (DIY) solution, two of the leading technologies include

- X10
- Z-wave

The following sections discuss these technologies in greater detail.

Understanding X10 Technology

X10 technology is the foundation of most do-it-yourself home automation and control systems. X10 uses the AC power lines in your wall to transfer signals from an X10 transmitter to an X10 receiver. Many vendors sell X10-compatible hardware, and you can mix and match products from various firms. You can use X10 to control

- Lamps and home lighting
- Appliances
- Home heating and cooling
- Sprinkler systems
- Garage doors

...and that's just a few of the possibilities.

A basic X10 home control configuration is simple and requires the following:

- *An X10 receiver*—Plug it into an AC outlet and plug in the device you want to control (for example, a lamp). Each receiver is configured with a House Code and a Unit Code (Figure 9.1). If you want two or more receivers to activate at the same time, program them with matching House and Unit Codes. House codes range from A–P, and Unit codes range from 1–16.

- *An X10 transmitter*—Plug it into an AC outlet. It can control one or more X10 receivers. You configure which button controls which device by selecting the House Code and Unit Code to activate.

Figure 9.1 shows typical House and Unit code dials. Use a coin or small flatblade screwdriver to adjust the dials to the desired values.

FIGURE 9.1

Typical house and unit dials used by X10 receivers. X10 transmitters must send a matching House/Unit code to activate a device connected to the receiver.

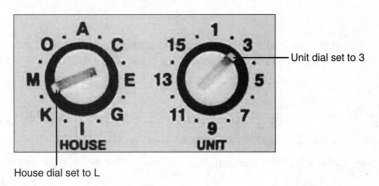

Unit dial set to 3

House dial set to L

Originally, X10 automation required you to install one or more X10 transmitters to perform tasks for you at the push of a button. However, this has several drawbacks:

- You might need to go to the room to press the correct X10 transmitter button.

- You might want to activate multiple events at the same time (open the drapes and turn on the coffeepot).

Many X10 systems include a remote control to select which X10 receiver to activate. The remote control sends radio signals to a transceiver that plugs into an AC outlet and relays X10 control signals to the selected device. The transceiver replaces the X10 transmitter.

Figure 9.2 shows a typical X10 home automation system, which controls a lamp and a washing machine.

FIGURE 9.2

An X10 home automation system that uses a multibutton remote to control a lamp (top center) and a washing machine (bottom right).

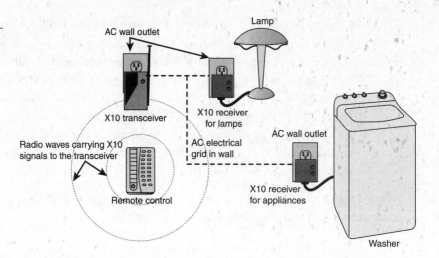

You can program multiple receivers to work at the same time or program handheld remotes to trigger events in sequence, but if you want to get the most out of X10, it helps to have a computer do the hard work for you.

Controlling Your Home with X10 and Your Home Network

By connecting a computer to your X10 network, you can

- ▓ Control X10 devices remotely via your home network or the Internet.

- ▓ Create macros that can activate multiple events at the same time, such as turning on the lights in the kitchen and turning on your coffee maker at a particular time or on demand.

X10 installations are relatively inexpensive, but because X10 was not originally designed with PCs, home networks, or Internet access in mind, you need to add the following to an existing X10 home control system to make it PC-friendly:

- ▓ *A PC to X10 interface*—This enables a PC to control X10 devices. Originally, most of these devices plugged into a PC's serial (COM) port, but with so many systems now abandoning serial ports for USB ports, you can get USB to X10 interfaces as well.

- ▓ *A method of storing X10 commands for playback (such as turning on or turning off lights at particular times)*—Low-cost PC-to-X10 interfaces require that the PC be turned on at all times to provide control. However, some newer PC-to-X10 interfaces include a clock and built-in memory. This enables you to program the interface and shut down the PC.

Figure 9.3 illustrates a typical X10 home control configuration that uses a USB-based PC-to-X10 interface in place of the X10 remote control.

FIGURE 9.3

Using a PC-to-X10 interface to control X10 devices.

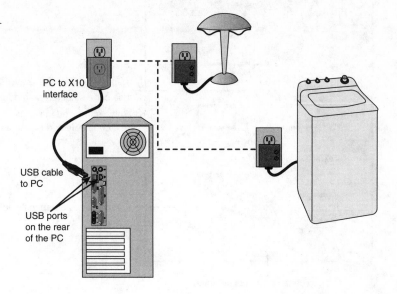

PC to X10 interface

USB cable to PC

USB ports on the rear of the PC

To program the PC-to-X10 interface, you need to use software that creates command sequences (macros) for playback by the X10 interface. Most PC-to-X10 interfaces include software, but you can purchase third-party programs if you prefer.

Figure 9.4 illustrates setting up a device using a popular third-party software program for X10 control, HomeSeer (http://www.homeseer.com).

After you set up a device, you can assign one or more events to it; an event activates one or more devices. The events possible with a PC to X10 interface go well beyond simply turning on or turning off the device: they can also involve time of day, lamp brightness, interaction between devices, and much more. For example, if you are using a bedroom lamp that can be dimmed, you can create an event that uses the lamp as a visual alarm clock: Gradually adjust the brightness on the lamp from 10% to 100% (full power) every few minutes at scheduled times in the morning.

tip

TRY BEFORE YOU BUY

Many X10 control programs are available on a trial basis, so if you're not satisfied with the program included with your PC-to-X10 interface, you can try different programs.

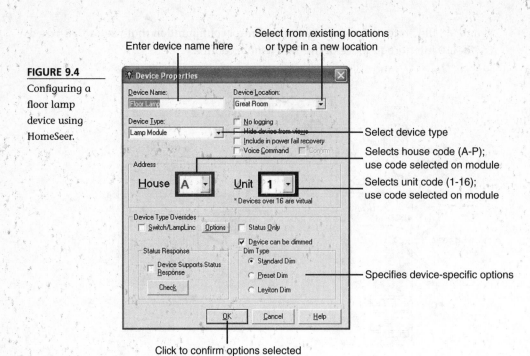

FIGURE 9.4
Configuring a
floor lamp
device using
HomeSeer.

Enter device name here

Select from existing locations
or type in a new location

Select device type

Selects house code (A-P);
use code selected on module

Selects unit code (1-16);
use code selected on module

Specifies device-specific options

Click to confirm options selected

Figure 9.5 shows an event that turns on the garage light when the motion sensor in
the garage is activated.

Device Actions tab

FIGURE 9.5
Configuring an
event using
HomeSeer.

Device actions

Click to confirm devices selected

After you have set up your devices and events, you can control your devices through the PC connected to the X10 network. However, to control your devices from other PCs on your home network, you need to run the web server included in many X10 home control programs. The web server enables other PCs on the home network to control X10 devices.

To view the web interface from another PC on your home network, enter the IP address for that PC in the address line of your browser and provide the username and password if necessary.

Figure 9.6 illustrates using the HomeSeer web control to adjust the lighting in the Great Room.

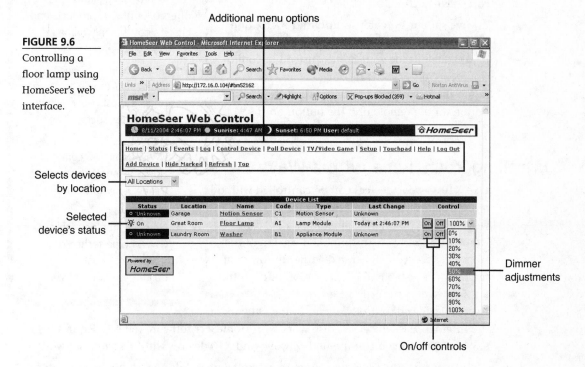

FIGURE 9.6

Controlling a floor lamp using HomeSeer's web interface.

If your home network includes broadband Internet access, you can also access the web interface from any web browser. To learn more about configuring this option, see "Setting Up a Dynamic DNS Server to Enable Remote Access," p. 274, this chapter.

If you're new to X10, many vendors offer kits that combine lamp modules, tabletop or keychain remote controls, a PC to X10 interface module (I recommend USB, but serial is also available), and control software. These kits are frequently far less expensive than purchasing the same components separately. Check the vendors in the following tip for pricing.

Understanding Z-Wave Technology

Z-wave is a proprietary wireless technology sold by HomePro and Sylvania. Z-wave is faster and more reliable than X10 and natively supports two-way communications. Z-wave can control lamps, home lighting, and appliances, and it can coexist with X10.

Z-wave supports greater security than X10, and unlike X10, Z-wave devices cannot be controlled by anyone outside your home. Instead of configuring two sets of codes for each device, you configure the Z-wave remote control by pressing a button on the remote and the button on the Z-wave device module.

Controlling Your Home with Z-Wave

Like X10, Z-wave devices can be controlled with a remote control or with a PC interface module. Z-wave uses a USB interface module for PC control. HomeSeerSE software, a simplified version of the HomeSeer software illustrated earlier in this chapter, provides web-based configuration and control for Z-wave devices. You can access the HomeSeerSE web control via your home network or the Internet. Z-wave devices also work with HomeSeer software (refer to Figures 9.4, 9.5, and 9.6), so you can use both Z-wave and X10 devices with the same software.

A Z-wave starter kit including HomeSeerSE software, a lamp module, the USB interface, and a handheld remote control is around $200. Z-wave products are available from HomeSeer and many vendors of X10 products.

tip

XPLORING THE WORLD OF X10

You've probably heard of X10.com (www.x10.com)—its pop-up ads have interrupted lots of your web browsing. Although it offers a lot of X10 products and kits, it's not the only game in town. Also check out

- SmartHome (www.smarthome.com)—a huge, almost overwhelming array of products

- HomeToys (www.hometoys.com)—the Home Technology emagazine (a new issue every month online)

- Home Technology Store (www.home-technology-store.com)—customized build-to-order quotes

Commercial Home Control Systems and Home Networks

Most commercial home control systems, like the do-it-yourself X10 and Z-wave systems described in earlier sections of this chapter, use a home network and a broadband Internet connection primarily to enable web-based monitoring and control of the systems' features. If you don't have a home network, you can use control panels or remote throughout your home to activate, adjust, or deactivate features such as HVAC, lighting, security, and other options. If you don't have a broadband Internet connection, many of these systems offer you telephone-based remote access.

Although you don't need a home network to make home control possible, a home network makes home control easier. You can adjust options with a web-based interface from any PC on your network. And, if you add broadband Internet access, you can also control your home from remote locations, such as your office or vacation spot.

Commercial home control systems are sometimes based on X10 technology or might use various proprietary interfaces. These systems typically offer the following benefits:

- Tight integration between software and device controls
- Single source for products
- Professional installation
- Whole-house lighting, security, or HVAC control

Some potential drawbacks include

- High cost, especially for installed systems
- Potential lack of compatibility with already installed home control devices. Ask about compatibility with X10 or other home control devices you already use.

Some of the leading vendors of commercial home control products that offer home network/Internet control options are discussed in the following sections.

HAI Omni Series

The HAI Omni series sold by Home Automation, Inc.(www.homeauto.com) offers three levels of comprehensive home control (lighting, HVAC, security) based on your home's square footage, HVAC requirements, and other factors:

- Omni LT is designed for homes up to 2,000 square feet.
- Omni II is designed for homes up to 3,000 square feet.
- Omni Pro II is designed for homes with more than 3,000 square feet.

All Omni systems support connection to X10 automation products, and all support remote access via touch-tone telephone or the Internet. Remote Internet access is provided by Web-Link II, a web-based configuration utility that also supports PDA and smart phone clients. It works with home networks and broadband Internet access. Figure 9.7 illustrates a sample Web-Link II session. See a demonstration of Web-Link II at http://www.homeauto.com/Web-Link/demo/ie/main.htm.

FIGURE 9.7

HAI's Web-Link II provides comprehensive home control via the Internet or your home network.

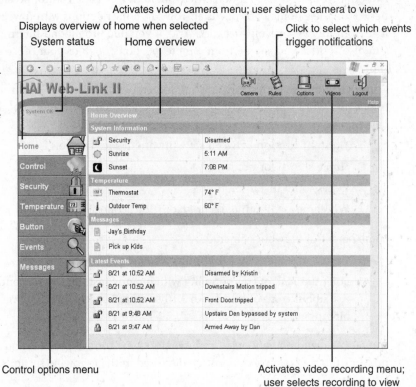

A typical HAI Omni home control system ranges in price from $1 to $2/square foot (including installation), based on the options you select. See the HAI website for more details.

iTouch

The iTouch home automation system provides a PC/LCD TV with touchscreen front end to a variety of home automation products including Lutron, HAI, and others. It has built-in lighting, home theater, video camera, irrigation, and HVAC control features.

iTouch can be controlled remotely via a web browser. You need to log in to the iTouch owner section and enter your username and password. This triggers the download of an ActiveX control that is used to access your iTouch system. Get more information from www.itouch.ws.

Vantage Controls

Vantage Controls (www.vantagecontrols.com) offers a variety of home automation including lighting, climate, home theater, and pool/landscape options. Although the system is professionally designed, you can control the system through PCs, PDAs, and smart phones in one of two ways:

- Designer Toolbox creates customized controls using Macromedia Flash. See an interactive demo at http://www.vantagecontrols.com/CES_preview/index.html.

- WebPoint provides Internet access to the system. To access an interactive demo, go to http://webpoint.vantagecontrols.com and enter demo for the username and the password. Figure 9.8 illustrates adjusting HVAC settings using the online demo.

See the Vantage Controls website for dealer information.

Xanboo

Xanboo bills itself as the leading developer of Internet-enabled devices. Unlike most other home control systems, this does *not* mean that you need to tie up a PC to run Xanboo-based home automation products. Instead, Xanboo enables you to access and control Xanboo devices remotely through its iG3 Internet gateway, which can be connected to a broadband Internet connection using cable or DSL connections.

Xanboo's major focus for home control is on home security of property and residents. Xanboo has developed a variety of product packages to meet various specialized requirements, such as child safety, pet safety, senior safety, and others.

Xanboo can also connect to X10 Pro devices through its XSK205 controller, which enables you to control both X10 and Xanboo through a single web-based interface. Visit www.xanboo.com for more information.

Selected menu   Top-level menu

FIGURE 9.8

Vantage
WebPoint pro-
vides web access
to your Vantage
Controls home-
automation
settings.

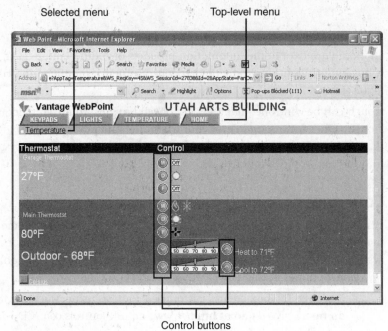

Control buttons

Using a Webcam for Home Security

If you're not interested in a full-blown home control or security system, but you'd like to keep an eye on your home when you're away, you're not alone. Webcams on home networks have been responsible for catching burglars, intruders, and bad babysitters in the act.

Although you can connect a webcam to an always-on computer and log in to it remotely, you should also consider using a wireless webcam that has its own web server. You can locate this type of webcam anywhere in your home, whether it's near a PC or not, and access it via your broadband Internet connection or your home network. Thus, you can keep an eye on an important part of your home whether you're in a different part of your house, at your office, or on the road. The following sections discuss how to use a Linksys WVC11B wireless webcam (Figure 9.9).

Setting Up a Wireless Webcam

The setup process for the Linksys WVC11B wireless webcam is similar to that used for configuring other wireless ethernet/Wi-Fi devices. You use a wizard on the CD packaged with the webcam to

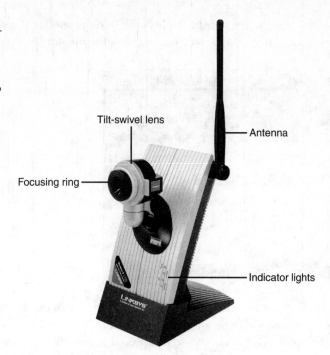

FIGURE 9.9
The Linksys WVC11B wireless webcam supports 802.11b and 802.11g wireless networks and wired ethernet networks. Photo courtesy Linksys.

Tilt-swivel lens

Antenna

Focusing ring

Indicator lights

- Specify the network type (infrastructure or ad-hoc; use infrastructure to enable Internet access).
- Specify the SSID.
- Encrypt information.
- Specify IP address type (fixed or via DHCP).

For details, see Chapter 6, "Installing and Configuring a Wi-Fi Network," and Chapter 11, "Troubleshooting Your Home Network."

Because the webcam contains a web server, which enables the webcam to run without a host PC, you also need to set up the following for the location where the camera will be used:

- Date
- Time
- Time zone
- Webcam name (change the default if you want an easier name to type or have more than one webcam)

caution

JOT DOWN THAT IP ADDRESS!

The setup wizard displays the IP address assigned to the webcam. Be sure to note this address, because you will access the webcam on your home network by entering this address in your web browser.

At the end of the process, the wizard displays the settings selected (Figure 9.10) and prompts you to save them to the webcam's nonvolatile memory.

The Linksys WVC11B's setup wizard after completion.

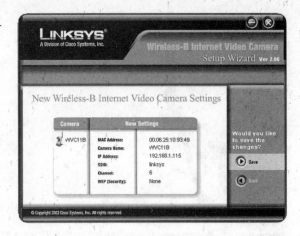

The next step in preparing the webcam for use is to install viewer software on the PCs on the home network. Depending on the webcam, you might have more than one option. For example, the Linksys webcam used in this chapter can install an ActiveX control in your Internet Explorer browser the first time a PC logs in to the camera's built-in web server, or you can install a standalone program. The standalone program can be used to access your choice of webcams on the home network, so if you use more than one webcam, consider installing it as well.

Figure 9.11 shows the Linksys Viewer and Recorder utility supplied with the WVC11B wireless webcam.

When you select a webcam, a live video window appears on your desktop (Figure 9.12). Use the buttons to start the camera, record video to the hard disk, or stop the camera.

From your home network, you can also access a webcam that has a built-in web server by opening a supported web browser (this webcam supports Internet Explorer) and entering the webcam's IP address. Figure 9.13 illustrates how a webcam appears on a typical home network.

In the example shown in Figure 9.13, the webcam has an IP address of 172.16.0.100. To access the webcam from another computer on the home network, enter http://172.16.0.100 into the address bar of a web browser.

Figure 9.14 illustrates how the Linksys WVC11B wireless webcam's built-in web server displays video.

FIGURE 9.11
The Linksys Viewer and Recorder program detects Linksys webcams on your home network so you can use them.

Selected webcam

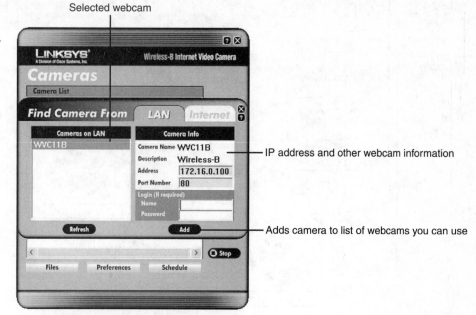

IP address and other webcam information

Adds camera to list of webcams you can use

FIGURE 9.12
Live video from the WVC11B webcam can be recorded to disk with the control buttons at the bottom of the screen.

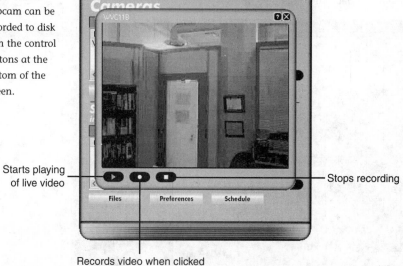

Starts playing of live video

Stops recording

Records video when clicked

FIGURE 9.13
To access a web-cam on your home network, enter its IP address in the web browser of another PC on the network.

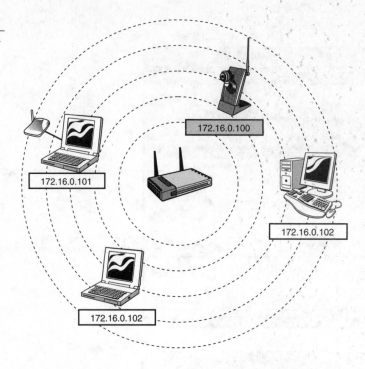

FIGURE 9.14
Using the Linksys WVC11B's built-in web server to display live video.

IP address of webcam

Click to display live video; installs viewer in web browser on first use

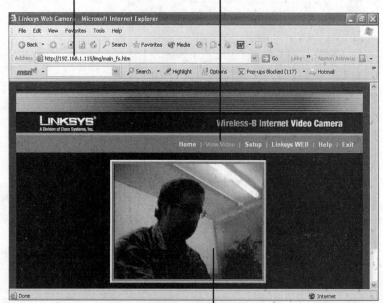

Live video playing in window

To set up options for motion detection, image quality, and other settings with the Linksys WVC11B, click Setup and provide the correct username and password.

Use the Basic menu to adjust time, webcam name, network, and wireless network settings. Use the Image menu to adjust color balance and image size. Use Password to change the webcam's default administrator name and password; this helps prevent an unauthorized user from hijacking your webcam. The Users menu enables you to specify which users of the home network have access to the webcam. Click Status to see the camera's current settings and to view a log of camera events. Click Advanced (Figure 9.15) to configure the camera to detect motion and send you email notifications. You need to know your email account information to set up these fields; check your email client setup if you don't know your email server or other information required.

tip

ASK A FRIEND FOR HELP IN ACHIEVING SHARP FOCUS

Webcams use manual focus. To adjust a webcam in a remote location for the best view of the subject, ask a family member or friend to focus the camera for you while you view live video through your web browser or viewing program. Use two-way radios or cell phones to stay in touch until you have sharp focus on the most important part of the subject.

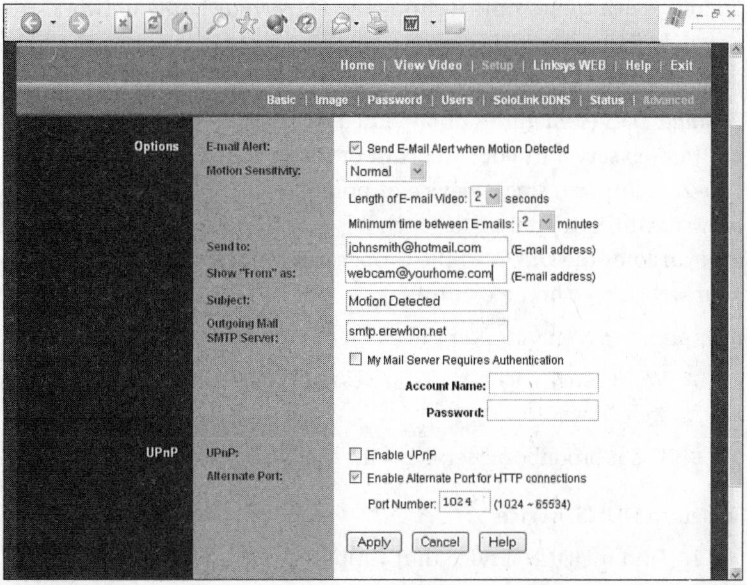

FIGURE 9.15

Configuring a Linksys WVC11B wireless webcam to provide email alerts when motion is detected.

After you complete the setup menus, your webcam can be used to keep an eye on whatever it sees. However, if you want to use it to capture a criminal while you're away from home, as a Washington state family did in the summer of 2004, you might need to set up a Dynamic DNS server.

Setting Up a Dynamic DNS Server to Enable Remote Access

It's easy to access a webcam with a built-in web server on your home network. As Figures 9.13 and 9.14 demonstrate, you enter the IP address of the webcam and you can view live video. A similar process enables you to access a home control web server on your home network. The problem is that your webcam or the PC with home control software, like the rest of your home network, uses a private IP address. To access your webcam or home control web server from the Internet, you need to know the public IP address that corresponds with the specific device on your home network.

> **tip**
>
> **TRIAL AND ERROR FOR BEST RESULTS**
>
> The Linksys WVC11B wireless webcam offers five sensitivity settings. If you set up the webcam to detect motion, you might need to try several settings to find the best one for your situation.

The trouble is that just as home networks typically use DHCP to assign IP addresses on a first-come, first-served basis, Internet providers also give your router different IP addresses using the same technology. Thus, your home network's router might have one public IP address this week and a different one next week. If you want to access your webcam or home control system remotely, you need a solution.

Dynamic DNS (sometimes abbreviated as *DDNS*) is the solution you need. By signing up the web server in your webcam or home control PC with a DDNS service (around $20–25/year for a single device at home), you can access the device from any web browser with a friendly URL, such as http://mywebcam.myhome.ddns.com. The DDNS service translates the URL into the proper combination of commands needed to reach your webcam or home control PC.

Keep in mind that you don't need DDNS unless you

- Want remote web-based access of home control or other devices that have a web server
- Use a broadband service with a dynamic IP address

To set up DDNS service:

1. Find a DDNS service that supports web servers (some support clients only).

2. Determine what TCP service port is used by your device's web server. A service port is not a physical device, but rather a virtual port used to enable the device to respond to certain types of Internet traffic. This information is provided in the documentation for the software or device. For example, typical home control web servers use TCP port 80, and the Linksys WVC11B wireless webcam uses TCP port 1024. This information is needed by the DDNS service and for the configuration of your router.

3. Use a static IP address for your webcam, home control PC, or other device that contains a web server. This ensures that your router can locate your device and pass the correct data to it. See Chapter 11 for more information about setting up static IP addresses.

4. During the DDNS service configuration process, provide the information needed to enable the service to identify your hardware (Figure 9.16).

caution

DDNS SERVICE SEARCH STARTS HERE

You can get DDNS service from the following vendors among others:

- Linksys (SoloLink) (www.linksys.com)
- Dynamic Network Services, Inc. (www.dyndns.org)
- Tzolkin (www.tzo.org)

To locate other vendors, use a search engine such as Google with the search term "DDNS service" or "DDNS service provider."

Before you can use DDNS to access the web server remotely, you must set up port forwarding on your router. Port forwarding transfers information on the specified TCP port to the IP address of the device expecting it. For example, Figure 9.15 shows that the TCP port used by the Linksys WVC11B wireless webcam is 1024. If the webcam is located at IP address 172.16.0.100, traffic on TCP port 1024 must be routed to the webcam's IP address, as shown in Figure 9.17.

To access the webcam shown in Figure 9.17 via DDNS, enter the URL http://wvc11b.selsys.ourlinksys.com in a web browser. The DDNS service redirects the URL to the actual private IP address of your web server so you can use the webcam or home control web server located there. Figure 9.18 illustrates the process.

The process shown in Figure 9.18 is also used if you set up DDNS to access a web server running home control software on your home network. Although DDNS adds a modest additional cost to your home network, your ability to access webcams and home control software on your home network from any location via the Internet helps you keep your home secure. It's a worthwhile feature to add to your configuration if you use home control or wireless webcams.

Domain name (device name+domain name create
the URL needed to access the web server)

Username and password used to manage account

FIGURE 9.16
Completing the
setup of the
SoloLink DDNS
service (supports
Linksys wireless
webcams).

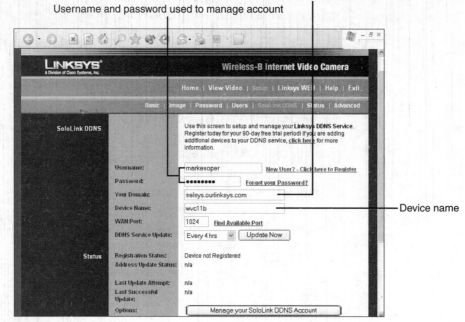

FIGURE 9.16
Completing the
setup of the
SoloLink DDNS
service (supports
Linksys wireless
webcams).

Device name

Protocol type

Service port range   IP address of webcam

FIGURE 9.17
Setting up port
forwarding to
a wireless
webcam.

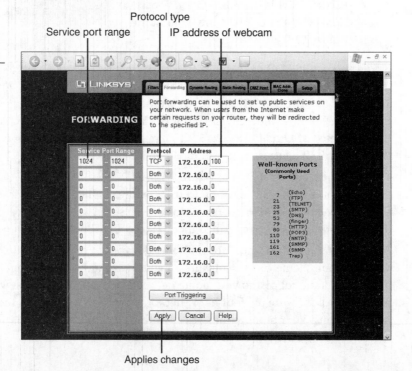

Applies changes

FIGURE 9.18

DDNS enables a remote system to access a webcam or other web server on a home network with an easy-to-remember URL.

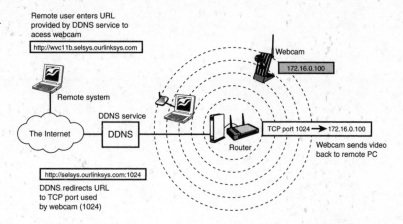

Remote user enters URL provided by DDNS service to acess webcam

http://wvc11b.selsys.ourlinksys.com

Remote system

The Internet

DDNS service

DDNS

http://selsys.ourlinksys.com:1024

DDNS redirects URL to TCP port used by webcam (1024)

Router

Webcam

172.16.0.100

TCP port 1024 ➔ 172.16.0.100

Webcam sends video back to remote PC

THE ABSOLUTE MINIMUM

You can control almost any part of your home if you're willing to spend the money to do it or the time to learn how to do it.

X10 is the leading home control system, supported by DIY and professional installers alike.

Z-wave is a low-cost wireless rival to X10, supported by HomeSeer and Sylvania.

X10 was not designed for computer interfacing, so you must use a PC to X10 interface to connect your PC to a X10 system.

Many commercial home control systems, as well as X10 and Z-wave, can be controlled via a web browser.

The Xanboo home security system uses a standalone controller rather than depending upon a PC. It connects to your broadband Internet connection via your home network.

Webcams have been credited with capturing many criminals. They can be triggered by motion and will send you video instantly via the Internet.

Webcams with a built-in web server can be accessed via a home network, via special viewing software, or via the Internet.

To connect to some home control systems or webcams, you might need to sign up for a dynamic DNS service.

PART IV

Managing and Troubleshooting Your Network

10

SECURING YOUR HOME NETWORK

If you have a home network, particularly if you have wireless ethernet, a broadband Internet connection, or both, you're in a war against an invisible army. Intruders ranging from the bored teenager down the street with a Wi-Fi–equipped laptop to the creators of sophisticated viruses want to get access to your home network. Casual snoopers might just want access to say "yeah, I did it," but the creators of viruses, worms, malware, and fraudulent emails hope to fool you into giving them access to your personal data, your identities, and even your childrens' innocence. In this chapter, you learn how to keep your network, your data, and your family safe from network and Internet intruders.

Securing Your Wireless and Wired Ethernet Networks

If your home network is 100% wired ethernet, it's pretty simple to spot an unauthorized connection: Do you see an extra cable to your switch or router? However, fewer home networks today are 100% wired. Wireless ethernet, as you saw in Chapter 6, "Installing and Configuring a Wi-Fi Network," is a great way to avoid the hassles of wiring your home. But, with the convenience of wireless networking comes additional risk.

Figure 10.1 shows the results of a brief stroll through my office building with NetStumbler (http://www.stumbler.net), a popular utility used to detect wireless networks.

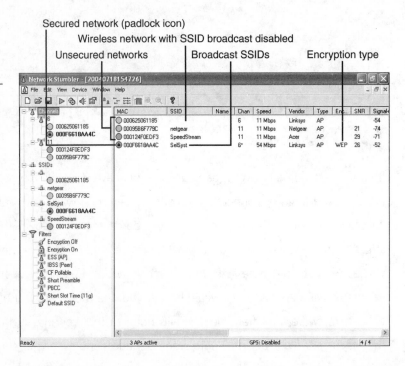

FIGURE 10.1
NetStumbler detecting wireless networks near my office. Most are unsecured.

Only one of the wireless networks I detected used encryption, and another one did not broadcast its SSID. Others broadcast their SSIDs, and they used the default SSID name provided by the vendor. I saw similar results when checking residential neighborhoods. Sooner or later, wireless networks that are not secured in some fashion are likely to be compromised.

You learned how to block casual intruders in Chapter 6 by enabling basic WEP security, but there are more and better ways to secure your wireless network, including the following:

- Higher levels of WEP encryption
- Concealing the identity of your wireless access point
- Upgrading to WPA encryption
- Continued upgrades to wireless security

Whether you have a wired, wireless, or mix-and-match network, you can also use the following techniques:

- Control access by network adapter MAC addresses
- Limit IP address ranges
- Check router configuration screens

The following sections cover these techniques in detail.

Enabling 128-bit WEP Encryption

In Chapter 6, I suggested using 64-bit WEP encryption for your wireless network for just one reason: It's easy to enable and configure on your network. I wanted you to get your network running as quickly as possible with some basic security enabled.

However, you shouldn't be satisfied with 64-bit WEP for one simple reason: there aren't enough digits in the WEP key. The fewer the digits, the easier it is for an intruder to determine the key. As with a house or car, the person with the key has access.

To switch to 128-bit WEP encryption, follow this outline (see Chapter 6 for details):

1. Make sure wireless clients aren't using the network.
2. Start the web-based configuration utility on the WAP.
3. Enable 128-bit WEP encryption and provide the WEP key (or generate one if your WAP supports passphrase) (see Figure 10.2).
4. Record the new WEP key.
5. Save the changes.
6. Configure each wireless network adapter on your network (don't forget game systems, media adapters, print server, and so on) with the new encryption setting and WEP key (see Figure 10.3).
7. Reconnect to the WAP from a wireless client to verify everything is working correctly.

FIGURE 10.2

Enabling 128-bit encryption on a U.S. Robotics wireless router, which supports entering a WEP key in ASCII or hex modes.

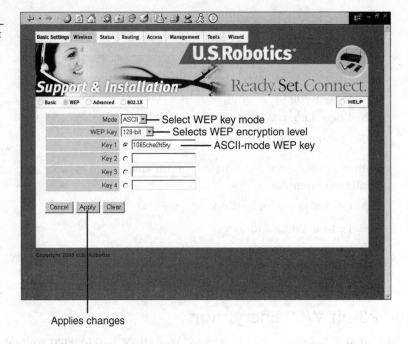

Select WEP key mode
Selects WEP encryption level
ASCII-mode WEP key

Applies changes

FIGURE 10.3

Enabling 128-bit encryption with Windows XP.

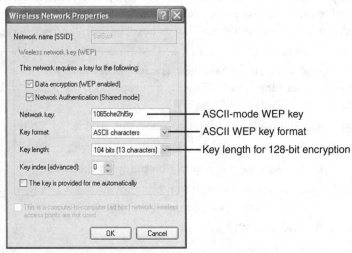

ASCII-mode WEP key
ASCII WEP key format
Key length for 128-bit encryption

Hiding Your Wireless Access Point from Intruders

Unfortunately, even if you upgrade to 128-bit WEP encryption, the longer key isn't as secure as you'd like. The problem is that any WEP key stays the same until you change it. Given enough time and enough data transmitted, a really determined intruder with the right analysis software can figure out what your WEP key is—if your wireless network can be detected. That's why it's important to follow these procedures as well:

- Change the default SSID of your WAP.
- Change the administrative password.
- Disable broadcast of your SSID.

These tasks are performed using the web-based configuration tool built in to your WAP (Figure 10.4).

FIGURE 10.4
Default wireless
settings on a
Linksys WAP.

Click to open the password dialog

The default SSID
shown should
be changed

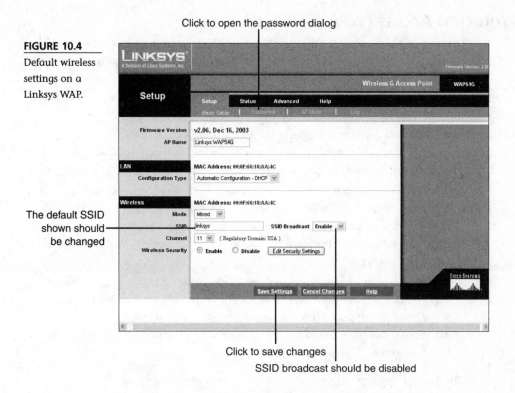

Click to save changes
SSID broadcast should be disabled

Why are these security procedures so important?

- The default SSID identifies the brand of WAP your wireless network uses to everyone. If your WAP broadcasts your network's SSID as shown in Figure 10.1, it's easy for a would-be intruder to look up the documentation for your WAP, determine the default settings, use the default password (unless you've changed it) and lock you out of your own network (at least, until you reset your WAP).

■ Changing the default administrative password makes it much harder for a would-be intruder to take over your WAP, even if you didn't change the default SSID.

■ Disabling SSID broadcast keeps snooping tools such as NetStumbler from finding your wireless network's SSID. An "invisible" network is a difficult network to compromise.

However, it pays to take further approaches to security if you can.

Wi-Fi Protected Access (WPA)

Wi-Fi Protected Access provides a big boost in wireless network security over WEP. WPA uses encryption keys that are re-created frequently, making key cracking much more difficult (although not yet impossible). WPA is a worthwhile upgrade for any wireless network. What might stop you from switching your wireless network from WEP to WPA encryption?

■ *Spotty vendor support*—Although WPA was approved in 2003, many vendors of wireless products haven't rolled out WPA upgrades for all their hardware yet. A firmware upgrade might be required for adapters and WAPs.

■ *PCs safer than specialty devices*—In Chapters 7, "Home Networks at Play," and 8, "Home Networks at Work and School," I showed you how to add home theater systems, game consoles, network storage, and print servers to your wireless network. The problem is that almost all of these devices still support only WEP encryption.

■ *Operating system support issues*—If you use Windows XP, you need to install Service Pack 1a and the Wireless support rollup package (see Table 10.1). Some vendors support WPA encryption only for Windows 2000 and Windows XP, leaving out older Windows versions that might still be in use on your home network.

If *all* the devices on your wireless network support WPA, you can use it for security instead of WEP. However, if even one device doesn't have WPA support, your home network must be content with WEP security.

To assure WPA support on all your network devices, you need to

■ Verify that your wireless router or WAP supports WPA. Upgrade the firmware on your router if necessary. See Chapter 11, "Troubleshooting Your Home Network," for details.

■ Verify that your wireless adapters support WPA. Upgrade the firmware on adapters if necessary.

- Download WPA-compatible drivers for your wireless adapters. Note that some vendors support WPA encryption only for Windows 2000 and Windows XP.

- Install Windows XP Service Pack 1a on systems running Windows XP (Home Edition or Professional) (see Table 10.1).

- Install the Wireless Update Rollup package on systems running Windows XP Service Pack 1 or greater (see Table 10.1 and Figure 10.5).

Table 10.1 Windows XP Upgrades Required for WPA Support

Install Order	Update Name	Website URL
First	Service Pack 1a	http://www.microsoft.com/windowsxp/downloads/updates/sp1/default.mspx
Second	Wireless update rollup package KB#826942	http://support.microsoft.com/default.aspx?scid=kb;EN-US;826942

To determine whether your system already has Windows XP Service Pack 1 or 1a, right-click My Computer and select Properties. Information about your computer's processor, memory size, and Windows version is displayed (see Figure 10.5).

This system is using original Windows XP

This system has Service Pack 1 installed

FIGURE 10.5

Systems running Windows XP Service Pack 1 (left) and original Windows XP (right). Use Service Pack 1 or higher with WPA.

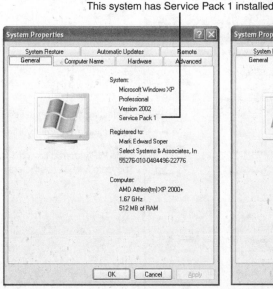
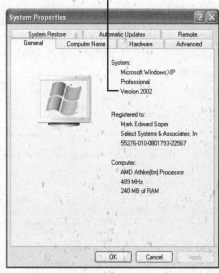

If you can use WPA encryption, you enable it on both your wireless router/WAP (Figure 10.6) and your wireless adapters (Figure 10.7) in a manner similar to that used for WEP encryption.

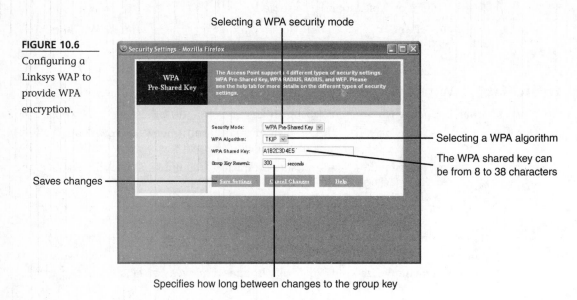

Selecting a WPA security mode

FIGURE 10.6
Configuring a
Linksys WAP to
provide WPA
encryption.

Selecting a WPA algorithm

The WPA shared key can
be from 8 to 38 characters

Saves changes

Specifies how long between changes to the group key

Type in the SSID if it not broadcast

FIGURE 10.7
Using Windows
XP to configure
a wireless
adapter to
use WPA.

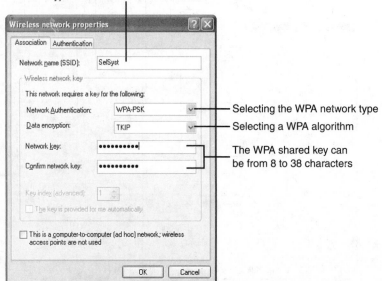

Selecting the WPA network type

Selecting a WPA algorithm

The WPA shared key can
be from 8 to 38 characters

On a home network, choose WPA Pre-Shared Key, as shown in Figure 10.7. The other method, WPA Radius, is used by corporate networks that have a Radius identity server. Select the TKIP algorithm; it rewrites the shared key periodically as determined by the group key renewal setting.

After you configure the wireless router or WAP with the new WPA settings, configure one of your adapters and test the connection. If all goes well, continue with the remainder of your wireless network.

However, even if you can't enable WPA, you can still make your network a tough one to compromise. And, all that's required to make the bad guys leave you alone is to be tougher than the network down the street.

MAC-based Access Control Lists

Every network adapter—whether it's built in to a PC, an add-on card, or built in to a specialized device such as a media adapter or a networked personal video recorder—has a unique identification. The media access control address, better known as the MAC address or physical address, is a list of six two-digit hexadecimal numbers (0–9, A–F).

With most wireless routers and WAPs, you can specify the MAC addresses of devices on your network. Only these devices can access your network. This is a very effective method for keeping unauthorized users away from your network.

Before you can use MAC filtering, you need to create a list of MAC addresses used by devices on your network. The MAC address is usually found on a label on the side of the network adapter, as shown in Figure 10.8. Depending on the device, the MAC address might be labeled MAC, MAC address, or ID No. Many devices that have integrated network adapters also list their MAC address on a label. Note that MAC addresses are sometimes listed as 12 digits rather than in six groups of 2 digits.

Using `ipconfig` and `winipcfg` to Look Up MAC Addresses

How can you determine the MAC addresses for network adapters that are already installed in a PC or are built in to a device? To find the MAC address for a network adapter that is already in a PC, you can use one of the following utility programs:

- With Windows XP or Windows 2000, use `ipconfig`.
- With Windows 9x or Windows Me, use `winipcfg`.

The utility program `ipconfig` requires you to open a command-prompt window. To run it follow these steps:

00-0F-66-6E-0F-AD

FIGURE 10.8

Typical locations
for MAC
addresses on
wireless
adapters.

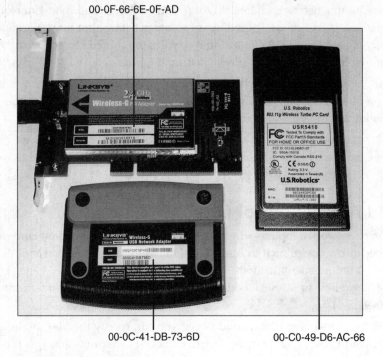

00-0C-41-DB-73-6D   00-C0-49-D6-AC-66

1. Click Start, Run.

2. Type cmd and press the Enter key.

3. Type ipconfig /all to display the MAC addresses for the network adapter(s) in your computer, as shown in Figure 10.9.

4. After you record the MAC addresses, type Exit to close the window.

Repeat this process for each computer on your home network.

To run winipcfg:

1. Click Start, Run.

2. Type winipcfg and click OK.

3. Select your network adapter from the pull-down menu.

4. The Adapter Address listed (see Figure 10.10) is its MAC address.

5. After you record this address, click OK to close the program.

Ethernet adapter

FIGURE 10.9

Using ipconfig /all to determine MAC addresses for installed network adapters.

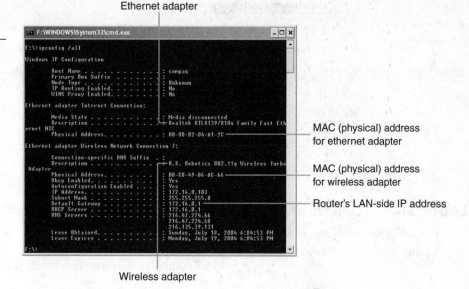

MAC (physical) address for ethernet adapter

MAC (physical) address for wireless adapter

Router's LAN-side IP address

Wireless adapter

Determining MAC Addresses for Entertainment Devices

If you have video game systems, media adapters, personal video recorders, or other specialized network devices on your home network, you also need to record their MAC addresses. External network adapters, including USB, game adapters, and media adapters have labels listing their MAC addresses similar to those shown in Figure 10.8. Some devices with integrated network ports list the MAC address on the rear of the unit.

Table 10.2 shows you how to determine the MAC address for other types of networked entertainment devices.

tip

RECORD *ALL* THE MACS

If you have a wireless adapter in a computer that also has an ethernet adapter, as in Figure 10.9, each network adapter has a unique MAC address (listed as a physical address). If your wireless router has an ethernet switch that you use for some of the PCs on your network, you need to list both wireless and wired MAC addresses to enable a PC using the ethernet switch to connect to your network. For the same reason, you should also determine the MAC addresses of PCs with wired ethernet, HomePlug or HomePNA adapters.

FIGURE 10.10

Using winipcfg to determine MAC addresses for installed network adapters.

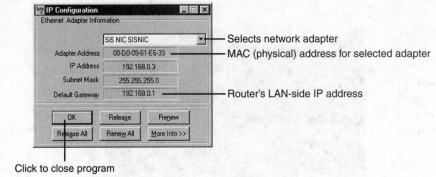

Selects network adapter

MAC (physical) address for selected adapter

Router's LAN-side IP address

Click to close program

Table 10.2 Determining the MAC Address for Specialized Devices

Device Type[*]	Brand & Model	Procedure
Video Game	Microsoft Xbox	Start Xbox Live, Select Settings, Network Settings. The MAC address is listed on the bottom right of the screen.
Video Game	Nintendo GameCube	The MAC address is on a sticker on the bottom of the GameCube Network Adapter.
Video Game	Sony PlayStation2	Use the Startup Disc to start the game system. Press Select on the controller for help after the connection test fails. The MAC address is displayed onscreen.
Personal Video Recorder	ReplayTV	Assign the device a static IP address (see Chapter 7). Open a command prompt on a PC connected to the home network. Type ping *xxx.xxx.xxx.xxx* and press Enter. (Replace *xxx.xxx.xxx.xxx* with the IP address used by the ReplayTV device.) Type arp -a to display the physical (MAC) address of the device. Type Exit to close the command prompt. See Figure 10.11.
Personal Video Recorder	TiVo Series 2	Uses external ethernet or wireless adapter; get MAC address from adapter label.

[*]*If you use a wireless ethernet bridge to connect a video game or other device to your home network, you need to record only the MAC address of the bridge. The network "sees" the ethernet port in your entertainment device only if you connect it directly to the network.*

Pinging the IP address of the ReplayTV PVR

FIGURE 10.11

Using `ping`
and `arp` to deter-
mine the MAC
address of a
ReplayTV PVR.

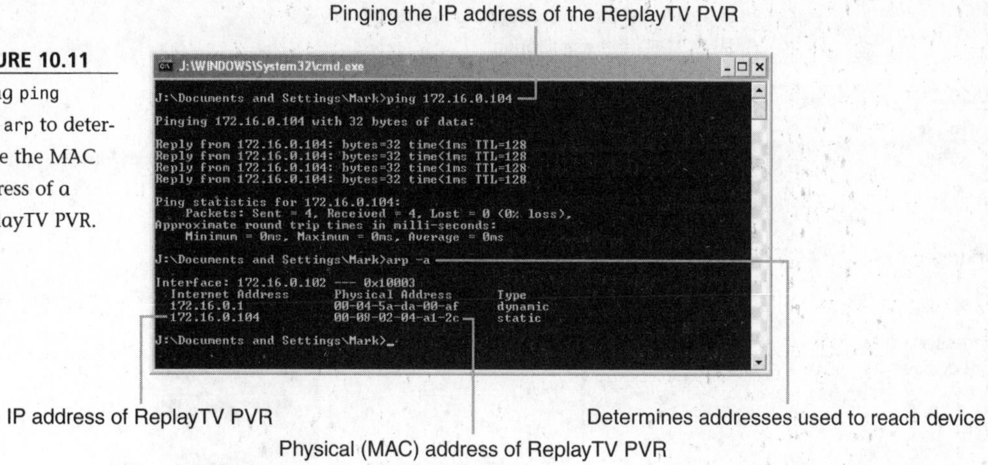

```
J:\WINDOWS\System32\cmd.exe                                    _ □ X

J:\Documents and Settings\Mark>ping 172.16.0.104

Pinging 172.16.0.104 with 32 bytes of data:

Reply from 172.16.0.104: bytes=32 time<1ms TTL=128
Reply from 172.16.0.104: bytes=32 time<1ms TTL=128
Reply from 172.16.0.104: bytes=32 time<1ms TTL=128
Reply from 172.16.0.104: bytes=32 time<1ms TTL=128

Ping statistics for 172.16.0.104:
    Packets: Sent = 4, Received = 4, Lost = 0 (0% loss),
Approximate round trip times in milli-seconds:
    Minimum = 0ms, Maximum = 0ms, Average = 0ms

J:\Documents and Settings\Mark>arp -a

Interface: 172.16.0.102 --- 0x10003
    Internet Address      Physical Address      Type
    172.16.0.1            00-04-5a-da-00-af     dynamic
    172.16.0.104          00-08-02-04-a1-2c     static

J:\Documents and Settings\Mark>_
```

IP address of ReplayTV PVR   Determines addresses used to reach device

Physical (MAC) address of ReplayTV PVR

Configuring Your WAP or Wireless Router to Provide MAC Filtering

After you have created a *complete* list of MAC addresses, it's time to open your WAP or wireless router's web-based configuration utility to establish the access list. Log in to the WAP or router and look for a menu item such as Advanced, Filtering, MAC Filtering, or similar. Figure 10.12 depicts MAC filtering setup on a Linksys WAP54G.

If you use a wireless router that has both wireless and wired clients, you might need to indicate which type of connection is being made by a particular device. See Figure 10.13 for an example.

After you enable MAC address filtering to permit only listed devices on the network, devices with unlisted MAC addresses can't connect.

caution

DON'T FILTER OUT YOUR NETWORK

Figure 10.12 shows that MAC addresses filter work in two ways: They can be used, as in this example, to permit only listed addresses to access the network. However, if you select Prevent instead of Permit, all the MAC addresses you list will be blocked from the network. If you goof up and select Prevent by mistake, use the reset button on your WAP or wireless router to reset its configuration to the factory defaults and start over.

Select to enable MAC addresses listed to use network

Enables MAC address filtering

FIGURE 10.12

Configuring a
Linksys WAP54G
wireless access
point to use
MAC address
filtering.

MAC addresses of
network devices

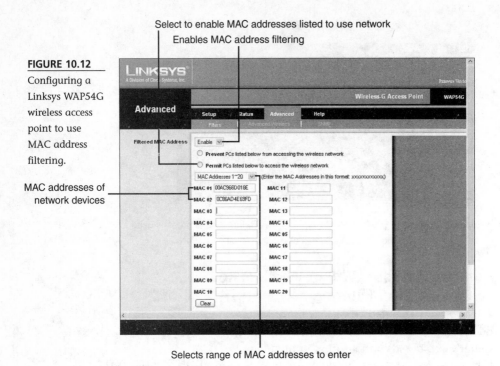

Selects range of MAC addresses to enter

Enter descriptive name of computer

Enables listed MAC addresses to access network

FIGURE 10.13

Configuring a
U.S. Robotics
wireless router to
use MAC address
filtering.

Saves changes

Adds computer
to list

Already-added
computers

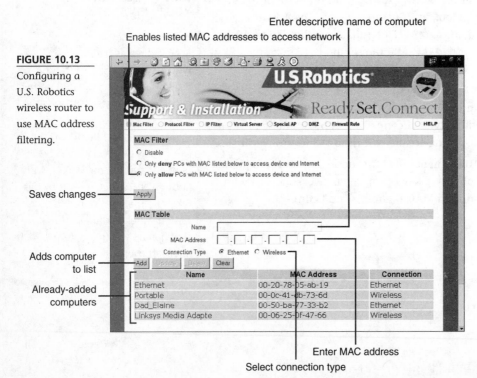

Enter MAC address

Select connection type

Limiting the Number of Dynamic IP Addresses

Another method of limiting access to your wireless network is to adjust the number of dynamic
IP addresses provided by the router. Most home
networks use *dynamic host configuration protocol
(DHCP)*, also known as *server-assigned IP
addresses*, to provide IP addresses for the home
network. This is far easier than assigning an IP
address to each device on your network (see
Chapter 11 for details). However, most routers
are configured to provide dozens of IP addresses
by default, even if you have only a few PCs and
other devices on your home network. Excess IP
addresses can be grabbed by intruders if you
don't use WEP encryption or other types of security. After they're on your home network, they
can access any unprotected shared folders and
steal bandwidth from your Internet access.

To limit the number of IP addresses your router
provides to the network, log in to the router's web-
based configuration utility and look for the menu
listing for LAN, DHCP server, or a similar name.
Depending on the router, you might specify the
number of DHCP users (each user = one IP
address) or specify a range of IP addresses. In the
example shown in Figure 10.14, the router provides IP addresses from 172.16.0.100 to
172.16.0.109.

Following these suggestions will help you protect
your home network, but don't forget to secure
your Internet connection.

tip

**AS YOU ADD TO YOUR
NETWORK, ADD TO
YOUR LIST**

As soon as you receive a new
network device, write down
its MAC address and add it
to the router or WAP's
configuration table. That will
ensure that it can access the network as soon as you complete its
configuration.

caution

**OUT OF IP
ADDRESSES? NO
NETWORK FOR
NEWCOMERS!**

Just as you need to update
the list of MAC addresses when you
add new network devices, you
might also need to add additional IP
addresses before you add new
devices. If you don't have enough IP
addresses for newcomers, additional
devices will assign themselves a private IP address that will isolate them
from the rest of the network.

Enables DHCP

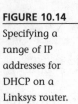

FIGURE 10.14

Specifying a range of IP addresses for DHCP on a Linksys router.

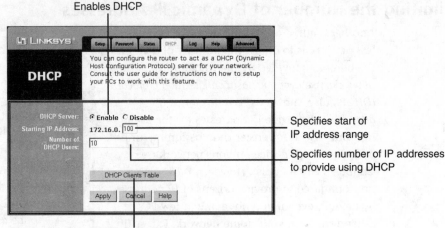

Specifies start of IP address range

Specifies number of IP addresses to provide using DHCP

Click to list computers with DHCP-assigned IP addresses

Securing Your Broadband Internet Connection

For all the concerns about Internet security since cable and DSL modems first became popular, it's horrifying how many home Internet users have essentially unsecured broadband connections. Adding a home network to share an Internet connection only makes security issues worse, because most broadband security still depends on how you configure each individual computer. You need to guard each PC sharing an Internet connection against the following:

- Unauthorized access
- Viruses, worms, and Trojan horse programs
- Spyware and malware
- Deceptive email

To do so successfully, you need a combination of hardware, software, and informed common sense. To improve your Internet security, keep reading.

Internet Firewalls

One of the most important defenses against intruders is some type of Internet firewall. You've probably read about firewalls, but you might not understand what a firewall can do for you. What is a firewall?

In network terms, a *firewall* is a barrier between one network and another. Just as a firewall in a building helps prevent a fire from spreading to an adjacent building, an Internet firewall is intended to prevent unauthorized programs or data from accessing your system.

It's common among many home network and Internet users to assume that an ordinary router is a true firewall. It's true that a router prevents the Internet from seeing the true IP address of PCs on your network. Routers use a feature called *network address translation (NAT)*, to translate the private IP addresses used on a network into the public IP address that the router uses to connect to the Internet. Figure 10.15 shows how NAT works.

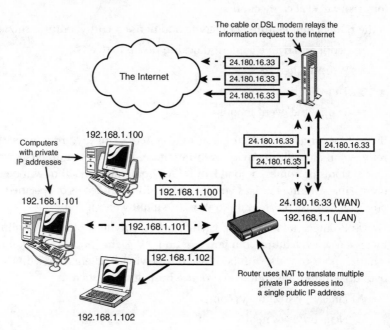

FIGURE 10.15
With NAT, the router makes page requests for multiple PCs, each with its own IP address, but displays only a single IP address to the Internet.

Although a router using NAT hides local network IP addresses from direct access by outside intruders, it isn't designed to cope with types of attacks against the router itself, such as denial of service or attempts to open unauthorized network services.

To improve security beyond the level that NAT translation in a basic router provides, there are three levels of firewall protection to consider:

- Routers with stateful packet inspection and other security features
- Firewall appliances
- Personal firewall software

The following sections examine each of these in greater detail.

SPI Routers and Firewall Appliances

For greater security, you can get a router that uses a feature called stateful packet inspection (SPI). SPI examines network traffic to determine whether incoming traffic was actually requested by the network and blocks unsolicited traffic. A router that features SPI is often referred to as a *firewall router* or a *VPN router* because most of these routers also add support for two or more VPN connections and provide support for inbound VPN connections.

Some routers that feature SPI include additional security features such as

- Script and active content blocking (Java, ActiveX)
- Website filtering
- Time filtering
- Traffic and event logging

If you have problems with users installing ActiveX or Java programs, some firewall routers can block this activity. Website filtering enables you to block websites based on keywords or names, a good feature for home networks that will be used by children. Time filtering enables you to shut off Internet access at specified times of the day; you can use this feature to stop late-night web surfing.

Firewall routers are more expensive than basic routers. Many firewall routers don't include wireless features, but you can add a WAP to enable a firewall router with ethernet ports to work with both wired and wireless clients. Firewall routers are available from firms that also produce basic routers, such as

- Linksys (www.linksys.com)
- Netgear (www.netgear.com)
- D-Link (www.dlink.com)
- Belkin (www.belkin.com)

A firewall appliance is similar to a firewall router, but typically adds features such as

- Notification of intrusion attempts
- Requirement that connections run an up-to-date version of antivirus software
- Support for multiple VPN connections inbound and outbound
- Automatic firmware updates

A firewall appliance is more expensive than a firewall (SPI) router. Which should you choose?

- Choose a basic router for a small home network that's used for a mixture of work-from-home, educational, and recreational activities.
- Choose a firewall router if you need to have two or more VPN connections running at the same time or have a small business that uses your home network. Firewall routers also support recreational and entertainment uses.

■ A firewall appliance is overkill for a home network, unless you want maximum control over network activity and want to pay for self-managing features such as automatic antivirus and intrusion warnings. If you have entertainment devices that need Internet access such as personal video recorders or video game consoles, contact the vendor to see whether such devices are supported by a particular firewall appliance.

Some of the leading vendors of firewall appliances include

■ Cisco (http://www.cisco.com)

■ HotBrick (http://www.hotbrick.com)

■ SonicWall (http:/www.sonicwall.com)

■ Symantec (http://www.symantec.com)

Windows XP Internet Connection Firewall

Windows XP features an Internet Connection Firewall. To enable it in the original version and in Service Pack 1, click the Advanced tab on the properties sheet for Network Connections and click the Protect My Computer and Network check box.

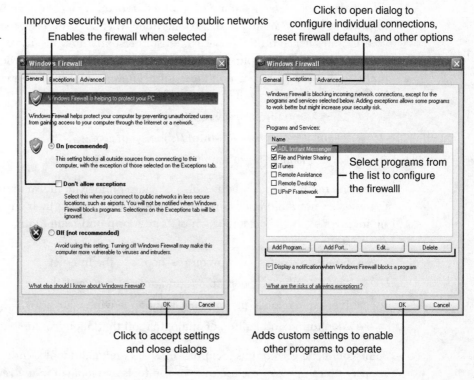

FIGURE 10.16
Enabling and configuring the Windows XP Internet Connection Firewall.

Improves security when connected to public networks

Enables the firewall when selected

Click to open dialog to configure individual connections, reset firewall defaults, and other options

Select programs from the list to configure the firewalll

Click to accept settings and close dialogs

Adds custom settings to enable other programs to operate

In Service Pack 2, Windows XP is equipped with a more powerful and more configurable firewall. To verify whether firewall, antivirus, and automatic updates through Windows Update are enabled, open the Security Center icon in Control Panel. To configure the Windows XP SP2 Firewall (Figure 10.16), open the Windows Firewall icon in Control Panel.

Compared to the original Windows XP Firewall, SP2's Firewall is much improved:

- Configuring the firewall for network and Internet-compatible programs is much easier
- The firewall works with home and small-business networks
- The firewall can log activity

However, neither the original Windows XP firewall nor the SP2 version checks outgoing traffic. As a result, they permit spyware or Trojan horse programs installed on your computer to send data to remote computers. For full protection, I recommend using a third-party firewall instead.

Third-Party Firewall Software

If you have a basic router, you can greatly improve the security of the computers on your home network by installing firewall software on each computer. Basic firewall software inspects incoming traffic to determine whether it has been requested by your PC; unsolicited traffic is rejected. Most third-party firewalls also alert you to programs that are attempting to access the Internet, providing you with the opportunity to stop programs you don't recognize. Firewalls also hide your computer from intruders. Free basic firewall software includes

- Zone Alarm (http://www.zonelabs.com)
- Sygate Personal Firewall (http://soho.sygate.com)
- Kerio Personal Firewall limited version (http://kerio.com)

These and many other companies also provide commercial firewall programs. Commercial firewall programs provide more protection than their crippled freeware siblings. For example, a comparison of Zone Alarm and Zone Alarm Pro reveals that Zone Alarm Pro adds

- Enhanced control over programs' access to the Internet
- Protection against pop-up ads and adware cookies
- Protection against personal information leaving your system
- Monitoring and halting of outgoing mail that might contain viruses

Some commercial programs integrate antivirus and additional security features into security suites. You can use the comparison tools available at many vendors' websites to determine which firewall or firewall suite is best for you.

Some of the leading commercial firewall software and security suite products include

- Zone Alarm Pro, Zone Alarm Security Suite (http://www.zonelabs.com)
- Norton Personal Firewall, Norton Internet Security Suite (http://www.symantec.com)
- PC-Cillin Internet Security (http://www.trendmicro.com)
- McAfee Personal Firewall, McAfee Internet Security Suite (http://www.mcafee.com)
- Sygate Personal Firewall Pro (http://soho.sygate.com)
- Kerio Personal Firewall (http://kerio.com)

The best way to find out what a firewall can do for you, as well as show you what you need to do to use it effectively, is to try it. Some of the commercial products listed offer limited time trials. In the following section, I show you how to use ZoneAlarm, the best known (and one of the best) free (for noncommercial use) software firewalls.

Using ZoneAlarm

ZoneAlarm divides network traffic into two categories:

- Internet Zone
- Trusted Zone

By default, it permits your installed web browser to connect to the Internet. All other online and network traffic is placed in the Internet Zone (allowing minimal interaction with your PC) until you manually select programs and activities that can be placed in the Trusted Zone.

ZoneAlarm identifies programs when they try to access the Internet for the first time and pops up a dialog asking you whether the program should be allowed access or denied access, as in Figure 10.17. Expect to see several of these dialog boxes as you use your computer for the first few days.

Before granting access, look carefully at the program. To stop repeated alerts, click the check box next to Remember This Setting before you allow or deny the program.

Attempts by others to access shared resources or other network/Internet intrusion attempts on your system will trigger an alert such as the one in Figure 10.18.

FIGURE 10.17

A ZoneAlarm alert triggered by a program.

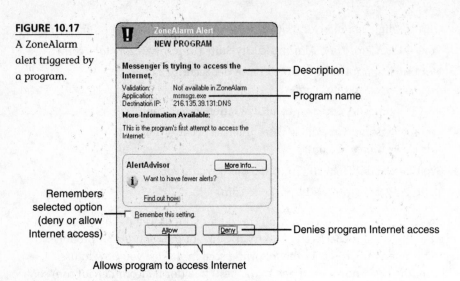

Description — Description

Program name — Program name

Remembers selected option (deny or allow Internet access)

Denies program Internet access

Allows program to access Internet

FIGURE 10.18

A ZoneAlarm alert triggered by an attempt to access your system remotely.

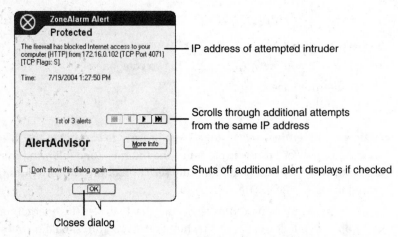

IP address of attempted intruder

Scrolls through additional attempts from the same IP address

Shuts off additional alert displays if checked

Closes dialog

Look carefully at the IP address in an alert like the one in Figure 10.18. This IP address is on your home network (compare to the list of IP addresses in Figure 10.14). However, until you instruct ZoneAlarm to permit access from your home network to the system, ZoneAlarm blocks all attempts to view or use shared resources. If a system running ZoneAlarm attempts to use another computer's shared resources, a Windows error appears indicating that the resource is not available. The solution? Add your home network to the list of Trusted Zones.

To add your home network to the Trusted Zone:

1. Open the ZA icon in the system tray.

2. Click Firewall.

3. Click Add.

4. Select IP Range to bring up a dialog box similar to the one shown in Figure 10.19.

FIGURE 10.19

Adding the IP addresses of your network to the ZoneAlarm Trusted Zone list.

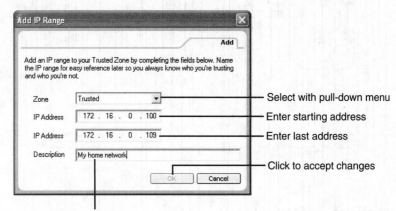

Enter descriptive name for your network

5. Make sure Trusted is selected in the pull-down menu.

6. Enter the starting address of your home network in the first IP address line. If you use DHCP to provide your network with IP addresses, use the first IP address specified in your router's DHCP settings. Refer to Figure 10.14.

7. Enter the last IP address on your network in the second IP address line. Use the last IP address provided by your router's DHCP server unless you manually assign addresses to other devices.

8. Type a descriptive name for your home network.

9. Click OK. The specified IP addresses on your network are listed as Trusted in the Firewall listing (Figure 10.20).

10. Click Apply to complete the process.

After adding your home network's list of IP addresses, you can access other computer's shared resources and they can access yours while being protected from intruders outside the network.

FIGURE 10.20

The ZoneAlarm Firewall list after adding the IP addresses used by your network to the Trusted Zone.

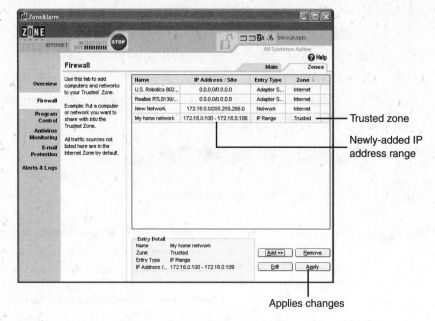

Trusted zone

Newly-added IP address range

Applies changes

Using Antivirus Software

Antivirus software is essential for both individual PC users and home network users. With the most recent versions of antivirus applications from leading vendors such as Norton (www.symantec.com) and McAfee (www.mcafee.com), you protect your network from

- Computer viruses carried by floppy disks and other media
- Emails that include hostile scripts or have attachments with other types of harmful programs

Automatic protection (which updates your antivirus software for you) should be enabled during installation. Figure 10.21 shows a typical status screen from the Norton Antivirus component in Norton System Works 2004.

As you can see from Figure 10.21, this system needs a full system scan. You can schedule these to take place during off hours (such as during the day when you're at work). Depending on the antivirus application and version of Windows you use, you can use the program's own scheduler or the scheduler built in to most versions of Windows.

Click to check for updates if desired
Indicates status is acceptable

FIGURE 10.21
Norton
SystemWorks'
Antivirus status
screen.

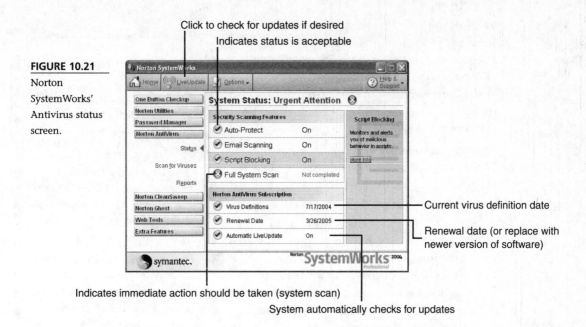

Indicates immediate action should be taken (system scan)

System automatically checks for updates

Current virus definition date

Renewal date (or replace with newer version of software)

Don't make the all-too-common mistake of assuming that once you've installed antivirus software you don't need to maintain it. Automatic updates help keep detection features up-to-date, but most antivirus programs today include only one year of updates. On the system shown in Figure 10.21, the last date for updates without additional charges is March 26, 2005.

Remember that you need up-to-date antivirus for each PC on your network. To save money, consider the following:

- Buying multipacks
- Buying programs that provide a license for two PCs
- Getting bundles that include antivirus with other network/Internet security tools

Stopping Adware/Spyware Programs

Pop-up ads, mailbox spam, browser hijacking, and slow system performance are just a few of the problems caused by so-called adware or spyware programs. Adware programs display pop-up ads (and might also send ads to your email box or take over your browser's home page) based on your browsing behavior. Spyware refers to programs that are designed to monitor and transmit reports about your online behavior to remote websites for marketing or other purposes. These programs are often installed as part of the process of installing "free" programs from the Internet, such as screensavers, customized cursors, weather display programs, password helpers, and many more. Some websites offer such free programs through pop-up ActiveX installers, such as the one shown in Figure 10.22.

How should you deal with pop-up installers? These rules of thumb are your first line of defense:

- If you didn't click on a link to download something, click No! *Never* take an unsolicited download. If the program offered is required to view the contents of a particular website (such as a new version of Macromedia Flash or Apple Quick Time), visit the vendor website yourself and download the update.

- *Always* read the privacy or user policy presented before you accept a download.

- *Consider* searching for other programs with similar features and less obnoxious marketing techniques.

- *Never* click the check box Always Trust Content, no matter what vendor. The security certificates used to identify the source of downloaded programs have occasionally been stolen or forged.

Your second line of defense is to adjust how your web browser handles downloaded programs and other content. By default, Internet Explorer offers various security zones that adjust how the browser handles different types of content. By default, the Internet zone (includes all websites until you use other categories) uses Medium security (Figure 10.23). To display this dialog, open the Internet properties sheet in Control Panel and click Security.

> **tip**
>
> **WHY UPGRADING ANTIVIRUS BEATS UPDATING**
>
> I have *never* purchased a renewal to an installed antivirus program. Instead, I purchase the newest version and use it until it's time for the next version. Here's why:
>
> - Renewals provide continued updates to virus signatures (the behavior and clues used to detect viruses and other threats) but they don't provide enhancements to the basic virus-detection program.
>
> - Buying the latest version of an antivirus program adds new features that you won't get if you renew your subscription to the previous year's version.
>
> You'll pay a bit more doing it this way, but you get better protection and more features.

FIGURE 10.22

A typical pop-up installer offering a (fictitious) "free" program.

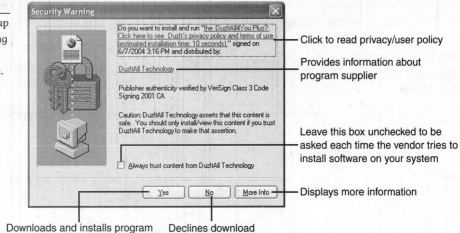

Click to read privacy/user policy

Provides information about program supplier

Leave this box unchecked to be asked each time the vendor tries to install software on your system

Displays more information

Downloads and installs program   Declines download

FIGURE 10.23

The Internet Explorer Security tab uses a default Medium setting for Internet sites.

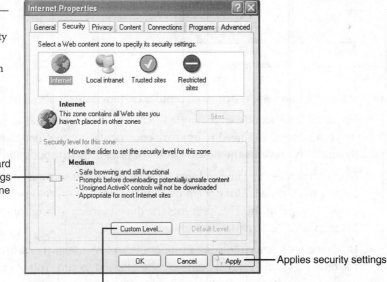

Adjusts standard security settings for selected zone

Applies security settings

Displays detailed settings for editing

You can increase the security of your browser two ways:

- Adjust the sliding bar upward to High to disable active content.
- Create a custom level.

Using High disables ActiveX program downloads, file downloads, and Java programs among others. This sounds useful, but unfortunately this setting prevents many legitimate websites from working properly.

You can create your own customized security settings by clicking Custom Level and adjusting the settings (Figure 10.24).

FIGURE 10.24

Adjusting settings for ActiveX controls in Internet Explorer.

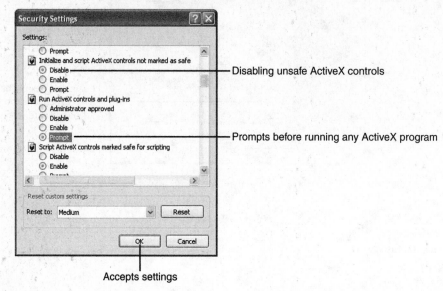

I suggest the following approach to creating a custom security level:

- Use Prompt when offered for signed ActiveX, Java, and other active content on your system. You need to approve each active content program that tries to run. This prevents the downloading of programs without your consent.

- On systems used by your children, set active content settings (ActiveX, Java, scripts) to Disabled. Make them ask you for permission to download that "cool" new program. This prevents the downloading of programs that are likely to contain spyware or malware.

- Unsigned programs and content (doesn't display a security certificate such as the one in Figure 10.22) should *never* be allowed to run. You wouldn't take candy from a stranger, and you shouldn't accept programs from strangers either.

- If you visit reputable websites frequently that use a lot of active content, add those URLs to the Trusted sites zone. This eliminates the need to constantly approve active content when you visit the websites in the Trusted Zone, without affecting security settings for other sites.

Even if you're already following these precautions, your system might already be infected. Two of the most effective ways to clean up adware/spyware infections are

- Spybot Search & Destroy
  (http://www.safer-networking.org/
  en/index.html)

- Lavasoft AdAware
  (http://www.lavasoft.de/)

These free programs use different methods to
detect and remove spyware and adware from
your system. AdAware is also available in a
commercial Plus version that prevents adware/
spyware infections.

Avoiding "Phishing" Expeditions

One of the biggest problems in Internet and
home network security today is *phishing*—a term
that refers to the widespread use of bogus emails
intended to entice you into revealing personal
information. You might have already gotten fake
emails, but if more people in your home are now
online as a result of your home network, the odds
of somebody being conned have increased—
unless you take precautions.

Many of these emails purport to come from
major institutions—such as Citibank, U.S. Bank,
or eBay—but a careful analysis of the email
reveals that the credit card, account, password
information, and so forth that you provide to the
sender will go somewhere else.

These types of emails have some characteristics in
common, as shown in Figure 10.25.

tip

**FOR MORE ABOUT
BROWSER SECURITY,
SURF THESE**

Find a great visual guide to
completing the Internet
Explorer security dialog at
http://www.dslreports.com/
forum/remark,1333507~mode=
flat.

Microsoft doesn't enable you to
save custom security settings.
Consider add-on browser software
that enhances IE's security settings, such as Secure IE
(http://www.winferno.com),
Norton Internet Security 2004
(http://www.symantec.com), and
McAfee Security Suite
(http://www.mcafee.com).

Find a concise guide to configuring IE and Mozilla (a popular
open-source browser) at
http://cybercoyote.org/security/
settings.htm.

Note the misspelling of the URL at the bottom of Figure 10.25. To see the actual URL
for a link in the status line, move your mouse over the link. The actual CitiBank
online banking URL is https://web.da-us.citibank.com/cgi-bin/citifi/scripts/login2/
login.jsp (https:// indicates a secured site). The fake email has Iogin2 instead of
login2, but you can't tell in the body of the message because l and I look about the
same in a sans serif font.

Poor grammar and sentence structure—often indicates the
writer of the message is not using his or her native language

Not personalized—your bank should know your name

FIGURE 10.25

A fraudulent
email purporting
to come from
Citibank.

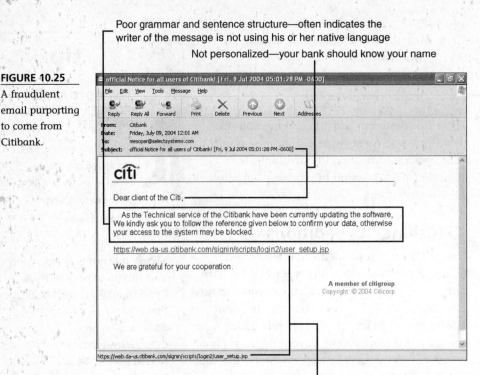

URL appears correct in the body of the message, but the status bar shows it's misspelled

Even before you open such an email, you can often tell a phony from the real deal by looking at the details of the email. For example, the fake email shown in Figure 10.25 purports to be from <u-support@citibank.com> if you right-click the email, select Properties, and look at the General tab (Figure 10.26, left). Click the Details tab, though, and it's clear from the Return-Path (Figure 10.26, right) that Citibank has never had anything to do with this email.

If anyone in your home gets an alarmist message like this, contact your financial institution to see whether there's really a problem; *don't* use the convenient link in the message because it's probably a fake. Disregard any messages purporting to come from an institution you don't do business with. Fake messages from eBay run the highest risk of catching an unwary user, because so many people shop and sell on eBay. ZoneAlarm's free version even has a special eBay setting designed to alert you if you try to surf to a fake eBay site.

Actual return-path to sender indicates message not from Citibank
Faked return address

FIGURE 10.26
More details
about a fraudu-
lent email pur-
porting to come
from Citibank.

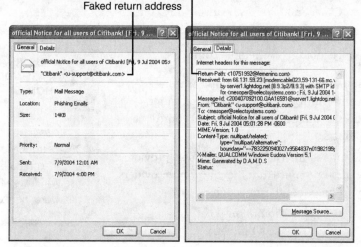

Protecting Your Family

A home network is a wonderful way for your family to enjoy the Internet. Unfortunately, it's also a wonderful way for all types of assorted evildoers to cause problems for your family. Here are some ways to protect your family while you all enjoy home networking and Internet access.

You can control the websites your children visit in a variety of ways. As I discussed earlier, many firewall routers have provisions for blocking undesirable websites. That's good as far as it goes, but in a world of billions of web pages, that requires a lot of maintenance. Better options include the following:

- Using the parental control features provided by some commercial broadband ISPs
- Using add-on parental control packages
- Using filtered Internet service in conjunction with your existing broadband service

To find out whether your broadband provider offers parental controls, check online help for your ISP or call its helpline. Note that some providers offer email filtering, but not website filtering.

Leading parental control packages include

- Cyber Snoop (www.pearlsoftware.com)
- CyberPatrol (www.cyberpatrol.com)
- Netopia (www.netopia.com)

Some Internet security suites also feature parental control features, and some router vendors also partner with parental control developers.

Some filtered Internet access providers provide only dial-up service, but the following providers support broadband connections:

- Covenant Promotions (http://www.covpro.net/)
- CIS Internet (http://www.wv-cis.net/)
- Family-Surf.com (http://www.internetfilters.net)

tip

USERNAMES AND PASSWORDS KEEP USERS HONEST

To keep kids whose computers have filtered access away from adults' unfiltered computers, make sure to use Windows XP's username and password login option.

Trial versions of some products and services are available. Try several out before you settle on one. Some of these vendors also provide email and chat protection.

The Absolute Minimum

Unsecured wireless networks can be accessed by anybody with a wireless network adapter and a scanning utility, such as NetStumbler.

You should use 128-bit WEP encryption if your network does not support WPA encryption.

To prevent your wireless network from being detected by most intruders, you should change the default SSID, change the default password, and disable SSID broadcast.

Wi-Fi Protected Access (WPA) is much better than WEP encryption, but all the devices on your network must support it or you can't use it.

Windows XP must be updated with Service Pack 1 or greater and the Wireless update rollup package before it can use WPA encryption.

Driver and firmware updates might be needed to make some WAPs and adapters WPA-compatible.

You can use MAC address filtering to allow only listed network adapters to use your wired or wireless network.

Configure your router to provide only the number of IP addresses actually needed for your network to prevent additional users from borrowing your Internet connection.

Routers provide basic protection against intrusion with a technique called network address translation (NAT).

Better routers offer stateful packet inspection (SPI) to accept or reject information going to or from the network, and they might add additional security features.

Firewall appliances provide centralized management of security but are generally designed and priced for business rather than home use.

Free firewalls, such as ZoneAlarm and others, provide inbound and outbound protection for your home network, but require configuration to work properly.

Commercial firewalls help protect against adware, spyware, and snatching of personal information.

Antivirus programs should be configured to perform automatic updates for best protection.

You can adjust your browser configuration to stop some adware and spyware programs from being installed.

Bogus email often has telltale signs that it doesn't come from the purported sender.

You can protect your children from harmful online content with parental controls and filtered Internet access.

11

TROUBLESHOOTING YOUR HOME NETWORK

Home networks are simpler than ever before, but they're a long way from being foolproof. Some of the typical problems you might run into can include

- Difficulties playing online games
- Inability to access the Internet
- Problems with different versions of Windows running on the same network

Use this chapter to help you keep network protocols, software, and hardware working properly so you can work and play the way you like.

The Home Networker's Guide to TCP/IP

If you're going to build a home network, you need to understand something about TCP/IP, the protocol that makes the Internet and your home network work. TCP/IP enables different brands of computers and different operating systems to share the same network. If TCP/IP is not installed or configured properly, your computer can't connect to the Internet

You don't need to know everything about TCP/IP, but knowing nothing about it isn't a good idea either.

In the following sections you learn

- The difference between private and public IP addresses
- How devices on your network get an IP address
- When and how to assign an IP address manually
- How to refresh and renew IP addresses
- How to use Windows XP's network troubleshooters
- What Windows XP's network repair tool does and when to use it
- How to get older and newer versions of Windows to talk to each other
- How to add MacOS and Linux PCs to your home network

Let's get started!

Understanding Private and Public IP Addresses

IP addresses are used to identify devices on the Internet. Every device that uses the Internet must have an IP address. An IP address acts like a street address or telephone number to uniquely identify a particular computer or device. Most IP addresses are used by devices that are directly visible to the Internet (these are called public IP addresses). Home networks use private IP addresses, which are not directly visible to the Internet. Home networks use one of these private IP address ranges:

- 172.16.0.0—172.31.255.255
- 192.168.0.0—192.168.255.255

(A third range, 10.0.0.0–10.255.255.255, is also available for private networks, but is not usually supported by home network routers.)

A private IP address, by definition, can't be used on the public Internet. How does a router make the connection between the Internet and your home network? As you learned in Chapter 8, "Home Networks at Work and School," routers use a feature called network address translation (NAT) to convert private IP addresses to public IP addresses that work on the Internet. The router keeps track of which information requests were sent by which device on the network and makes sure that the right device gets the information when the Internet transmits the data back to the router.

To enable the router to connect to a home network and the Internet connection at the same time, the router uses two types of network connections:

■ The WAN port connects the router to a device such as a cable modem and, thus, the Internet. The WAN port has an IP address it receives from the cable modem, or it might require you to configure an IP address manually (see next section). The WAN port's address is a different address than the one your network uses.

■ The LAN side of the router might have a single port, which connects the router to an ethernet switch, or multiple ports if the router has a built-in ethernet switch. The LAN side of the router has a private IP address that is known as the gateway address. Figure 11.1 helps you visualize this.

FIGURE 11.1
A router has two IP addresses: a WAN address (left) that connects to the Internet, and a LAN address (right) that connects to the devices on the home network.

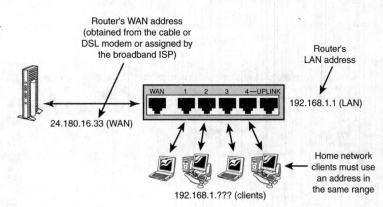

Router's WAN address
(obtained from the cable or DSL modem or assigned by the broadband ISP)

Router's LAN address

WAN 1 2 3 4—UPLINK

24.180.16.33 (WAN)

192.168.1.1 (LAN)

Home network clients must use an address in the same range

192.168.1.??? (clients)

So, how do devices on the network get their IP addresses? There are two ways to assign IP addresses:

■ Manually

■ Automatically

Home networking would be just about as difficult as office networking if you had to assign IP addresses manually. I show you how to do it in a later part of this chapter because it can be helpful in special situations. However, most of the time you don't need to do it yourself because almost all routers feature dynamic host configuration protocol (DHCP). DHCP takes care of the hard work of providing IP addresses for your computer.

DHCP for Easy Networking

DHCP is enabled through your router's web-based configuration program (Figure 11.2). Generally, the router's LAN setting is factory-configured with an IP address in the 192.168.*xxx.xxx* range and a subnet mask (always 255.255.255.0—why isn't important for this discussion). Some routers are just about foolproof because they enable you to select only the last set of digits in the starting and ending IP address ranges. However, if your router enables you to type in anything you like for the range of DHCP-assigned IP addresses, as in this example, make sure you enter an IP address range that

- Uses the first three groups of numbers as in the router's LAN address (in this case, 192.168.123.*xxx*).

- Provides a range of digits for the fourth group that doesn't overlap the router's LAN address. In this example, the router's address is 192.168.123.254, and the DHCP address range is 192.168.123.100–105.

FIGURE 11.2

Enabling DHCP and providing a range of valid IP addresses on a U.S. Robotics 8054 wireless router.

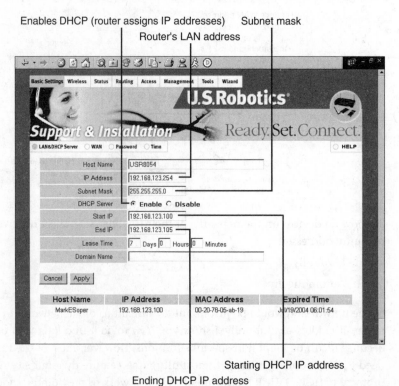

Enables DHCP (router assigns IP addresses) Subnet mask

Router's LAN address

Starting DHCP IP address

Ending DHCP IP address

By default, Windows PCs are configured to look for a server-assigned IP address. You can also configure other types of network devices to use DHCP-assigned IP addresses. So, when you turn on a network device connected to a router with DHCP enabled, the first device to connect to the network gets the first IP address listed. The second device gets the second address, and so forth. The process is the same whether the devices connect via an ethernet cable, with wireless ethernet, or through HomePlug or HomePNA networking: It's first come, first serve.

APIPA-Assigned IP Addresses

Actually, there are two different ways that a Windows PC (starting with Windows 98) can get an IP address. The second method is known as automatic private IP addressing (APIPA). Windows PCs assign themselves an APIPA IP address if they're configured to get a server-assigned IP address but can't find a DHCP server to connect to.

How can you tell whether your system is using APIPA? The most obvious sign is that you can't connect to the Internet. Systems with APIPA-assigned IP addresses can still communicate with each other to share printers and network resources, but they cannot access the Internet.

To determine whether APIPA IP addressing is the reason you can't connect to the Internet, run `ipconfig` or `winipcfg` as discussed in Chapter 10, "Securing Your Home Network." These utilities display the IP address of your system. A system that is using APIPA will have an IP address starting with 169.254.

Systems that have assigned themselves an APIPA periodically check for a DHCP server to come on line. If they see one, they are supposed to dump their APIPA address and get a DHCP address instead. However, in my experience, you're better off to take action right away when you determine that one or more systems have an APIPA IP address. If you don't, systems that have a DHCP-assigned IP address can't communicate with systems that have an APIPA-assigned IP address. In effect, you have two networks—and one "notwork."

Recovering from an APIPA-Assigned IP Address

Try the following solutions:

- Check network cable connections to the PC and switch or router; see "Troubleshooting Cabling Problems," p. 335, this chapter, for details. Restart the computer after reattaching or replacing cables.
- Make sure the router is configured as a DHCP server; see "DHCP for Easy Networking," p. 318, this chapter, for details. Be sure to save any changes to the router configuration and restart PCs after resetting the router.

■ Make sure the router is powered up and running.

■ Make sure the router is configured to assign enough IP addresses for all your network devices. If you use MAC address filtering, make sure the list of MAC addresses is up to date. Be sure to save any changes to the router configuration and restart PCs after resetting the router.

■ On a wired network, restart the computer to see whether it can obtain an IP address from DHCP.

■ On a wireless network, make sure you have a working connection to your WAP or wireless router; see "Configuring Your Wireless Adapters," Chapter 6, "Installing and Configuring a Wi-Fi Network." p. 159, for details.

■ On a wireless network, verify that your system is connected to the correct WAP or router. Windows XP's Zero Configuration Utility is notorious for connecting to the wrong WAP; see "Using the Windows XP Wireless Configuration Utility," p. 159, Chapter 6, and "Using a Vendor-Supplied Wireless Network Configuration Tool," p. 162, Chapter 6, for solutions.

■ On a wireless network, make sure you are getting a strong signal (50% or greater) from your WAP or wireless router. Low signal strength can cause your system to connect to the WAP or wireless router, but not get a valid IP address from the DHCP server. Without a valid IP address, you can't access the Internet or other devices on the network.

■ On a non-PC device such as a print server, video game system, or PVR, restart the device or rerun its configuration routine.

Releasing and Renewing IP Addresses

If you move your laptop computer between a home network and an office network that both use DHCP to provide IP addresses, your laptop might try to use the office IP address at home or the home IP address at the office.

You can use the release and renew IP address options in `ipconfig` or `winipcfg` to discard the incorrect IP address and get a new one.

To use `ipconfig` (Windows XP and Windows 2000):

1. Click Start, Run.

2. Type `cmd` and press Enter.

3. Type `ipconfig /release all` and press Enter to release the old IP address. The IP address is listed as 0.0.0.0.

4. Type `ipconfig /renew all` and press Enter to get a new IP address from the DHCP server in your router.

5. Type `exit` and press Enter to close the window.

See Figure 11.3 for an example of using `ipconfig /release all` and `ipconfig/renew all`.

Command to release IP address

FIGURE 11.3

Using `ipconfig`
to release and
renew an IP
address.

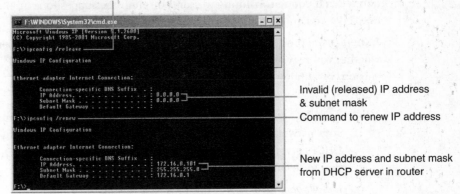

Invalid (released) IP address
& subnet mask
Command to renew IP address

New IP address and subnet mask
from DHCP server in router

To use `winipcfg` (Windows 9x/Me):

1. Click Start, Run.

2. Type `winipcfg` and click OK.

3. Click Release All to drop the old IP address. The IP address and subnet mask change to all zeros.

4. Click Renew All to get a new IP address from the DHCP server in the router.

See Figure 11.4 for an example of using `winipcfg`.

FIGURE 11.4

Using `winipcfg`
to release and
renew an IP
address.

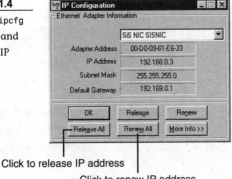

Click to release IP address

Click to renew IP address

If your laptop uses a user-assigned IP address at the office, at home, or both, this trick won't work. Instead see "Dealing with Multiple TCP/IP and Network Configurations," p. 328, this chapter.

Manual IP Address Configuration

If you find that some devices on your home network have problems with picking up a server-assigned IP address, you can assign them an IP address manually. Consider doing this if you're constantly working through the suggestions in "Recovering from an APIPA-Assigned IP Address," p. 319, this chapter.

Although the process of configuring a manual IP address differs depending on whether you're working with a PC running Windows 2000 or XP, a PC running older versions of Windows, or a non-PC device, the information you need to provide is the same:

- *IP address and subnet mask*—Use an IP address in the same range as the rest of your network. It must *not* overlap the IP address range used by your router's DHCP server or the router's LAN address. Check the router's DHCP configuration to see allowable address ranges.

- *Default gateway*—This is the LAN address of your router.

- *DNS servers*—These are the IP addresses of the servers that translate hostnames such as www.erewhon.net into IP addresses.

Determining Available IP Addresses

To determine what IP address to use, reopen your router's DHCP configuration screen and note the IP address range it provides. Use a non-conflicting address in the same range. For example, if the router uses 192.168.0.1 for its LAN address and provides IP addresses from 192.168.0.100 to 192.168.0.105 to clients, any IP address from 192.168.0.2 through 192.168.0.99 and from 192.168.0.106 through 255 would be acceptable.

The easiest way to get the rest of the information you need is to go to a computer that is working correctly and use our old friends `ipconfig` or `winipcfg` to display network information. Figure 11.5 provides an example using `ipconfig`, used by Windows XP and Windows 2000.

> **tip**
>
> **LEAVE ROOM FOR DHCP RANGE EXPANSION**
>
> You'll probably want to use DHCP for most network clients, so to leave room, make sure the IP addresses that you assign are not directly after or directly before the IP addresses provided by the router. Leave 5 to 10 addresses open before the first IP address provided by the router or after the last IP address provided by the router.

FIGURE 11.5

Using `ipconfig` to determine the subnet mask, default gateway, and DNS server addresses to use for manual IP address configuration.

Subnet mask; must be the same for all computers in your home network

Default gateway (router) IP address; use this value

DNS server IP addresses; use these values

If you use Windows 9x/Me, you use `winipcfg`. Click the More Information button to see a display similar to Figure 11.6.

DNS server IP address

FIGURE 11.6

Using `winipcfg` to determine the subnet mask, default gateway, and DNS server addresses to use for manual IP address configuration.

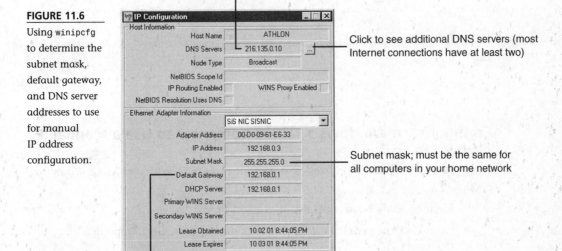

Click to see additional DNS servers (most Internet connections have at least two)

Subnet mask; must be the same for all computers in your home network

Default gateway (router) LAN IP address (must be the same for all computers in your home network; the gateway connects your computer to the Internet)

Use Tables 11.1 and 11.2 to list the information you need for any manual IP addresses you decide to use on your network.

Table 11.1 Available IP Address Configuration Worksheet

IP Address Used by Router (LAN address)	IP Addresses Used by DHCP Server in Router	Available IP addresses Range #1	Available IP Address Range #2

Table 11.2 Manual IP Address Configuration Information

Device Description	Available IP Address (from Table 11.1)	Subnet (from `ipconfig` or `winipcfg`)	Default Gateway (Router LAN address from Table 11.1)	DNS Servers (from `ipconfig` or `winipcfg`)

Configuring a Windows XP/2000 Computer to Use a Manual IP Address

To configure a manual IP address on a computer running Windows XP or Windows 2000:

1. Right-click My Network Places and select Properties.

2. Right-click the connection you are configuring and select Properties (Figure 11.7).

3. Scroll through the list of network components to Internet Protocol (TCP/IP) and select it.

4. Click Properties (Figure 11.8).

FIGURE 11.7

Selecting a network connection in Windows XP.

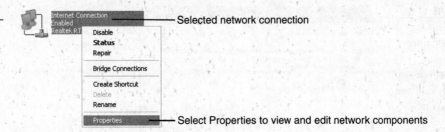

Selected network connection

Select Properties to view and edit network components

FIGURE 11.8

Selecting TCP/IP for configuration in Windows XP.

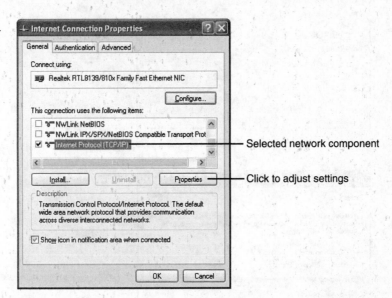

Selected network component

Click to adjust settings

By default, Windows 2000 and XP are configured to Obtain an IP Address Automatically (Figure 11.9). To change this configuration, click Use the Following IP Address and enter the information requested from your worksheet (Table 11.2):

- IP address
- Subnet mask
- Default gateway

To add the DNS server information, click Use the Following DNS Server Addresses and enter the DNS servers' addresses from Table 11.2.

Figure 11.9 shows a typical configuration before making changes, and Figure 11.10 shows the same system after adding configuration information based on the network shown in Figure 11.4.

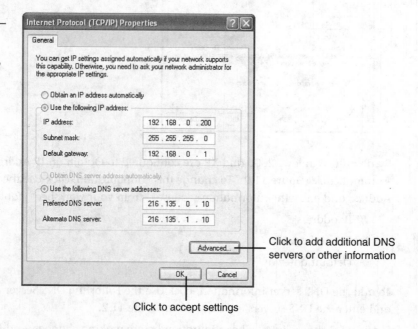

Click to add additional DNS
servers or other information

Click to accept settings

After you click OK, you might need to reboot your computer before the settings take
effect.

Configuring a Windows 9x/Me Computer to Use a Manual IP Address

To configure a manual IP address on a computer running Windows 9x or Me:

1. Click, Start, Settings, Control Panel.

2. Open Network.

3. Scroll through the list of network components to TCP/IP->*your network card* and select it.

4. Click Properties (Figure 11.11).

By default, Windows 9x and Me are configured to Obtain an IP Address Automatically. Click each tab of the TCP/IP properties sheet as shown in Figure 11.12 and make changes based on your worksheets. The values in Figure 11.12 are based on the network shown in Figure 11.6.

Click OK after completing the changes. Reboot your computer when prompted, and the changes take effect when your system restarts.

caution

DON'T CHANGE YOUR CORPORATE NETWORK CONFIGURATION

If you open your laptop's TCP/IP configuration and discover it's already completed with information from a different network than your home network, don't change anything on this screen. See "Dealing with Multiple TCP/IP and Network Configurations," p. 328, this chapter, for help.

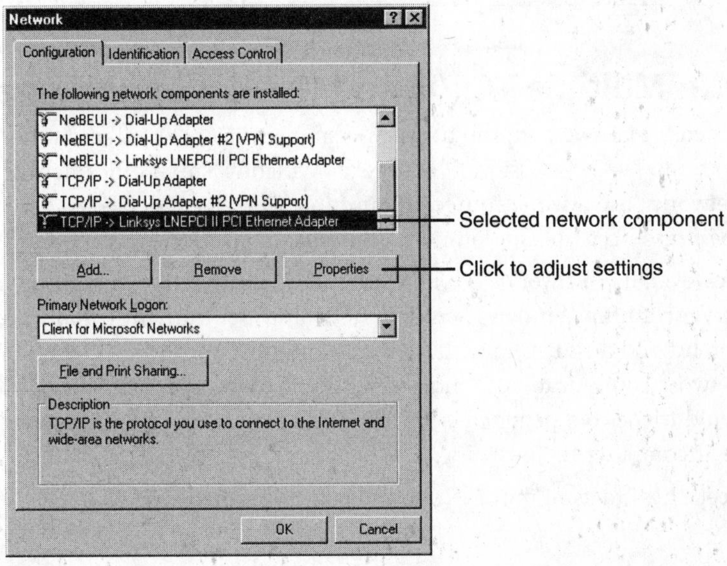

FIGURE 11.11

Preparing to configure TCP/IP in Windows 98.

Selected network component

Click to adjust settings

FIGURE 11.12

Configuring
TCP/IP with
user-assigned
values in
Windows 98.

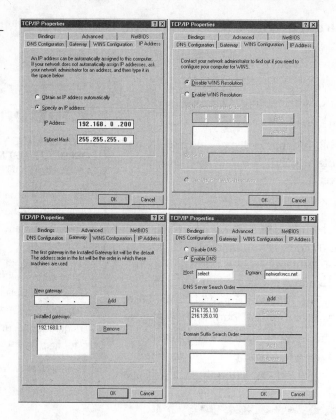

Dealing with Multiple TCP/IP and Network Configurations

It's easy to move a laptop between a small office network and a home network when
both use DHCP to assign IP addresses. Typically, small office networks, like home
networks, use a workgroup configuration: There's no dedicated server and PCs share
their resources (folders, printers, scanners, and so forth) with other PCs.

However, if your workplace network is a domain, not a workgroup (it has a domain
server running Windows Server or a similar user-authentication method), be very
careful about tinkering with your network configuration. Fiddle around with your
network configuration to make your home network easier to navigate, and you
could trigger big headaches for the IT folks back in your office when you bring in
your computer the next day.

Keep these facts in mind as you move between networks:

- You *don't* need to change from a domain to a workgroup to share your home Internet connection. If you use DHCP at both work and home, just refresh your IP address when you get home and you should be able to get on the Internet. If you have problems, find out what changes were made to your web browser settings at the office and reset your web browser's configuration.

- If you are a member of a domain at work, you can't use the domain configuration to connect to your network at home. Consider using network management software to enable you to switch back and forth between a domain (office) and a workgroup (home).

- If you use a fixed IP address at the office and DHCP to connect to your home address, you don't need to fiddle around with your network settings manually to get things working. One of these suggestions should help:

  - If you use a wired network at work and a wireless network at home (or vice versa), you should be able to connect to each network without any difficulty because each network connection is configured separately.

  - If you use the same network adapter in both locations on a system running Windows XP, you can use the Alternative Configuration tab shown in Figure 11.10 to configure your home network settings. You can't use DHCP with the Alternative Configuration tab, but you can set up a user-assigned IP address, as discussed in "Configuring a Windows XP/2000 Computer to Use a Manual IP Address," p. 324, this chapter.

  - You can store multiple network configurations (home/office, main office/branch office/home, and so on) with a variety of third-party programs whether you use Windows XP or earlier versions of Windows.

note

FEELING TECHY? DO IT YOURSELF WITH NETSH

Windows 2000 and XP contain a command-line utility called `netsh`, which can be used to automate switching between home and office networks. Ask your IT department about it or see the following websites for more information:

- Mike Rose—Windows on Multiple Networks http://www.tcm.phy.cam.ac.uk/~mr349/win_multi_net.html.

- Use `netsh` to configure your laptop for different networks http://is-it-true.org/nt/nt2000/utips/utips46.shtml.

Third-party network configuration management programs include

- Select-a-Net (http://www.select-a-net.com/)
- IP Switcher (http://www.softmate.co.kr/UK/ipswitcher/index.htm)
- Net Switcher (http://www.netswitcher.com)
- Mobile Net Switch (http://www.mobilenetswitch.com/)

Troubleshooting Your Network

Use the following sections to get your network up and running after problems.

After You Swap Network Adapters, You Can't Connect to the Internet

Some routers "remember" the network adapters that have requested an IP address via DHCP, even if you have removed or disconnected the adapter. To see which devices the router has provided an IP address to, open the router's DHCP configuration and look at the DHCP clients table. If you see an adapter that is not in use, select it and delete it (Figure 11.13).

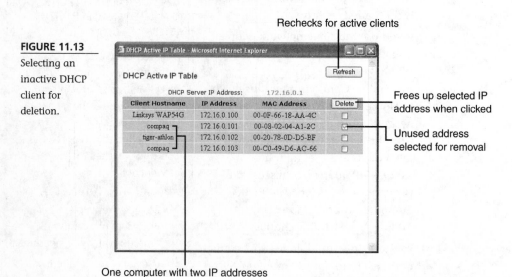

FIGURE 11.13
Selecting an inactive DHCP client for deletion.

The situation shown in Figure 11.13 can happen if you switch from a wired to a wireless ethernet connection or remove one USB or PC Card/CardBus adapter and insert another.

You can also use this feature to kick unknown devices off your wireless network (at least temporarily). If you see unfamiliar devices showing up in your DHCP clients table, you'd better enable security or use stronger measures. See Chapter 10 for details.

Using Windows XP's Network Troubleshooters

Windows XP includes several troubleshooting tools for home networks. To view the list:

1. Click Start, All Programs, Help and Support Center.

2. Click Networking and the Web.

3. Click Fix Networking or Web problems.

Windows XP's Help and Support Center displays network troubleshooters and other support tools (Figure 11.14).

FIGURE 11.14

Network troubleshooters and tools included with Windows XP.

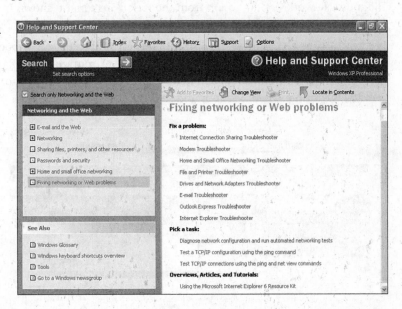

To start a troubleshooter, click it. Most of the troubleshooters start by asking you a question. Depending on your answer, the troubleshooter might

- Suggest a course of action.

- Offer to run a Windows tool such as Device Manager. These options are listed with a curved arrow.

- Ask another question.

- Offer to investigate the settings on your computer.

To get the most out of the network troubleshooters:

- Make sure your network cable or wireless network adapter is connected to your computer, even if your network connection is not working.
- Make sure you select the right troubleshooter for your problem.
- Answer the questions carefully.
- If you are asked to change network settings, write down the old settings before you change them.

In the following sections, I show you how to use some of the tools introduced in this section.

Network Diagnostics

The Network Diagnostics tool scans your network hardware, browser, email, and other network settings to see whether they're working correctly. To start it, click Diagnose Network Configuration from the Pick a Task menu shown in Figure 11.14.

Click Scan Your System to start the process. A status bar informs you of the tests' progress. Figure 11.15 shows the results of a successful test. FAILED appears in place of passes on a system with problems. Click the check mark next to the category for more information. Details for each item vary by the item type, such as hardware, website, operating system version, and so on.

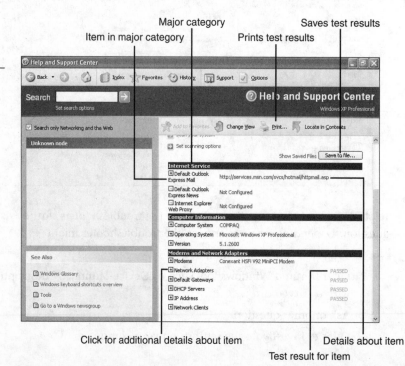

FIGURE 11.15

The results of a scan with Network Diagnostics.

Follow the suggestions given for FAILED test results.

Troubleshooting with `ping`

The `ping` command is used to send a signal to a specified IP address or website and receive a response back from that address or website. You can "ping" your own computer, your router or gateway, your broadband Internet connection, or your ISP.

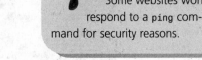

note

Some websites won't respond to a `ping` command for security reasons.

The `ping` command is run from the command line in Windows.

To open a command-line window in Windows 9x/Me:

1. Click Start, Run.
2. Type `command` and click OK.

To open a command-line window in Windows 2000/XP:

1. Click Start, Run.
2. Type `cmd` and click OK.

To ping a particular address, type `ping` *xxx.xxx.xxx.xxx* and press Enter. (Replace *xxx.xxx.xxx.xxx* with the actual IP address.) To ping a particular website, type `ping` *Websitename* and press Enter (replace *Websitename* with the actual website).

Here's how to use `ping` to test your home network configuration:

1. To make sure your system has TCP/IP installed, type `ping` `127.0.0.1` (also called the *local loopback*). Regardless of the IP address assigned your computer by your ISP or DHCP server, your system uses this IP address for testing. If your system responds as seen in Figure 11.16 with Reply From, you have the TCP/IP protocol installed. If you get an Unknown Host message, reinstall TCP/IP. Reconfigure your IP address if you assigned the computer a manual IP address.

2. To see whether you can connect with your router, ping its LAN IP address.

3. To see whether you can ping another device on the network, including non-PC network adapters, ping the device's IP address. If you are unable to ping a particular device, check cabling and then check your IP address setup.

4. To see whether you can connect with the Internet, ping a favorite website, as in Figure 11.17.

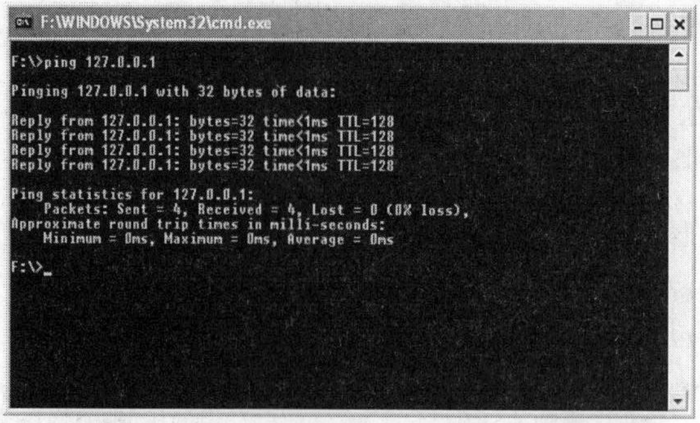

FIGURE 11.16

Using ping to test your own system's TCP/IP installation.

FIGURE 11.17

Using ping to test your connection to the Internet; note that the ping command specified the website, but the output also lists the site's IP address.

Error messages you might see include the following:

- Unknown Host—You might have misspelled the IP address or website, but if you spelled them correctly, this error indicates that you can't reach the address or website specified. Check cabling and then IP configuration.

- Host Timed Out—A normal message for some sites that don't respond to ping commands for security reasons; if all IP addresses that you ping display this information, your Internet connection has a speed problem beyond your control.

Troubleshooting with Windows XP's Network Repair Option

If you are having problems with a network connection, you can run the Windows XP Repair option. Right-click the network connection in the Network Connections folder and select Repair. This releases and renews the IP address, refreshes domain name system information, and performs other tasks. If the repair option fails, it usually indicates that you don't have a valid connection to a DHCP server. This could be caused by cable failure, problems with your wireless ethernet adapter, or a problem with your router. See the respective other sections of this chapter for details.

Troubleshooting Slow Connections Between Windows 9x/Me and Windows 2000/XP Systems

Windows 2000 and XP have an additional network component called Quality of Service Packet Scheduler (QoS Packet Scheduler), which is enabled by default (Figure 11.18). This service is not supported in older versions of Windows, and as a result, connections between a Windows 9x/Me system and a system running QoS are extremely slow; it can take a minute or more just to view the contents of a shared folder.

If your network has a mixture of Windows 9x/Me and Windows 2000/XP clients, disable QoS by clearing the check mark in the properties sheet for your network connection.

Clear checkmark in this box to disable QoS

FIGURE 11.18
Disabling QoS for better network performance on a mixed Windows network.

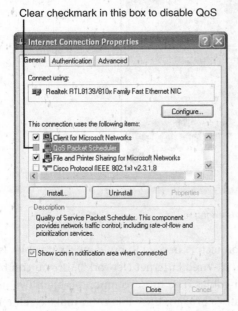

Troubleshooting Cabling Problems

Even if you have a wireless network, your router connects to your broadband Internet device with a cable, and a cable connects the broadband Internet device with the world. If your network has additional cabled connections, the odds of cable problems increase. Use the following sections to help you conquer cable problems.

Detecting and Solving Problems with UTP and Ethernet Cable

The most obvious reason for a wired network connection to fail is a loose cable. Although ethernet, DSL, and telephone cables have locking tabs, if they're not pushed in firmly enough to lock the tab in place, the connection will fail sooner or later. Compare the cables in Figure 11.19.

Loose cable; lock is not engaged

FIGURE 11.19

Loose (top) and properly con-nected (bottom) CAT5 Ethernet cables.

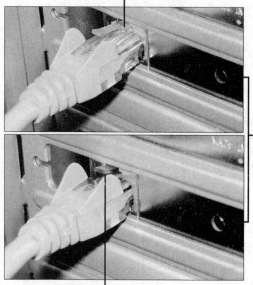

Link light; it is visible only when the cable is properly attached and both ends of the cable are energized

Fully inserted cable; lock is engaged

If you have the tools and connectors needed to build ethernet cables (see Chapter 5, "Installing and Configuring a Wired Ethernet Network"), or you can borrow them, you can fix broken ethernet cables. The most common problem I've seen is a broken locking tab. If the locking tab is broken, the cable can't make a reliable connection. To fix this problem, cut off the end of the cable with the broken locking tab and attach a replacement RJ-11 connector, as described in Chapter 5.

A cable that has good connectors and locking tabs but doesn't connect reliably might have sustained internal damage. Don't step on network cables! To determine whether the cable has failed, connect it to another computer. If the cable works correctly on another computer, the original computer's ethernet card or port may have failed. See "Troubleshooting Ethernet Port/Card Problems," p. 340, this chapter.

Detecting and Solving Problems with Coaxial Cable

Cable modems use a coaxial cable connection to the cable TV network. If the cable isn't tight enough or has been damaged, you won't have a reliable connection. See Figure 11.20 for a comparison between loose and properly connected coaxial cables.

If your coaxial cable connections to the cable modem appear sound, look at the cable itself. If there are several splices in the cable, this can cause a loss of signal quality from the CATV network to your cable modem. If the cable has cracks or tears in the outer jacket, it should be replaced.

To determine whether the cable running to the cable modem is at fault, disconnect the splitter from the CATV cable coming into your location and connect the cable modem directly to the CATV cable. If you can now synchronize with the network and make a connection, the splitter or the cable running from the splitter is defective and should be replaced.

Properly connected CATV cables should be immune to weather problems, but if you find that you're having loss of connection problems with your cable modem (or cable TV, for that matter) when it rains or snows, you may have unprotected connections between cable segments or bad splices on your cable. Ask the cable provider to check your outside cable and its connection to the fiber-optic cable for problems. Rubber boots and tape can be used to secure splices and connections against weather problems.

caution

GET THE RIGHT CABLE FOR YOUR ROUTER

If you need to replace the CAT5 cable running from your broadband Internet device to your router, be sure to choose a cable that's the same standard or better. CAT3 cables use the same connector, but are designed to handle 10Mbps signals instead of the faster 100Mbps signals supported by CAT5 cables. Also, be sure to check the cable type. Although most cable modems use a standard Cat 5 cable, some might use a crossover cable (which reverses the order of some wire pairs). Both types are available at most computer stores and departments. Installing the wrong type of cable will prevent data transfer between the device and your router. Some routers automatically detect the cable type and adjust for it, or use a manual switch, but others don't.

Loose coaxial cable; note large amount of screw thread visible

FIGURE 11.20
Loose (left) and
properly con-
nected (right)
coaxial cables.

Coaxial cable correctly screwed into place

Correcting Broadband Internet Device Problems

Most broadband Internet access devices are external units. The signal lights on the front of the unit can help you diagnose connection problems. Table 11.3 shows you how the signal lights on the Toshiba PCX1100 and PCX1100U cable modems can be used to diagnose problems (shown in shaded boxes). Your cable or DSL modem and connection type will vary, so see your manual for details.

Table 11.3 Signal Lights on the Toshiba PCX1100 Series Cable Modem

Signal Light	Color	Off	Blinking	On	Items to Check
Power	Green	No power	N/A	Power on	AC adapter, AC cord plugged into unit
Cable	Green	No cable signal from CATV network if power on	Synchronizing and registering with network	Cable modem ready	Coaxial cable to cable modem; coaxial cable into splitter
PC	Green	No Ethernet or USB connection to computer if power on	N/A	Ethernet or USB connection to computer is present	Verify USB or Ethernet cable properly plugged into cable modem and PC; correct type of Ethernet cable used; check USB or Ethernet port on PC for proper operation

Signal Light	Color	Off	Blinking	On	Items to Check
Data	Green	No data transfer in progress if power on	Data transfer in progress	N/A	No problem apparent unless light stays off during web page opening, email sending/ receiving, or file downloads/uploads
Test	Amber	Self-test OK if power on	Self-test in progress	Self-test failed	Reset cable modem

DSL modems use similar signals to those shown in Table 11.3, except that the connection to the DSL modem is made with a UTP cable instead of a coaxial cable.

As you can see from Table 11.3, when signal lights are off, it's usually bad news. However, if the Test/TST signal light stays on, this also indicates a problem with the cable modem.

Loose cables, or using the wrong cable between the cable modem and the Ethernet card in the computer or the router's WAN port, will cause loss of signal. Loss of signal will result in most of

tip

Because the process of synchronizing the cable modem with the CATV network can take as long as 30 minutes if the cable modem is turned off, it should be left on at all times.

the problems listed in Table 11.3. If the cables are the correct type, appear in good condition, and are attached correctly to the cable modem and the PC, check the Ethernet adapter or USB port on the PC as discussed in the following sections. A self-test failure can sometimes be cured if you reset the cable modem by either pressing the reset switch on the cable modem (if available) or by turning off or unplugging the cable modem, waiting for 30 seconds, and turning it on/plugging it back in again. If the self-test continues to fail, contact your ISP or cable modem vendor for repair or replacement.

If your modem spontaneously reboots, which will cause it to go through the Power On Self Test (POST) and force it to resynchronize to the cable network, look for these interference sources nearby:

- Power spikes coming from refrigerators, vacuum cleaners, or air conditioners
- EMI (electromagnetic interference), such as cordless phones

Troubleshooting Your PC's Ethernet and USB Connections

If the network adapter connecting your PC to the home network fails or the USB port used for external adapters malfunctions, the computer cannot connect to the home network.

Problems with your Ethernet, wireless ethernet, and USB connections can come from any of the following sources:

- Hardware and device driver failure
- Incorrect port configurations
- Resource conflicts with another device

Here's how to solve these problems.

Troubleshooting Ethernet Port/Card Problems

If the Ethernet port, card, or adapter has failed, you may be able to determine this from one of the following symptoms:

- The signal lights on the back of the Ethernet card don't light up when the computer is on and a cable from a working cable modem, switch, or router is plugged into the card (refer to Figure 11.19).
- The Windows Device Manager doesn't list the card, or displays the card with a red x across the card listing (see next section).
- The card is not displayed as a PCI/PnP device when you turn on your system.

If your Ethernet card fits into a slot, you can replace it. In Windows, be sure to remove it from the Device Manager before you physically remove the card from your system. Be sure to install the correct drivers for your new card.

If your Ethernet port is built in to your system and you have an open PCI expansion slot, you may be able to install a replacement 10/100 Ethernet card as an alternative to repairing your system or replacing your motherboard. If you use a notebook computer with a built-in Ethernet port, you can use a PC Card or CardBus-based

tip

CHECK THE MAC ADDRESS BEFORE YOU CONCLUDE IT'S BROKEN

If you use MAC address filtering (see Chapter 10), make sure the MAC address for the computer's network adapter has been added to the router's table of valid MAC addresses. If not, fix that problem first and your connection might begin to work.

10/100 Ethernet adapter as a replacement. Remember, you can also use a USB/ethernet adapter if you don't like fiddling with the interior of your PC.

Using the Windows Device Manager

Although hardware failures can take place, it is more likely that problems with your Ethernet port or adapter come from a resource conflict with another card or from a problem with your drivers. The Windows Device Manager can help you determine which of these is the problem.

To open the Windows Device Manager:

1. Click Start, Control Panel (Windows 2000/XP) or Start, Settings, Control Panel (Windows 9x/Me).

2. If the System icon is not visible in Windows XP, click Switch to Classic view.

3. Click the System icon. The General tab (listing Windows version and RAM) is displayed.

4. In Windows XP or Windows 2000, click the Hardware tab and then the Device Manager button. Click the Device Manager tab in Windows 9x/Me. A yellow-circled exclamation mark (!) symbol next to a device indicates a conflict with other devices or a driver problem. A red x indicates the device has failed or has been disabled. The Windows 98 Device Manager is shown in Figure 11.21. The Windows XP Device Manager is shown in Figure 11.22.

FIGURE 11.21
The Linksys
EtherPCI LAN
Card has a con-
figuration prob-
lem, as shown
by the yellow !
symbol.

Yellow ! indicates
problem device

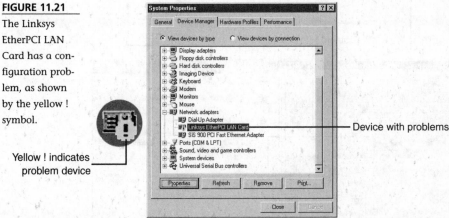

Device with problems

FIGURE 11.22
The Realtek eth-
ernet adapter
has been dis-
abled, as indi-
cated by the red
X symbol.

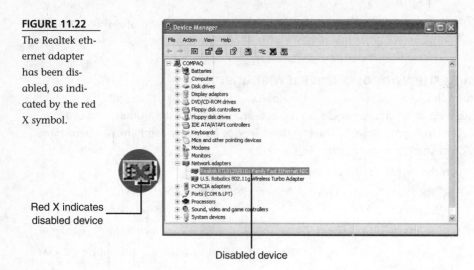

Red X indicates
disabled device

Disabled device

5. Double-click the device icon to display the properties sheet. Click the solution button on the General tab to fix the problem with the device (Figure 11.23).

6. Follow the prompts onscreen to update drivers, enable the device, resolve resource conflicts, or provide other solutions. Restart the system if prompted to do so.

Click to view driver details, update driver or (Windows XP only) roll back driver

Click to adjust power management
or other advanced settings

Problem with device

FIGURE 11.23
Using the
Solution button
to solve a net-
work adapter
problem in
Windows 98
(left) and
Windows XP
(right).

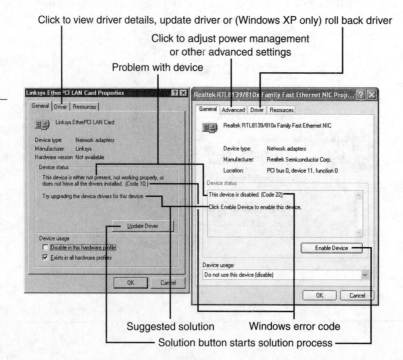

Suggested solution   Windows error code

Solution button starts solution process

Troubleshooting USB Port Problems

The USB port is an increasingly popular way to connect a network adapter to your PC, particularly a wireless ethernet or HomePlug adapter. Although USB support is universal among PCs built in the last few years, you might encounter one or more of these problems:

- USB port not enabled in system BIOS
- High-speed USB (USB 2.0) support not enabled in system BIOS
- USB drivers not loaded
- Not enough power provided by the USB port for device

If your network adapter doesn't work when you plug it into a USB port, your USB port might not be enabled or working. Check the following:

- *USB port status*—Open the Windows Device Manager as discussed in the previous section and scroll down to the bottom of the hardware listing. You should see a category called Universal Serial Bus Controllers. Click the plus (+) sign next to this category to display its contents. As with other devices, a red x indicates the device has been disabled; check its Properties sheet for an option to reenable it. A yellow ! indicates a driver or conflict problem.

- *USB hub power issues*—Because many external devices connect to the USB port, and most systems have only two, four, or six USB ports, many users prefer to attach multiple devices to an external USB hub. Most standalone USB hubs come with a small AC adapter to make sure that all USB

note

ONE BUTTON, MANY USES

The solution button performs various tasks depending on the device's problems. For example, if the device needs a new driver, the solution button reads Update or Reinstall Driver. If the device is disabled, the solution button reads Enable Device.

tip

If the Universal Serial Bus category is not displayed in the Windows Device Manager but your system has USB ports present, they have been disabled in the system BIOS. See your system documentation for details on how to access your system BIOS (you normally press a particular key during startup to access the setup program) and enable these ports.

devices have plenty of power (500mA per port); such hubs are called *self-powered hubs*. USB hubs built in to monitors, keyboards, and other devices are usually bus-powered, drawing power from your system's USB ports and providing only 100mA per port. Bus-powered hubs might not provide adequate power for some devices. For example, some USB network adapters require 500mA of power. If your network adapter won't work when you plug it in through a bus-powered hub (you might see an error message), connect it directly to a USB port on your system, or purchase a self-powered hub and use it for your network adapter and other USB devices. To determine how much power a device uses and how much power is available per port, click the Power tab for a USB root hub or Generic hub (external hub) in Device Manager.

■ *USB port type*—USB 1.1 ports have a maximum speed of only 12Mbps, far slower than the 100Mbps provided by fast ethernet or the 480Mbps speed of USB 2.0. You might not notice the difference in speed in a home network, but your system will display an error message (Figure 11.24) if you connect a USB 2.0 network adapter to a USB 1.1 port. If you see this message on a system that has USB 2.0 ports, you might have plugged the network adapter into the wrong port or you might need to install USB 2.0 drivers or configure the system BIOS to provide USB 2.0 support. See your system manual for details.

FIGURE 11.24

Windows displays a warning if you plug a USB 2.0 (Hi-speed USB) device into a USB 1.1 port. The device works, but at reduced speed.

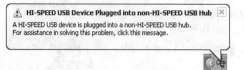

Solving Routing Problems

A router has two functions:

■ It enables your home network to connect to the Internet.

■ It helps prevent hostile traffic from reaching your network.

To perform the second task, routers block, by default, certain types of Internet traffic. Different types of Internet traffic use different logical ports provided in each Internet connection. For example, your web browser uses TCP port 80 to view HTTP web pages, and your email program connects with the POP3 email server using TCP port 110. Routers permit traffic between so-called well-known ports like these and others. Software firewalls also watch these logical ports and block or allow traffic based, in part, on which programs are using the Internet connection. Web browsers are allowed to use the Internet connection, but you must grant permission to other programs before they can use the connection.

However, some online games, video chat, and other functions might not work on a home network because the router or software firewall prevents access to the TCP ports or UDP ports used by the application.

There are two ways to deal with this problem:

- Determine which ports are needed by the application and configure the router or software firewall to allow the traffic.

- Disable firewall protection for the client by placing the client's IP address into the demilitarized zone (DMZ).

Some routers are preconfigured with options to permit traffic for certain programs. Figure 11.25 shows the Special Apps configuration screen for a U.S. Robotics wireless router.

FIGURE 11.25

Configuring a U.S. Robotics wireless router to provide customized TCP/UDP port handling for special applications.

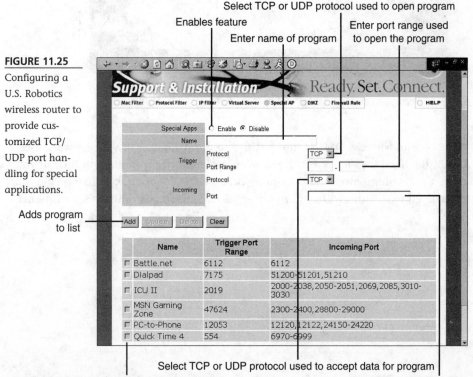

Select TCP or UDP protocol used to open program

Enables feature

Enter name of program

Enter port range used to open the program

Adds program to list

Click box to activate preconfigured setting

Select TCP or UDP protocol used to accept data for program

Enter port range used by program

This method enables the router to protect the client while permitting programs that use nonstandard ports to run correctly. It does take time to configure, but the advantage is that these settings work for any IP address on the home network.

The second method is quicker, but potentially more dangerous. The DMZ zone turns off router protection for the specified IP address (Figure 11.26). The specified IP address has full access to the Internet—and the Internet has full access to that IP address!

FIGURE 11.26

Configuring a Linksys router to place an IP address into the DMZ.

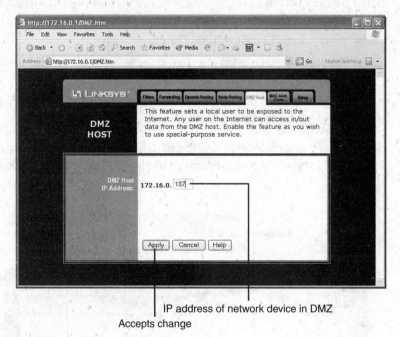

IP address of network device in DMZ

Accepts change

One problem with the DMZ is that it is tied to the IP address. If your network uses DHCP, the IP address for particular devices might change from time to time. If you have a particular network device that *must* have DMZ support, consider giving it a static IP address. Otherwise, you might expose the wrong computer to the Internet.

More Help from Many Places

In addition to the specific suggestions in this chapter, be sure to check the following:

- *Vendor websites for network adapters and routers*—The latest drivers and firmware updates can solve many problems, especially with wireless connections.

- *The Microsoft Windows Knowledge Base*—Check it out at http://support.microsoft.com.

- *Software vendor websites*—If you're having problems getting software to work with a router or firewall program in place or have other network/Internet-related problems, software vendor websites can help.

- *Third-party home network information sites*—I particularly recommend Practically Networked (http://www.practicallynetworked.com), Tom's Networking (http://www.tomsnetworking.com/), and Dux Computer Digest (http://www.duxcw.com/).

tip

SOFTWARE FIREWALLS AND PORT CONFIGURATION

Don't forget to disable a software firewall (such as Zone Alarm) if you are playing a game or other program that needs access to non-standard TCP or UDP ports. It doesn't matter whether you configure the router to permit traffic if the software firewall stops it. If you put a computer in the DMZ, run a commercial software firewall on it at all times other than when you run a program that requires DMZ service. A commercial firewall program helps protect the computer from hostile intruders (see Chapter 10).

THE ABSOLUTE MINIMUM

Home networks use private IP addresses that are converted to public IP addresses by a router.

A router has two IP addresses; the WAN address is the connection to the Internet access device, and the LAN address is the connection to the local network.

Routers can provide IP addresses to the local network using a feature called DHCP.

If a Windows computer can't get an IP address from the router, it gives itself a private IP address starting with 169.254.

If your computer has a DHCP-assigned address from a different network, you can release the old address and renew a new address for the current network.

Manual IP address configuration makes sense for devices that can't get a DHCP-provided address in a reliable fashion or need a fixed IP address for other reasons.

You need to provide the IP address, subnet mask, default gateway IP address, and DNS server IP addresses when you assign a manual IP address.

If you need to connect to a domain-based network at work but want to use shared network resources at home, you can get a program that stores multiple network configurations for easy switching.

You don't need to connect to a workgroup at home to share an Internet connection.

Windows XP features a variety of network troubleshooters you can use to solve hardware, software, and configuration problems.

Problems with network and coaxial cable can cause network or Internet connections to fail.

The signal lights on the front of cable and DSL modems help you diagnose connection problems.

You can use the Windows Device Manager to diagnose problems with ethernet and USB ports and wireless ethernet adapters.

You can configure most routers to provide special TCP and UDP port handling for programs that might otherwise fail, or you can turn off router protection for a particular address by using DMZ.

Index

F

T

How can we make this index more useful? Email us at indexes@quepublishing.com

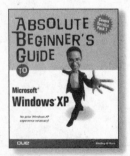